To my wonderful son
on his 25th birthday :)
— Enjoy !
love, mom
May 5, 2012

PUERTO RICAN
COOKERY

Puerto Rican Cookery

A NEW APPROACH
OF A REVISED AND ENLARGED EDITION OF
THE ART OF CARIBBEAN COOKERY

Carmen Aboy Valldejuli

PELICAN PUBLISHING COMPANY
Gretna 2011

First printing, March 1975
Second printing, August 1976
Third printing, October 1977
Fourth printing, September 1978
Fifth printing, December 1979
Sixth printing, October 1980
Seventh printing, March 1981
First Pelican printing, March 1983
Ninth printing, April 1984
Tenth printing, June 1985
Eleventh printing, June 1986
Twelfth printing, November 1987
Thirteenth printing, May 1988
Fourteenth printing, June 1989
Fifteenth printing, June 1990
Sixteenth printing, June 1991
Seventeenth printing, June 1992
Eighteenth printing, May 1993

Nineteenth printing, February 1994
Twentieth printing, September 1994
Twenty-first printing, June 1995
Twenty-second printing, March 1996
Twenty-third printing, September 1997
Twenty-fourth printing, July 1998
Twenty-fifth printing, September 1999
Twenty-sixth printing, January 2001
Twenty-seventh printing, July 2001
Twenty-eighth printing, April 2002
Twenty-ninth printing, March 2003
Thirtieth printing, December 2003
Thirty-first printing, January 2005
Thirty-second printing, April 2006
Thirty-third printing, September 2007
Thirty-fourth printing, February 2009
Thirty-fifth printing, January 2011

Library of Congress Cataloging in Publication Data

Valldejuli, Carmen Aboy, 1912-2005
      Puerto Rican cookery.
      ISBN: 9780882894119
      "A new approach of a revised and enlarged edition
of the art of Caribbean cookery."
      Includes indexes.
      1. Cookery, Puerto Rican. I. Title.
TX716.P8V34 1983 641.597295 83-2149

Designed by Joseph L. Smongeski

Manufactured in the United States of America

Published by Pelican Publishing Company, Inc.
1000 Burmaster Street, Louisiana 70053

TAINO INDIAN PETROGLYPH

One of the principal manifestations of the art of the Taino
Indians of Puerto Rico are the petroglyphs, or engravings on
stone. They carved them on the walls of the caves that served
as sanctuaries, in the monoliths that demarcated their cere-
monial grounds (*plazas*), and in the large rocks frequently
found along our river beds.

The figures represented in the petroglyphs are geometric symbols and human or animal forms. The Indians attached great
magical value to these symbols.

DR. RICARDO E. ALEGRÍA

OTHER BOOKS BY
CARMEN ABOY VALLDEJULI

Cocina Criolla

Also published in Braille by
The American Printing House for the Blind
Louisville, Kentucky

Cucuyé

children's storybook

JUNTOS EN LA COCINA

Fifty years of love, sharing, and cooking

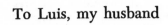

To Luis, my husband

ACKNOWLEDGMENTS

Miguel Pou, famous Puerto Rican artist, is the artist of the watercolor on the jacket of this book. It depicts the manner in which our people prepare the typical and savory *lechón asao* (roast suckling pig), gently barbecuing it over slowly glowing charcoal embers.

Born in 1880 in Ponce, Puerto Rico, he died in 1968. Exposed to the old Spanish tradition, as well as to the new trends, he can be described as a product of both the nineteenth and twentieth centuries. His work as a portrait painter has been outstanding. His interpretation of the Puerto Rican countryside is considered an unique merge of the realistic and the impressionistic schools. He loved his native land and its people, as shown by his portrayals of our folklore, our traditions, and our typical Puerto Rican *jíbaros* (peasants) and plain folk. I am proud to include this masterful touch of Puerto Rican art in the presentation of Puerto Rican cookery.

Joseph L. Smongeski, a graduate of the Art Institute of Chicago, Illinois, designed the book, and jacket. He is a noted painter, whose work has been exhibited in the Boston Museum of Fine Arts, the Art Institute of Chicago, in Madison and Milwaukee, Wisconsin, as well as in New York City, Parish Museum, Long Island, N.Y., and throughout other cities in Massachusetts. At present, he designs books for D. C. Heath and Company in Boston, Massachusetts, and is a member of *Who's Who in American Art.*

Dr. Ricardo E. Alegría is responsible for the establishment of eleven museums in Puerto Rico. As founder and Executive Director of the Institute of Culture of Puerto Rico, he has made possible the preservation and restoration of the nation's oldest city, Old San Juan, where he was born. He was educated at the University of Puerto Rico, the University of Chicago and Harvard University. Dr. Alegría was awarded the Louise duPont Crowninshield Award for his unflagging dedication and superlative achievement in the preservation of the architecture of the previous four hundred and fifty years in Puerto Rico.

Rafael Tufiño is a well known Puerto Rican artist. He has contributed with the chapter illustrations of the petroglyphs carved by the Taino Indians on the rocks and caves around the towns of Jayuya and Lares in Puerto Rico.

Eileen Gaden is a leading food consultant and co-author of cookbooks. She has contributed with the color photograph of the tropical vegetables, spices and herbs in a bed of *achiote* (annato) seeds shown on the frontispiece.

Ramón Aboy, a nephew of the author, has contributed with the photograph on the back of the jacket. Born in San Juan, Puerto Rico, he studied photography at the Maryland Institute College of Art. At present, he has his studio in Old San Juan, and teaches at the School of Plastic Arts of the Institute of Culture of Puerto Rico.

Walter Murray Chiesa, Coordinator of the Program of Plastic Arts of the Institute of Culture of Puerto Rico, helped in the research and selection of the Taino Indian petroglyphs.

CONTENTS

INTRODUCTION

When I was a girl in Puerto Rico, most of the young women I knew were taught in the Spanish tradition that proper young ladies never performed menial household chores. Cooking was one of those chores. Servants were plentiful in those days and my father, who loved fine food, made certain that his kitchen was staffed with the finest cooks in the island. It was lovely food, always, a rare combination of European and domestic cuisine. But only rarely was I permitted to enter the vast room where those *comidas* were actually prepared, and how I regretted that!

In 1936 I married a charming young man named Luis F. Valldejuli, recently graduated from Yale University, who though a mechanical engineer by profession, was himself a devotee of the culinary arts in private. From the beginning of our courtship I shared his enthusiasm for dining well, and his restless curiosity as to how it was all done. By the time we returned to Puerto Rico from our honeymoon, we were launched on a lifetime adventure—collecting recipes of dishes which are representative of Puerto Rican cookery.

This special Caribbean cookery of ours has a fairly traceable family tree. One can seldom be exactly sure how any really ancient dish began, of course. But it is safe to say that our *cocina criolla* was initiated by the first human inhabitants of the islands, the native Indians. Not the cruel, marauding Caribs, who in their sail-rigged war canoes invaded island after island, plundering or carrying off such gentler peoples as the Arawaks or the Tainos of our own Puerto Rico. These savages may have contributed something. By the same token, the last torment that many a dying Arawak captive knew may have been the tantalizing aroma of roasting *batatas* or *mazorcas de maíz* as the Caribs squatted down to supper.

For almost five hundred years the basic ingredients the native Indians used have been enriched by the culinary skills of newcomers who have chosen these blue-green islands as their homes—descendants of the original Spanish, British, French, Danish, and Dutch settlers, or of Negro slaves brought from Africa to toil in the sugar fields. As you will see from the recipes in this book, the time-honored ingredients are still at the bottom of almost every dish. Though they may be used with slight differences in the different islands, the result is that the delicate blends and innovations of five centuries have developed a genuine Caribbean cuisine.

It is an interesting fact that the ever-popular barbecue owes its origin to our Indians' barbecue, which they called *barbacoa*.

The Puerto Rican cuisine differs from that of the American mainland not only in cooking methods, but in seasonings and flavorings. You must think of delicious dishes prepared with fresh lime rind or lime juice, fresh ginger, *naranja agria* (sour orange), and many others. The favorite herbs are fresh *culantro* leaves and whole dried *orégano*.

In Puerto Rican cookery, two magical words are the secret to many unique and characteristic dishes with a Caribbean flavor. These words are: **Adobo** and **Sofrito.**

Adobo is a blend of ingredients crushed and mixed in a mortar and pestle and rubbed into poultry and meats to impart a unique seasoning.

Sofrito is a combination of ingredients used as a flavoring to give a distinctive taste to many native dishes.

One of the most versatile pots in Puerto Rican cookery is the *caldero* or cauldron, which is a cast-iron or cast-aluminum kettle, with round bottom and straight sides. The use of this pot is highly recommended, although it can be substituted by a heavy kettle or Dutch oven.

An important contribution to the Puerto Rican diet are plantains— the variety of bananas that are never eaten raw, known in the island as *plátanos*. When green, they are called *plátanos verdes;* when ripe, they are called *amarillos*. Plantains are fried, roasted, boiled, or baked, either whole or in slices in many interesting recipes. The leaves of the plantain plant also serve a useful purpose in Puerto Rican cookery. They are used to wrap up certain foods to be boiled or baked. Aluminum foil is a serviceable substitute for plantain leaves covering foods to be baked, while parchment cooking paper may be used in lieu of leaves to cover foods to be boiled, such as *pasteles*. A vast majority of all the ingredients used in the *cocina criolla* are available in Puerto Rican or Latin American markets which can be found in most metropolitan centers in the United States.

However, for the benefit of those who are unable to obtain some of the ingredients mentioned in this book, I have indicated substitutes and suggestions which will make possible the enjoyment of the recipes.

As a supplement to our many enticing typical recipes, I have included others which, due to their acceptance and popularity, have been adapted to our tastes and appear frequently in our menus.

Puerto Rican Cookery conforms to its Spanish counterpart, *COCINA CRIOLLA*, reprinted in over forty-three editions. Also I have been honored by The American Printing House for the Blind, in Louisville, Kentucky, by publishing *COCINA CRIOLLA* in Braille.

Luis has contributed with a special chapter on Puerto Rican rum

drinks, which I am sure will be a smash hit with your guests. Among his favorite recipes are *Daiquirí-on-the-Rocks* and *Pineapple Rum Punch.* The first is prepared in large quantities and kept in the freezer until ready to be served *on-the-rocks.* The other is also prepared in advance and kept in the freezer. It never congeals, but retains the consistency of a frozen *Daiquirí.* When ready to serve, it is scooped right into the glasses.

I trust that some day you will have the opportunity to visit Puerto Rico and taste the native foods and drinks in their natural setting. Meanwhile, may you spend many pleasant hours enjoying them in your home.

Carmen Aboy Valldejuli

Santurce, Puerto Rico
March 23, 1975

USEFUL INFORMATION

Due to modern technology, there are in the market many specialized appliances that save time and effort in the kitchen. Among these are Food Processors and Blenders.

Because of their versatility, they are highly recommended in this book for recipes that call for ingredients to be chopped, ground, crumbled or minced. (Follow manufacturer's instructions for their use.)

For accuracy in measuring ingredients and temperatures, the following kitchen utensils are recommended: a cooking scale, a set of cooking thermometers, a set of measuring spoons, either plastic or metal, and two sets of measuring cups (**glass** for liquid ingredients and **metal** for dry ingredients).

TABLE OF EQUIVALENT AMOUNTS

Apples	1 pound	3 medium
Bread	1 pound loaf	16 to 18 slices
Butter or oleomargarine	¼ pound stick	½ cup
Cheese	¼ pound	1 cup shredded
Chocolate, unsweetened	1 ounce	1 square
Coconut milk		(see Index)
Egg whites (large eggs)	About 8 egg whites	1 cup
Egg yolks (large eggs)	About 12 yolks	1 cup
Flour	1 pound, all-purpose	About 3½ cups
	cake flour	About 4 cups
Onions	1 pound, small	8 to 12
	medium	4 to 6
	large	2 to 3
Potatoes	1 pound, small	6 to 8
	medium	3 to 4
	large	1 to 2
Sugar	1 pound, granulated	2¼ cups
	brown	2¼ cups, packed
	confectioners'	3½ to 4 cups

TABLE OF EQUIVALENT MEASURES

Liquid Ingredients

60 drops	1 teaspoon
1 tablespoon	3 teaspoons
½ tablespoon	1½ teaspoons
1 tablespoon	½ ounce
2 tablespoons	1 ounce
4 tablespoons	2 ounces
4 tablespoons	¼ cup
16 tablespoons	1 cup
¼ cup	2 ounces
1 cup	8 ounces
2 cups	1 pint
4 cups	1 quart
1 pint	16 ounces
2 pints	1 quart
1 quart	32 ounces
4 quarts	1 gallon

Solid Ingredients

1 pinch	less than ⅛ teaspoon
1½ teaspoons	½ tablespoon
3 teaspoons	1 tablespoon
4 tablespoons	¼ cup
1 pound	16 ounces
1 square chocolate	1 ounce
1 pound butter	2 cups
1 pound sugar	2 cups
1 pound confectioners' sugar	3½ cups, unsifted
1 pound flour	4 cups, unsifted
¼ pound butter	½ cup, or 1 stick

Yield of ¼ Pound Butter

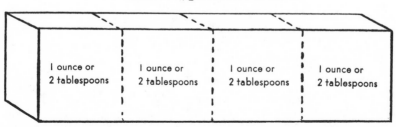

| 1 ounce or 2 tablespoons | 1 ounce or 2 tablespoons | 1 ounce or 2 tablespoons | 1 ounce or 2 tablespoons |

Note: ¼ pound butter is equivalent to 4 ounces, or 8 tablespoons.

TEST FOR CANDY SYRUPS

Consistency of syrups is determined by the use of a candy thermometer, or by dropping a small amount of syrup from the tip of a spoon into a small bowl with **very cold** water, and following the description of test and stage of syrup given below.

Description of Test	Stage of Syrup	Temperature on Candy Thermometer
Syrup thickens *lightly*	*Light*	220°F.–222°F.
Syrup thickens *heavily*	*Heavy*	223°F.–227°F.
Syrup spins a 2-inch thread as it falls from spoon	*Thread*	230°F.–234°F.
Syrup dropped into very cold water can be picked up as a ball that flattens when handled	*Soft Ball*	235°F.–240°F.
Syrup dropped into very cold water forms a firm ball that does not flatten when handled	*Firm Ball*	244°F.–248°F.
Syrup dropped into very cold water forms a firm, but *pliable* ball when handled	*Hard Ball*	250°F.–265°F.
Syrup dropped into very cold water separates into hard threads that are not brittle	*Soft Crack*	270°F.–290°F.
Syrup dropped into very cold water separates into hard and brittle threads	*Hard Crack*	300°F.–310°F.

ACHIOTE COLORING
(Lard or Vegetable Oil Colored with *Achiote*)

Achiote is the seed of a tropical tree, *Bixa orellana*, that produces a dye used for coloring. The **Achiote** (Annato) seeds were originally used by the aborigine Indians to paint their faces and bodies. Now, we use them for coloring certain food. The **Achiote** seeds are cooked in either lard or vegetable oil to extract their characteristic orange-red color. The seeds are strained out and the colored lard or vegetable oil is kept in a glass container in the refrigerator, to be used by table-spoons, as called for in some recipes. It is specially recommended to be used in the well-known and popular *Arroz con Pollo* (Rice with Chicken), as it imparts a very attractive color to the rice. If **Achiote** seeds are unavailable, substitute the amount of **Achiote Coloring** required in the recipe with regular lard or vegetable oil and color the dish with *paprika* or *saffron*.

BASIC RECIPE FOR ACHIOTE COLORING

A—2 cups lard or vegetable oil
  1 cup *achiote* (Annato) seeds, cleaned (see Glossary)

1—In a saucepan, heat fat. Turn heat to *low*, add *achiote* seeds and stir *occasionally* for 5 *minutes*, or until fat turns to a rich orange-red color.

2—Cool *thoroughly*. Strain through a colander with absorbent paper inside and pour into glass container. Cover, and store in the refrigerator, to be used by tablespoons, as called for in certain recipes.

ADOBO

Adobo is a blend of ingredients rubbed into
meat or poultry to impart a unique seasoning.
(Basic seasoning for **each pound** of trimmed meat)

A—1 peppercorn (whole black pepper) } crush and mix
¼ teaspoon dried whole *orégano*   in a mortar
1 clove garlic, peeled

B—1 teaspoon salt
½ teaspoon olive oil
½ teaspoon vinegar or fresh lime juice

1—Mix crushed ingredients included in *A* with ingredients included in
B.

2—Rub seasoning into meat **thoroughly** and set in the refrigerator for
several hours. (For seasoning poultry, see **Table for Seasoning
Chicken** on page 59.)

Note: Ingredients are optional and can be adjusted to taste.

SOFRITO

Sofrito is the seasoning used in flavoring many native dishes.
(Basic flavoring for recipes that serve 6 or 8)

A—1 ounce salt *pork* } washed and diced
2 ounces lean cured ham

B—1 tablespoon lard or vegetable oil
¼ teaspoon whole dried *orégano*

C—1 onion, peeled
1 green pepper, seeded
3 sweet chili peppers, seeded } washed and finely chopped
3 fresh *culantro* leaves
2 cloves garlic, peeled

1—In a small pan, brown **rapidly** ingredients included in *A*.

2—Reduce heat to *low*, add ingredients included in *B* and *C* and mix.
Sauté about *10 minutes*, stirring **occasionally.**

Note: Ingredients are optional and can be adjusted to taste.

PRACTICAL SOFRITO

Sofrito, if used frequently, can be prepared in accordance with the following recipe and kept in the freezer to be used as required

A — ¼ cup vegetable oil

B — ½ pound onions, peeled
  ½ pound green peppers, peeled
  ⅛ pound sweet chili peppers, seeded
  6 cloves garlic, peeled   washed and cut
  8 fresh *culantro* leaves   into pieces
  8 fresh *culantrillo* sprigs
  ½ pound leaned cured ham (*optional*)
C — 1 tablespoon whole dried *orégano*

D — ½ cup vegetable oil

1 — Pour vegetable oil included in A into the receptacle of an electric blender. Add ingredients included in B and grind **gradually**, alternating with the *orégano* included in C.

2 — In a *caldero* or heavy kettle, pour vegetable oil included in D. Add ground ingredients, mix and bring to a boil over *high* heat.

3 — Reduce heat to *moderate* and cook, *uncovered*, for *30 minutes*, stirring **occasionally**.

4 — Allow to cool **thoroughly** and distribute 2 tablespoons of *Sofrito* into each cube of ice-cube trays (reserved exclusively for this purpose).

5 — Set ice trays in the freezer until *Sofrito* is frozen. Remove ice trays from freezer, unmold the *Sofrito* cubes and keep in Freezer Bags in the freezer, to be used as required.

Note: Frozen *Sofrito* cubes will not stick together. Two or three *Sofrito* cubes can be substituted in recipes serving 6 to 8 that require *Sofrito*.

CHAPTER 1 *Soups*

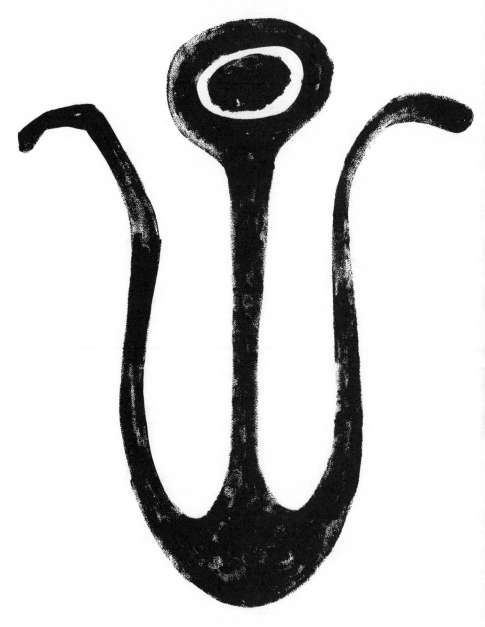

Soups

SOUP STOCK

Caldo Básico

(7½ to 8 Cups)

A—1 pound lean beef
   1 pound beef bone
   2 quarts (8 cups) water

B—1 onion, peeled
   1 green pepper, seeded   } coarsely chopped
   2 sweet chili peppers, seeded

C—1 tablespoon salt
   6 fresh *culantro* leaves
   1 fresh corn kernel, cut into pieces
   2 cloves garlic, crushed

1—Clean and wash both meat and bone. Cut meat into 2-inch cubes. Soak meat and bones in water included in A for *1 hour* in a covered pot.

2—Uncover and bring **rapidly** to a boil. Add ingredients included in B and C and bring to a boil again. Reduce heat to *low, cover,* and *simmer* for *1½ hours.*

3—Strain soup and use stock as a base in the preparation of different soups.

BLACK BEANS SOUP

Frijoles Negros

(See Black Beans Pottage on page 240.)

3

VEGETABLE PURÉE

Puré Básico

(Serves 8)

1—Prepare Soup Stock. (see Index) Peel 2 pounds of vegetables. Wash and cut into small pieces and add to Soup Stock. Bring **rapidly** to a boil. Reduce heat to *moderate, cover* and cook for *45 minutes.* Strain soup. Press vegetables through sieve.

2—Mix stock and vegetable purée well, season to taste, reheat, and serve **immediately.**

CHICKEN SOUP WITH RICE

Sopón de Pollo con Arroz

(Serves 8 to 10)

A—¼ cup short-grain rice | 1 cup water

B—2½ quarts (10 cups) water | 2 teaspoons fresh lime juice
5 teaspoons salt | 2 onions, peeled and halved

C—1½ pounds of large pumpkin pieces, peeled and washed
1½ pounds of diced *yautías* or potatoes, peeled and washed
3 pounds dressed-weight whole chicken, washed and drained

1—Wash rice. Soak in water included in A.

2—Meanwhile, in a large kettle, combine ingredients included in B and bring **rapidly** to a boil. Add ingredients included in C and bring **rapidly** to a boil again. Reduce heat to *moderate, cover* and boil for *1 hour.* Remove chicken and pumpkin pieces. Mash pumpkin and add to kettle.

3—Drain rice **throughly,** add to kettle, mix, *cover* and boil at *moderate* heat for *20 minutes.* In the meantime, discard bones from chicken and add chicken meat to kettle. Serve hot.

Note: 2 ounces very thin vermicelli can be substituted for rice.

CHICKEN SOUP WITH VEGETABLES

Sopa de Pollo con Vegetales

(Serves 6 to 8)

A—2 pounds dressed-weight whole chicken
or
2 pounds chicken pieces

B—2 quarts (8 cups) water
3½ teaspoons salt

C—½ pound potatoes
1 pound white *yautía*   peeled, washed,
½ pound yellow *yautía*   and diced
1 pound pumpkin or squash
¼ pound string beans, trimmed, washed, and halved
¼ pound carrots, scraped, washed, and cut into 1-inch rounds

1—In an 8-quart kettle, bring to a boil ingredients included in *B*.

2—Wash and drain chicken. Add chicken to kettle, together with ingredients included in *C*. Bring *rapidly* to a boil. Reduce heat to *moderate, cover,* and boil for *1 hour*.

Note: To serve soup as purée, remove chicken and blend rest of soup in an electric blender. Discard bones from chicken and add chicken meat to purée.

CHICKEN SOUP WITH VERMICELLI

Sopa de Pollo con Fideos

(Serves 6 to 8)

A—2 pounds dressed-weight whole chicken
or
2 pounds chicken pieces

B—2 quarts (8 cups) water
3½ teaspoons salt

C—1½ pounds potatoes, peeled and diced
2 small onions, peeled and halved
1 green pepper, seeded and quartered
2 sweet chili peppers, seeded
3 cloves garlic, crushed
3 fresh *culantro* leaves

D—2 ounces very thin vermicelli

1—In an 8-quart kettle, bring to a boil ingredients included in *B*.

2—Wash and drain chicken. Add to kettle together with ingredients included in *C*. Bring *rapidly* to a boil again. Reduce heat to *moderate, cover,* and boil for *45 minutes*.

3—Strain soup and return to kettle the chicken and potatoes. Mash and strain whatever remains in the sieve into the soup.

4—Crumble the vermicelli and add. *Cover* kettle and cook over *moderate* heat for *15 minutes*.

Note: To serve soup as purée, remove chicken and blend rest of soup in an electric blender. Discard bones from chicken and add chicken meat to purée.

CREAMED CORN SOUP

Sopa de Maíz a la Crema
(Serves 6)

A—1 ounce (2 tablespoons) butter   1½ teaspoon salt
2 tablespoons flour   Dash ground pepper

B—1 quart (4 cups) milk

C—1 small onion, peeled and coarsely chopped
1 can (1 pound) cream style corn
1 teaspoon sugar (*optional*)

1—In a kettle, melt butter *slowly*. Add flour, salt and pepper. Mix well.

2—Add milk *slowly*, stirring *constantly*, and bring to a boil.

3—Add ingredients included in *C* and cook over *low* heat for *15 minutes*, stirring *occasionally*.

FISH SOUP

Sopón de Pescado
(Serves 6)

A—4-pound cleaned and scaled white-meat fish, with head and tail intact

B—1 large clove garlic, peeled
  2 teaspoons whole dried *orégano*
  2 teaspoons salt   crush and mix
  2½ teaspoons olive oil   in a mortar
  1 teaspoon vinegar

C—7 cups water
  2 tablespoons salt
  6 cloves garlic, peeled
  1 bay leaf
  12 peppercorns (whole black peppers)

D—¼ pound butter
  1 pound onions, peeled and quartered
  2 sprigs fresh parsley or 1 teaspoon dry parsley flakes
  2 tablespoons olive oil
  1 tablespoon vinegar
  ½ cup pale dry sherry
  1 can (1 pound 12 ounces) whole tomatoes, including liquid

1—Wash fish. Remove head and **reserve**. Remove tail and discard. Cut rest of fish in slices. Weigh fish slices and **take note of weight.**

2—Rub seasoning included in B into fish slices.

3—In a large kettle, cook fish head with ingredients included in C over *low* heat, *covered,* for *1 hour.*

4—Strain soup, add to stock ingredients included in D, *cover,* and cook over *low* heat for *45 minutes.*

5—Add fish slices, *cover,* and cook over *low* heat for *12 minutes* for **each** pound of fish.

FRIED PLANTAIN SOUP

Sopa de Plátanos Fritos
(Serves 8)

A—7½ cups Soup Stock (see Index)

B—2 green plantains

C—¾ cup freshly grated Parmesan cheese

1—Prepare Soup Stock.

2—Peel plantains, cut into 1-inch slices, and soak in salted water for *15 minutes.*

3—Drain plantains and deep-fry in lard or vegetable oil for *15 minutes* at a temperature of *350°F.* Remove plantain slices from fat, mash in a mortar, and add to Soup Stock.

4—Cook over *moderate* heat for *10 minutes.*

5—Add grated cheese and boil for *1 minute.*

EGG AND GREEN BANANA SOUP

Ajo Pollo
(Serves 8)

A—7½ cups Soup Stock (see Index)

B—8 green bananas   2 tablespoons salt
   1 quart (4 cups) water

C—8 eggs   1½ teaspoons salt

1—Prepare Soup Stock, using, if preferred, one pound cleaned and dressed chicken instead of beef, and substituting the beef bone by ¼ pound cured ham bone. When ready, remove meat, strain soup, and return meat to stock.

2—Peel bananas and cut into halves. Soak for *15 minutes* in water with salt included in B. Drain, and deep-fry in lard or vegetable oil for *10 minutes* at a temperature of *350°F.*

3—Remove bananas from fat, mash in a mortar, and form into small balls.

4—Heat Soup Stock and drop balls into it. Break eggs into soup, being careful not to break yolks. Add salt included in *C.* Cook *rapidly* for *3 minutes.*

CASABE SOUP

Sopa de Casabe
(Serves 8)

A—7½ cups Soup Stock (see Index)

B—¼ pound *casabe* (Cassava Cakes) (see Glossary)
1 teaspoon salt

1—Prepare Soup Stock.

2—Crumble *casabe* and mix with Soup Stock. Add salt and bring
to a boil.

3—Turn heat to *low, cover,* and cook for *20 minutes.*

CARIBBEAN SOUP

Sancocho
(Serves 8)

A—3 quarts (12 cups) water
1 tablespoon salt
1 onion, peeled
2 tomatoes
1 green pepper, seeded   } coarsely chopped
1 sweet chili pepper, seeded
3 fresh *culantro* leaves
2 fresh corn kernels, halved

B—1 pound lean beef
½ pound lean pork meat with bone

C—½ pound white *yautía*
½ pound yellow *yautía*
½ pumpkin or squash
½ pound potatoes   } peeled and diced
½ pound *ñame*
½ pound sweet potatoes

D—1 large green plantain } peeled and quartered
1 large ripe plantain

E—1 tablespoon salt | ½ cup tomato sauce

1—In a large, 12-quart kettle, combine ingredients included in A. Bring *rapidly* to a boil.

2—Clean and wash meats. Cut into 1-inch cubes. Add meats and bone to kettle. *Cover,* reduce heat to *moderate,* and cook for *1 hour.*

3—Wash vegetables included in C and add to kettle.

4—Rinse green plantain *rapidly* in *salted* water. Drain and add to kettle, together with ripe plantain.

5—Add salt and tomato sauce and bring *rapidly* to a boil. *Cover,* and cook over *moderate* heat for *45 minutes.*

6—*Uncover,* remove pieces of green plantain, mash, turn into balls, and add to kettle. Boil *rapidly* for *1 minute.*

GALLICIAN BROTH

Caldo Gallego

(Serves 8)

A—½ pound dried white beans (soaked overnight)

B—2 quarts (8 cups) water
2 ounces salt pork, in one piece, with rind removed
2 pounds lean cured ham, washed, and diced
1 small bone from cured ham
3 *chorizos* (Spanish Sausages)
½ cup finely chopped onions

C—1 tablespoon salt
¼ teaspoon ground pepper
1 pound potatoes, peeled, washed and cut into ¼-inch slices
1½ pounds cabbage, cored and cut into 1-inch pieces
1 package (10 ounces) frozen chopped *berzas* (Collard Greens) or *grelos* (Turnip Greens)

1—Drain beans, wash under running water and drain again. Place in a large, 12-quart kettle.

2—Add ingredients included in *B*, and bring to a brisk boil over *high* heat. Reduce heat to *low, cover,* and cook **slowly** for 2 *hours.*

3—Add ingredients included in *C* and bring to a boil over *high* heat. Reduce heat to *low,* and cook, **partially covered,** for ½ *hour.*

4—Discard ham bone and salt pork. Remove *chorizos,* cut into ½-inch rounds and return to pot.

5—Cook over *low* heat, *uncovered,* for ½ *hour.*

SOLDIER'S SOUP
Rancho
(Serves 12)

A—½ pound *garbanzos* (Chick-Peas)
    5 quarts (20 cups) water
    1 tablespoon salt

B—1 pound lean beef
    1 *chorizo* (Spanish Sausage), halved
    2 tablespoons salt

C—1 onion, peeled
    1 tomato
    1 green pepper, seeded   } coarsely chopped
    1 sweet chili pepper, seeded
    3 fresh *culantro* leaves

D—1 pound cabbage, quartered
    ½ pound **fresh** white pea beans (see Note)

E—1 pound pumpkin or squash
    1 pound potatoes   } peeled and diced
    ½ pound either turnips, *apio*
        ñame or yautía

F—½ cup tomato sauce
    2 teaspoons salt
    1 tablespoon vinegar

G—2 ounces very fine vermicelli

1—Pick over *garbanzos* (Chick-Peas). Wash well and soak **overnight** in water and salt included in *A*. Next day, drain and place in a large, 12-quart kettle. Add 5 quarts (20 cups) water and bring **rapidly** to a boil. *Cover,* and cook for *1 hour.*

2—Wash meat and cut into 1-inch cubes. Add to kettle with *chorizo* and salt included in *B*.

3—Add ingredients included in *C*. *Cover,* and cook over *moderate* heat for *1 hour.*

4—Wash white pea beans, and add to soup. Add cabbage. *Cover,* and cook for *1 hour.*

5—Add ingredients included in *E* and *F*. *Cover,* and cook for *30 minutes.*

6—Crumble vermicelli and add. Stir well, *cover,* and cook for *15 minutes* longer.

Note: If **fresh** white pea beans are not available, use **dried** white pea beans, but soak overnight in unsalted water to cover.

CHICK-PEA SOUP WITH PIG'S FEET

Sopón de Garbanzos con Patas de Cerdo
(Serves 12)

A—1 pound *garbanzos* (Chick-Peas)
2½ quarts (10 cups) water
2 tablespoons salt

B—3 pounds pig's feet (see Instruction 2)

C—4½ quarts (18 cups) water

D—2¼ pounds pumpkin, peeled and diced
2 *chorizos* (Spanish Sausages), halved, with casings removed
1 ounce salt pork ⎫
2 ounces lean cured ham ⎬ washed and diced
1 green pepper, seeded ⎫
3 sweet chili peppers, seeded ⎪
1 onion, peeled ⎬ coarsely chopped
2 cloves garlic, peeled ⎪
4 fresh *culantro* leaves ⎭

E—2 pounds potatoes, peeled and diced
2½ pounds cabbage, quartered
1 tomato, halved
½ cup tomato sauce

1—Pick over *garbanzos* (Chick-Peas). Wash well and soak **overnight** in water and salt included in *A.*

2—There are two kinds of pig's feet: **salted** and **unsalted.** If using *salted pig's feet,* soak overnight in water to cover. Next day, drain and wash in different waters **four** times. Cover with water, bring *rapidly* to a boil and drain. Remove and discard any small loose bones. If using *unsalted pig's feet,* **do not soak or boil.** Wash in different waters at least **four** times.

3—In a large, 12-quart kettle, bring to a boil water included in *C.* Add drained pig's feet and bring *rapidly* to a boil again. Reduce heat to *moderate, cover,* and boil for *1½ hours. Uncover,* and skim off fat.

4—Drain *garbanzos,* cover with water and drain again. Add to kettle, together with ingredients included in *D.* Bring *rapidly* to a boil. Reduce heat to *moderate, cover,* and boil for *1½ hours.*

5—Mash pumpkin. Add ingredients included in *E.* (If using *unsalted pig's feet,* add 2 tablespoons salt.) Bring **rapidly** to a boil. Reduce heat to *moderate, cover,* and boil for *1 hour.*

6—*Uncover,* taste and adjust seasoning, and boil for *1 hour,* or until soup thickens to taste. When serving, discard any small loose bones.

TRIPE A LA CRIOLLA

Mondongo

(Serves 12)

A—4½ pounds beef tripe, trimmed
1 pound calf's feet, cut up | 6 limes, halved

B—¼ pound lean cured ham, washed and cut into ½-inch pieces
   1 pound pumpkin, peeled and diced
   2 medium onions, peeled ⎫
   2 green peppers, seeded ⎪
   8 sweet chili peppers, seeded ⎬ coarsely chopped
   4 cloves garlic, peeled ⎪
   6 fresh *culantro* leaves ⎭
   2 tablespoons salt
   2½ quarts (10 cups) water

C—1 can (1 pound) *garbanzos* (Chick-Peas) boiled in water
      with salt
   1 pound *apio* (see Glossary) ⎫
   1 pound *yautía* (see Glossary) ⎬ peeled and cut into
   1 pound pumpkin ⎭ 1½-inch pieces
   1 can (8 ounces) tomato sauce | 2 teaspoons salt

1—Wash tripe and calf's feet **thoroughly** under running water.
   Drain and dry. **Reserve** calf's feet.

2—Rub tripe with limes and place in a pot. Squeeze rest of
   juice from limes over tripe. Add water to cover tripe by **2
   inches** and bring **rapidly** to a boil. Reduce heat to *moderate*
   and boil, *uncovered,* for *10 minutes.*

3—Drain and rinse well in cold running water. Cut tripe into
   strips 1½-inch x 1-inch and place in a 10-quart kettle, together
   with calf's feet and rest of ingredients included in *B.* Bring
   rapidly to a boil, reduce heat to *moderate, cover,* and boil
   about *2 hours,* or until tripe is tender.

4—Add *garbanzos,* including liquid, and rest of ingredients included in *C* and bring to a boil over *high* heat. Reduce heat
   to *moderate, cover,* and boil until vegetables are fork-tender.

5—Taste and adjust seasoning. Boil, *uncovered,* over *moderate*
   heat, until thickened to taste.

CHAPTER II Meats

Meats

PUERTO RICAN BEEF STEW
Carne Guisada Puertorriqueña
(Serves 6)

A—1 tablespoon lard or vegetable oil

B—2 pounds trimmed beef top round, cut into 1-inch chunks

C—1 green pepper, seeded
4 sweet chili peppers, seeded
2 onions, peeled ⎫
4 cloves garlic, peeled ⎬ chopped
6 fresh *culantro* leaves, washed ⎭
2 tablespoons vinegar
½ teaspoon whole dried *orégano*, crushed
½ cup tomato sauce
2 bay leaves
1 tablespoon salt

D—½ pound carrots, scraped, washed and cut into ½-inch rounds
1 can (1 pound 1 ounce) green peas (*Petit Pois*)

E—½ pound potatoes, peeled, washed and cubed
12 olives, stuffed with pimientos
1 tablespoon capers
¼ cup seeded raisins (*optional*)
¼ teaspoon salt

1—In a large *caldero* or heavy kettle, heat fat included in A. Add chunks of beef and stir **constantly** over *moderate-high* heat until meat loses its red color.

2—Add ingredients included in C, mix and bring to a boil. Reduce heat to *low*, *cover*, and cook for *1 hour*.

17

3—Add carrots to *caldero*. Drain liquid from peas into *caldero* and mix (**Reserve** peas). Bring **rapidly** to a boil, reduce heat to *low, cover* and cook about *1 hour*, or until meat is **almost** fork-tender.

4—Add ingredients included in *E*, mix, bring **rapidly** to a boil, reduce heat to *low, cover* and cook about *1 hour*, or until meat is fork-tender and vegetables are done.

5—Add reserved peas and mix. Taste and adjust seasoning. (*Uncover*, and boil to thicken sauce to taste.)

SHREDDED BEEF STEW

Carne en Ropa Vieja
(Serves 6)

This dish makes a whole meal, since it yields a very nourishing soup and a delicious meat.

Soup:
A—3¾ quarts (15 cups) water
2 pounds beef, trimmed | 1 small cured ham bone, washed
2 ounces lean cured ham, washed and diced
1 tomato, halved ⎤
1 green pepper, seeded ⎬ chopped
1 onion, peeled ⎟
3 fresh *culantro* leaves ⎦

B—¾ pound potatoes ⎫ peeled and quartered
¾ pound pumpkin ⎬
1 fresh corn kernel, shucked and broken into 3 pieces
5 teaspoons salt

C—¼ pound vermicelli, broken into pieces
¼ teaspoon salt

1—Mix ingredients included in *A* in a 12-quart kettle. Heat to boiling, *cover*, and cook for *20 minutes*.

2—Add ingredients included in *B, cover*, and boil over *moderate* heat for *1 hour*.

3—Remove meat and **reserve.** Strain soup, returning to the stock the potatoes, pumpkin, corn and ham.

4—Bring soup again to a boil and add ingredients included in *C*. Boil *rapidly* for *20 minutes.* **Reserve** 1½ cups of broth to use with meat. (see below)

Meat:

A—1 ounce salt pork
   2 ounces lean cured ham } washed and diced

   1 onion, peeled
   1 green pepper, seeded } chopped

   1 tomato, quartered | ½ cup tomato sauce

B—Reserved meat
   1½ cups reserved broth
   1 can (8 ounces) green peas (*Petit-Pois*)

1—In a kettle, brown salt pork and ham *rapidly*. Turn heat to *low* and sauté rest of ingredients included in *A*, stirring *occasionally*, until tender.

2—Shred reserved meat, add to kettle and mix. Add reserved broth and green peas, **including** the liquid. Bring to a boil, remove from heat and serve.

SWEET-AND-SOUR MEAT

Carne Agridulce

(Serves 6)

A—1 quart (4 cups) water
   1 tablespoon salt
   1 bell pepper, seeded and quartered
   1 onion, peeled and halved
   2 cloves garlic, peeled and crushed
   3 fresh *culantro* leaves

B—2 pounds trimmed top round, cut into ½-inch cubes

C—¾ cup vinegar
   2 bell peppers, trimmed and cut into 1-inch squares

D—2 tomatoes
    4 canned pineapple slices } cut into ½-inch pieces
    ¾ cup brown sugar, firmly packed
    ¼ teaspoon salt | 3 tablespoons ketchup

E—3 tablespoons cornstarch
    1½ cups broth (see Instruction 1)

1—In a kettle, bring **rapidly** to a boil ingredients included in A. Add beef cubes and bring **rapidly** to a boil. Reduce heat to *moderate, cover,* and boil about *1½ hours,* or until meat is fork-tender. Strain, measure 1½ cups broth and **reserve. Reserve** meat.

2—In a large saucepan, combine ingredients included in C, *cover,* and cook over *moderate* heat for *15 minutes.*

3—Add ingredients included in D and bring **rapidly** to a boil. *Cover,* and cook over *moderate* heat for *5 minutes.*

4—Dissolve cornstarch in part of broth included in E. Add rest of broth and blend. Add to saucepan and stir **constantly** over *moderate-high* heat until boiling.

5—Add drained chunks of beef and mix over *moderate* heat until boiling.

6—Serve over Chow Mein Noodles.

MEAT BALLS WITH POTATOES

Albóndigas con Papas
(Serves 6)

A—1 pound lean ground beef
    2 sandwich bread slices, with crusts trimmed (about ⅔ cup sandwich bread slices, thoroughly crumbled)
    ¼ cup milk

B—1 clove garlic, peeled
    ¾ teaspoon whole dried *orégano*
    Pinch ground nutmeg   } crush and mix
    1½ teaspoons salt   in a mortar
    1 teaspoon olive oil
    2 teaspoons vinegar

C—1 egg

D—1 ounce salt pork
   2 ounces lean cured ham } *optional*

E—1 green pepper, seeded
   3 sweet chili peppers, seeded
   1 onion, peeled
   3 fresh *culantro* leaves } washed and finely chopped

F—6 olives, stuffed with pimientos
   1 teaspoon capers
   ½ cup tomato sauce
   ½ teaspoon salt
   3 cups water
   1 pound potatoes, peeled and quartered

1—Place meat in a bowl.

2—Apart, crumble bread finely over milk, soak and crush to mix **thoroughly**. Add to bowl.

3—Add ingredients included in *B* and mix. Add egg and blend with meat.

4—Take mixture by spoonfuls and turn into balls. Set in a large shallow baking pan and bake for *10 minutes* in preheated oven to *350°F.* (If preferred, coat balls with flour and brown **lightly** in lard or vegetable oil.)

5—Wash, dice and brown **rapidly** in a *caldero* or heavy kettle ingredients included in *D*. Add ingredients included in *E* and sauté over *low heat* about *10 minutes,* or until tender.

6—Add ingredients included in *F*, bring **rapidly** to a boil, turn heat to *moderate, cover,* and boil for *30 minutes.*

7—Add meat balls and boil, *covered,* about *15 minutes.* (**Uncover,** if necessary, to thicken sauce to taste.)

CARIBBEAN MEAT LOAF

Butifarrón Sabroso

(Serves 6 to 8)

A—1½ pounds lean ground beef

B—3 slices sandwich bread, crusts trimmed
1 cup water

C—1 green pepper, seeded
2 sweet chili peppers, seeded
2 cloves garlic, peeled
1 onion, peeled   } ground or
4 fresh *culantro* leaves   finely chopped
1 ounce salt pork, washed
2 ounces lean cured ham, washed
½ teaspoon whole dried *orégano*, crushed

D—2 teaspoons salt | 1 egg

E—Flour (*to coat Meat Loaf*)
¼ cup lard or vegetable oil

F—¼ cup tomato sauce | 1 can (10½ ounces) tomato soup

G—3 onions, peeled and sliced

1—Put meat into a bowl.

2—Apart, crumble bread over water and soak. Mix until well blended. Squeeze to drain excess water. Add soaked bread to bowl and mix.

3—Add ingredients included in *C* and *D*, and mix. Turn mixture into a loaf and coat *lightly* with flour.

4—In a *caldero*, heavy kettle or frying pan, heat fat and brown loaf *very lightly*.

5—Pour over ingredients included in *F* and bring *rapidly* to a boil. Reduce heat to *low, cover,* and cook for *1 hour*. Baste *occasionally*.

6—Add onions, *cover,* and cook for *30 minutes*.

SWEET-AND-SOUR MEAT LOAF
Butifarrón Agridulce

(Serves 6)

A—1½ pounds lean ground beef

B—¼ cup minced or ground onions
1 egg, lightly beaten
1½ teaspoons salt
⅛ teaspoon ground pepper
½ cup tomato sauce
1 cup bread or cracker crumbs

C—2 tablespoons prepared mustard
2 tablespoons brown sugar, firmly packed
2 tablespoons ketchup
2 tablespoons vinegar
½ cup tomato sauce
1 can (10½ ounces) tomato soup

1—Preheat oven to *350°F.* Grease a 12 x 7½ x 2-inch glass baking dish.

2—Place meat in a bowl and mix *thoroughly* with ingredients included in *B*.

3—Mound meat in center of baking dish, leaving a space of about 1-inch on all sides.

4—Combine ingredients included in *C* and pour over meat.

5—*Cover* and bake about *1½ hours.* Serve hot or cold, together with its sauce.

BASIC MEAT FILLING

Receta Básica para Rellenos de Carne

Filling:

A—1 ounce salt pork
   2 ounces lean cured ham } washed and diced

B—1 tablespoon lard or vegetable oil
   1 green pepper, seeded
   3 sweet chili peppers, seeded
   1 onion, peeled
   2 cloves garlic, peeled } chopped

C—1 teaspoon whole dried *orégano*
   1 teaspoon salt
   ¼ teaspoon vinegar
   1 pound lean ground beef or pork

D—6 olives, stuffed with pimientos
   1 teaspoon capers
   ¼ cup tomato sauce (see Note)

E—2 tablespoons seeded raisins
   6 dry prunes, pitted and chopped
   2 hard-cooked eggs, chopped
   2 canned pimientos, chopped } *optional*

1—In a *caldero* or heavy kettle, brown *rapidly* salt pork and ham. Reduce heat to *low*, add ingredients included in *B*, and sauté for *10 minutes*, stirring *occasionally*.

2—Add ingredients included in *C*, mix, and stir over *high* heat until meat loses its red color.

3—Turn heat to *low*. Add ingredients included in *D* and *E*, mix, *cover*, and cook *30 minutes* for beef or *1 hour* for pork.

Note: Amount of tomato sauce varies according to use given to filling. (For fritters and turnovers it should be quite dry.)

MEAT PIE

Pastelón de Carne

Filling:

A—1 ounce salt pork
 2 ounces lean cured ham } washed and diced

B—1 tablespoon lard or vegetable oil
 1 green pepper, seeded
 3 sweet chili peppers, seeded
 1 onion, peeled
 2 cloves garlic, peeled } chopped

C—1 teaspoon whole dried *orégano*
 1 teaspoon salt
 ¼ teaspoon vinegar
 1 pound lean ground beef or pork

D—½ cup tomato sauce
 6 olives, stuffed with pimientos
 1 teaspoon capers
 2 tablespoons seeded raisins
 6 dry prunes, pitted
 2 hard-cooked eggs
 Pimientos, 1 can
 (4 ounces) drained } chopped

1—In a *caldero* or heavy kettle, brown *rapidly* salt pork and ham. Reduce heat to *low,* add ingredients included in *B* and sauté until tender, stirring *occasionally.*

2—Add ingredients included in *C*, mix, and stir *constantly* over *high* heat until meat loses its red color.

3—Turn heat to *low*. Add ingredients included in *D*, mix, *cover,* and cook *30 minutes* for beef, or *1 hour* for pork.

Pastry:

A—3 cups flour
 4 teaspoons baking powder
 ½ teaspoon salt

B—½ cup vegetable lard, chilled
¾ cup milk, chilled

1—Heat oven to *350°F.*

2—Sift together ingredients included in A.

3—Cut in shortening with a dough blender or 2 knives, until mixture resembles coarse meal.

4—Add milk and mix *rapidly* with a fork, to make a dough. Knead *lightly,* handling dough *gently* and *quickly.*

5—Turn dough out onto a floured board. Shape into a ball and divide in half.

6—Roll out one half of the dough with a lightly floured rolling pin in a circle to fit a 9 or 10-inch pie plate.

7—Place a piece of waxed paper over dough and roll together with dough like a jelly roll. Unroll over the pie plate. Discard paper. **Do not stretch dough.** Prick bottom and sides of dough in several places.

8—Spoon filling into lined pie plate.

9—Proceed with other half of dough in the same way and cover filling. Prick top of dough in several places. Join edges by pressing together firmly with a fork moistened in milk.

10—Brush top *lightly* with milk.

11—Bake about *45 minutes,* or until golden brown.

MEAT-EGGPLANT CASSEROLE

Pastelón de Carne y Berenjena
(Serves 8)

A—¼ cup olive oil
  1 medium onion, peeled and chopped
  3 cloves garlic, peeled and thinly sliced
  ½ pound lean ground beef

B—1 large tomato, chopped
  1 can (8 ounces) tomato sauce
  ½ cup water | ¾ teaspoon salt
  ⅛ teaspoon ground black pepper
  ⅛ teaspoon paprika | 2 tablespoons flour

C—1 pound eggplants
  Flour (*to coat eggplants*)

D—¾ cup olive oil

E—¼ pound Swiss cheese, very thinly sliced
  1 ounce (2 tablespoons) butter

1—In a saucepan, heat olive oil included in A. Sauté onions over *low* heat until tender, stirring **occasionally.**

2—Add sliced garlic and mix. Add ground beef, turn heat to *high* and stir **constantly** until meat loses its red color.

3—Reduce heat to *low*, add ingredients included in B and mix. Cook over *moderate* heat, stirring **occasionally,** for 20 *minutes*. Remove from heat and **reserve.**

4—Meanwhile, peel eggplants and cut into ¼-inch rounds. *Cover* **lightly** with flour included in C.

5—In a frying-pan, heat olive oil included in D and fry eggplant slices over *moderate* heat for 3 *minutes on each side.*

6—In a broiler-proof dish, arrange layers as follows:
  (a) ⅓ of meat filling   (d) ½ of eggplant slices
  (b) ½ of eggplant slices   (e) ⅓ of meat filling
  (c) ⅓ of meat filling

7—Top with cheese slices and dot with butter included in E.

8—Set on preheated broiler for a few seconds, just until cheese melts and browns lightly.

FRIED BEEFSTEAK WITH ONIONS

Carne Frita con Cebolla

(Serves 6)

A—2 pounds trimmed loin or fillet of beef

B—6 peppercorns (whole black peppers)
   4 cloves garlic, peeled
   ¼ teaspoon whole dried *orégano*   crush and mix
   1 tablespoon salt   in a mortar
   3 tablespoons vinegar

C—¼ cup lard or vegetable oil
   8 onions, peeled and sliced

1—Wash meat with a damp cloth and cut into slices ¼-inch thick. Pound each slice with a mallet, to tenderize.

2—Rub the seasoning included in *B* into meat. Set meat in refrigerator until cooking time.

3—Heat fat in a frying pan. Add onions and sauté over *low* heat until tender. Remove onions, draining well, and **reserve.**

4—Add meat to oil remaining in skillet and fry *rapidly* about *3 minutes* on each side or until done to taste.

5—Add onions and cook for *1 minute* longer.

6—Serve meat, covered with onions.

BREADED BEEFSTEAK
Carne Empanada
(Serves 6)

A—2 pounds trimmed loin or fillet of beef

B—4 peppercorns (whole black peppers) ⎫
    2 cloves garlic, peeled
    1 teaspoon whole dried *orégano* ⎬ crush and mix
    2 teaspoons salt   in a mortar
    2 teaspoons olive oil
    1 teaspoon vinegar ⎭

C—4 eggs
    ½ teaspoon salt

D—2 cups bread or cracker crumbs

E—Lard or vegetable oil (*for deep-frying*)

1—Wash meat with a damp cloth and cut into slices ¼-inch thick. Pound each slice with a mallet, until slices are very thin.

2—Rub well into meat the seasoning included in *B*. Set meat in refrigerator until cooking time.

3—Beat eggs *lightly* with salt.

4—Bread meat slices as follows:
    a—Dip slices in beaten eggs and drain *rapidly*.
    b—Coat with crumbs and firmly pound with palm of hands.
    c—Dip again in beaten eggs and drain *rapidly*.
    d—Coat with crumbs and pound again.

5—Place breaded meat in a flat platter and chill for *20 minutes*, to make coating firmer for frying.

6—Deep-fry in fat, heated to *375°F.*, until golden brown. Drain on absorbent paper.

FILET MIGNON A LA CRIOLLA

Filete Mignon a la Criolla

(Serves 6)

A—1 beef tenderloin, trimmed | ½ pound bacon slices

B—2 peppercorns (whole black peppers) ⎫
   3 cloves garlic, peeled
   ¼ teaspoon whole dried *orégano*   crush and mix
   1 onion, peeled and chopped   in a mortar
   1¼ teaspoons salt for **each** pound
      of trimmed fillet
   ½ teaspoon fresh lime juice ⎭

C—1 pound onions, peeled and sliced
   1 can (8 ounces) "Broiled in Butter" mushroom crowns,
   drained
   2 ounces (4 tablespoons) butter

1—Wipe meat with damp cloth. Cut into slices 1½-inch thick.

2—Rub seasoning included in *B* well into both sides of meat. Encircle each fillet with a bacon slice and secure with wooden picks. Set in refrigerator until cooking time.

3—**Mushroom sauce:**
   In a frying pan, sauté onions included in *C* over *low* heat for *10 minutes.* Add butter and drained mushrooms. *Cover* and cook for *20 minutes,* stirring *occasionally.*

4—Preheat broiler *10 minutes* before using. Grease *lightly* broiling-pan rack, to prevent meat from sticking.

5—Place meat on rack of broiling-pan. Place pan on broiler, with top of meat about *4 inches* from heat, and broil for *12 minutes.* Turn meat over, and broil other side for *10 minutes,* or until done to taste.

6—Remove fillets from broiler, remove picks, dot with butter and serve with the mushroom sauce.

STUFFED BEEF EYE OF ROUND

Lechón de Mechar Relleno

(Serves 10 to 12)

A—5½-pound eye of round beef roast (about 5 pounds, trimmed)

B—1 small onion, peeled ⎫
   2 cloves garlic, peeled ⎪
   2 sweet chili peppers, seeded ⎬ chopped
   ½ green pepper, seeded ⎭
   1 teaspoon whole dried *orégano*, crushed
   1 teaspoon capers | 1 tablespoon olive oil
   1 teaspoon salt | 1 teaspoon vinegar

C—2 ounces lean cured ham, washed and diced
   2 hard-cooked eggs, whole
   12 olives, stuffed with pimientos

D—2 tablespoons lard or vegetable oil

E—1½ quarts (6 cups) water | 1 tablespoon salt

F—1 medium onion, peeled ⎫
   ½ green pepper, seeded ⎪
   3 sweet chili peppers, seeded ⎬ coarsely chopped
   2 cloves garlic, peeled ⎪
   6 fresh *culantro* leaves ⎭
   ½ cup tomato sauce
   1½ pounds potatoes, peeled, washed and quartered
   1 teaspoon salt

1—Trim meat, wash and dry. With a knife, make a long, deep pocket from both ends to center of meat.

2—Mix ingredients included in *B* and stuff meat, alternating with ingredients included in *C*. Skewer or sew openings on both ends.

3—Heat fat in a *caldero* or heavy kettle. Add meat and brown **lightly** over *moderate-high* heat.

4—Add ingredients included in *E* and bring **rapidly** to a boil. Reduce heat to *moderate, cover,* and boil about *3 hours* or until meat is **almost** fork-tender. (**Halfway,** turn meat over.)

5—Add ingredients included in *F* and bring **rapidly** to a boil. Reduce heat to *moderate* and boil, *covered,* about *1 hour,* or until meat is fork-tender. Taste and adjust seasoning.

6—Remove meat and boil sauce, *uncovered,* until thickened to taste.

7—Cut meat in slices and arrange on a serving platter, garnished with the potatoes. Pour sauce, separately, in a deep dish.

BEEF EYE OF ROUND IN SHERRY

Lechón de Mechar en Jerez

(Serves 12 to 14)

A—1 large or 2 medium-size eye of round beef roasts

B—8 peppercorns (whole black peppers)
4 cloves garlic, peeled
1 tablespoon whole dried *orégano*
1 teaspoon salt for **each** pound of **trimmed** meat
1 tablespoon olive oil
1½ teaspoons vinegar

    crush and mix in a mortar

C—1 tablespoon lard or vegetable oil

D—1½ quarts (6 cups) water | 2 bay leaves

E—1½ pounds carrots, scraped and cut into ½ inch rounds
1 pound whole tiny white onions, peeled
2½ teaspoons salt
½ cup sherry
⅓ cup brown sugar, firmly packed
8 dry prunes, pitted
2 tablespoons seeded raisins

F—1 package (9 ounces) frozen *alcachofas* (artichoke hearts)

G—6 tablespoons cornstarch | ½ cup sherry

1—Trim, wash and dry eye of round. Rub with crushed ingredients included in *B*. Set in refrigerator over night.

2—In a large *caldero* or heavy kettle, heat fat included in *C* and brown eye of round **lightly** over *moderate-high* heat.

3—Add ingredients included in *D*, and bring **rapidly** to a boil. Reduce heat to *moderate, cover,* and boil about *3 hours,* or until eye of round is **almost** fork-tender. (**Halfway,** turn meat over.)

4—Add ingredients included in *E*, and bring **rapidly** to a boil. Reduce heat to *moderate, cover* and boil about *1 hour* or until eye of round is fork-tender. (**Halfway,** turn meat over.)

5 Add artichokes directly from the freezer. *Cover* and boil at *moderate* heat for *10 minutes.* Taste and adjust seasoning.

6—Meanwhile, dissolve cornstarch in ½ cup sherry and add to kettle. Mix and cook, *uncovered,* until sauce thickens to taste.

7—Remove eye of round, cut in slices and serve in a deep dish, together with sauce.

BEEF EYE OF ROUND IN BLACK SAUCE

Lechón de Mechar en Salsa Negra

(Serves 6 to 8)

A—4-pound eye of round beef roast (about 3½ pounds, trimmed)
2 tablespoons salt
2 large onions, peeled and sliced
6 tablespoons lard or vegetable oil
¼ cup vinegar

B—8 olives, stuffed with pimientos
1 teaspoon capers
¼ cup seeded raisins
4½ teaspoons sugar (*optional*)
1½ quarts (6 cups) water

C—4 medium onions, peeled and halved
1½ pounds potatoes, peeled and quartered
¼ teaspoon salt

1—Trim, wash and dry eye of round. Place in a *caldero* or heavy kettle, together with rest of ingredients included in *A*.

2—Brown meat and onions over *moderate-high* heat, turning meat and stirring onions *occasionally,* until onions are **very dark brown, without burning.** Discard onions.

3—Add ingredients included in *B* and bring **rapidly** to a boil over *high* heat. Reduce heat to *moderate, cover,* and boil for *1½ hours.* (**Halfway,** turn meat over.)

4—Add onions included in *C, cover* and boil for *1 hour.* (**Halfway,** turn meat over.)

5—Add rest of ingredients included in *C*, and bring **rapidly** to a boil. Reduce heat to *moderate* and boil about *1 hour,* or until meat is fork-tender.

6 —*Uncover,* taste, adjust seasoning and boil, *uncovered,* until sauce thickens to taste.

7—Cut meat in slices and serve in a deep dish, together with sauce.

VEAL A LA PARMESANA

Ternera a la Parmesana

(Serves 6)

A—1 pound veal cutlets, cut into 6 serving pieces

B—2 peppercorns (whole black peppers)
  2 cloves garlic, peeled
  ½ teaspoon whole dried *orégano*   crush and mix
  1¼ teaspoons salt   in a mortar
  1 teaspoon olive oil
  ½ teaspoon vinegar

C—3 eggs
  ½ teaspoon salt
  ¾ cup bread or cracker crumbs

D—½ cup olive oil

E—½ pound onions, peeled and sliced
1 can (1 pound 12 ounces) whole tomatoes
½ cup tomato sauce
¼ teaspoon salt
½ teaspoon whole dried *orégano,* crushed

F—½ cup freshly grated Parmesan cheese
¼ pound shredded Mozzarella cheese

1—Wipe meat with a damp cloth. Rub with crushed seasoning included in *B.*

2—Beat eggs *lightly,* together with salt included in *C.* Dip meat slices *gradually* into beaten eggs. Coat with crumbs and pound. Chill for *20 minutes,* to make coating firmer for frying.

3—In a frying pan, heat olive oil included in *D.* Add *gradually* breaded slices of meat and brown *lightly* on both sides over *moderate* heat. Remove from frying pan and set slices, one next to the other, in bottom of a 13 x 9 x 2-inch glass baking dish.

4—Add onion slices to the frying pan, and sauté in the left-over oil over *low* heat about *10 minutes,* or until tender, stirring **occasionally.**

5—Meanwhile, drain can of tomatoes over a sieve and break up tomatoes in pieces while in the sieve. Allow to drain **thoroughly.**

6—Add to frying pan drained tomatoes and rest of ingredients included in *E.* Mix well and pour mixture over the meat.

7—Sprinkle with half of the Parmesan cheese. Top with the shredded Mozzarella cheese and sprinkle with remaining Parmesan cheese.

8—Bake, *uncovered,* in preheated oven to *350°F.,* for *30 minutes.*

BREADED CALF'S BRAINS

Sesos Empanados

(Serves 6 to 8)

A—2 pounds of fresh calf's brains
1 quart (4 cups) water
1 tablespoon salt
1 tablespoon fresh lime juice or vinegar
1 bay leaf

B—½ teaspoon salt
¼ teaspoon ground pepper

C—2 eggs
¼ teaspoon salt

D—Bread or cracker crumbs (*to coat brains*)

E—Lard or vegetable oil (*for pan-frying*)

1—Wash brain and place in a saucepan, together with rest of ingredients included in A. Bring to a boil over *high* heat, *cover*, reduce heat to *low* and simmer for *20 minutes*. Drain and plunge into cold water. Drain again, remove outer membrane and cut brain into thin slices.

2—Season brains with salt and pepper included in B.

3—Beat eggs **lightly** together with salt included in C. Dip brain slices **gradually** into beaten eggs. Coat with crumbs and pound. Chill for *20 minutes*, to make coating firmer for frying.

4—Fry on both sides in the hot fat until brown. Remove and drain on absorbent paper.

CALF'S KIDNEY STEW

Riñones Guisados

(Serves 6 to 8)

A—2 pounds fresh calf's kidneys, trimmed and halved
1 quart (4 cups) water
1 fresh lime

B—1 ounce salt pork
1 ounce lean cured ham } washed and diced

C—1 green pepper, seeded
2 sweet chili peppers, seeded
1 onion, peeled
1 tomato
1 clove garlic, peeled
6 fresh *culantro* leaves
} chopped

D—1 teaspoon whole dried *orégano*
½ cup tomato sauce
2 teaspoons capers
8 olives, stuffed with pimientos
2½ teaspoons salt
3 cups water
1 pound potatoes, peeled and quartered

1—In a pot, bring to a boil water included in A. Wash kidneys twice, drain and add. Boil over *high* heat for *5 minutes.* Drain and cut kidneys into ½-inch cubes. Sprinkle with juice of fresh lime.

2—In a *caldero* or heavy kettle, brown *rapidly* salt pork and ham. Reduce heat to *low* and sauté ingredients included in C, for *10 minutes* or until tender, stirring **occasionally.**

3—Add kidney pieces and ingredients included in D, mix, and bring *rapidly* to a boil. Reduce heat to *low*, cover, and cook about *1½ hours*, or until kidney pieces are fork-tender.

4—*Uncover*, and cook until sauce thickens to taste.

CALF'S LIVER STEW

Hígado Guisado

(Serves 4)

A—1 pound fresh calf's liver, with membrane and tubes or veins removed
1 fresh lime

B—1 ounce salt pork
2 ounces lean cured ham } washed and diced

C—1 small onion, peeled
½ green pepper, seeded
2 sweet chili peppers, seeded
1 clove garlic, peeled } chopped

D—¼ cup tomato sauce
⅓ cup canned whole tomatoes
8 olives, stuffed with pimientos
1 teaspoon capers
2 tablespoons seeded raisins
¼ teaspoon whole dried *orégano*
2 teaspoons salt
4½ teaspoons vinegar
2 cups water
½ pound potatoes, peeled and quartered

1—In a saucepan, set calf's liver in water to cover, with lime juice and bring **rapidly** to a boil. Drain and cut into cubes.

2—In a *caldero* or heavy kettle, brown **rapidly** salt pork and ham. Reduce heat to *low* and sauté ingredients included in C until tender.

3—Add liver and ingredients included in D, mix, and bring **rapidly** to a boil. Turn heat to *moderate, cover,* and boil for *1 hour.*

4—*Uncover,* and boil until sauce thickens to taste.

BREADED CALF'S LIVER
Hígado Empanado
(Serves 4)

A—1 pound fresh calf's liver, trimmed
Juice of 1 fresh lime

B—3 peppercorns (whole black peppers) ⎫
1 clove garlic, peeled   ⎪
¼ teaspoon whole dried *orégano*   ⎬ crush and mix
1 teaspoon salt   ⎪ in a mortar
1 tablespoon vinegar   ⎭

C—1 egg, lightly beaten ⎫
¼ teaspoon salt   ⎬ mixed
1 tablespoon water   ⎭

D—1 cup bread or cracker crumbs

E—Lard or vegetable oil (*for pan-frying*)

1—In a saucepan, set calf's liver in water to cover, with lime juice and bring **rapidly** to a boil. Drain and cut into thin slices.

2—Rub well liver slices with seasoning included in B.

3—Dip liver slices into beaten egg. Drain and coat with crumbs. Pound crumbs **firmly**. Chill for *20 minutes*, to make coating firmer for frying.

4—Heat fat in a frying pan and brown breaded liver over *moderate* heat for about *10 minutes*, or until no blood emerges when pierced with a fork. Drain on absorbent paper.

SMOTHERED BEEF TONGUE

Lengua Estofada

(Serves 8)

A—4-pound fresh beef tongue
Water—(measure by **quarts** to cover tongue freely)
Salt—(use **1 teaspoon** salt for **each** quart of water)

B—4 peppercorns (whole black peppers)
1 teaspoon whole dried *orégano,* crushed
3 cloves garlic, peeled
1 tablespoon salt
1 tablespoon vinegar
2 bay leaves
1 quart (4 cups) water

C—1½ cups sweet or dry wine (see Note)
¼ cup sugar
12 dry prunes, pitted
1 pound potatoes, peeled and cut into pieces
1 pound onions, peeled and sliced
½ teaspoon salt

1—Scrub the tongue with a vegetable brush under warm running water. Drain and dry. Place in a large deep kettle. Add water and salt included in *A*.

2—Bring **rapidly** to a boil, reduce heat to *low*, partially *cover* kettle, and *simmer* for *2 hours.*

3—Remove tongue and plunge into cold water. Remove from water and allow to cool **slightly.** Trim off bone and gristle at thick end. Peel tongue.

4—Place tongue in a large *caldero* or heavy kettle. Add ingredients included in *B* and bring **rapidly** to a boil. Reduce heat to *low, cover,* and **simmer** until tongue is **almost** fork-tender.

5—Add ingredients included in *C* and bring **rapidly** to a boil. Reduce heat to *low, cover,* and cook until tongue is fork-tender. Taste and adjust seasoning.

6—Remove tongue. Boil sauce over *moderate* heat until sauce thickens to taste.

7—Cut tongue in slices and arrange on a serving platter, garnished with potatoes. Serve sauce in a deep dish.

Note: Sweet wine imparts a distinctive flavor to the recipe, but it can be replaced, according to taste, by Burgundy or any other good dry red wine. Rest of ingredients included in C are optional.

STUFFED BEEF TONGUE

Lengua Rellena

(Serves 8)

A—4-pound fresh beef tongue
  Water—(measure by **quarts** to cover tongue freely)
  Salt—(use **1 teaspoon** salt for **each** quart of water)

B—½ green pepper, seeded ⎤
  1 tomato
  2 sweet chili peppers, seeded ⎬ chopped
  1 clove garlic, peeled
  1 small onion, peeled ⎦
  1 ounce salt pork ⎫ washed and chopped
  2 ounces lean cured ham ⎭
  6 olives, stuffed with pimientos
  1 teaspoon whole dried *orégano*, crushed
  1 teaspoon capers
  1¼ teaspoons salt
  1 teaspoon olive oil
  1 teaspoon vinegar

C—½ cup lard or vegetable oil

D—5 cups water
  ½ cup tomato sauce
  ½ green pepper, seeded ⎤
  1 onion, peeled
  2 sweet chili peppers, seeded ⎬ coarsely chopped
  6 fresh *culantro* leaves ⎦
  1 pound potatoes, peeled and quartered
  2 teaspoons salt

1—Scrub the tongue with a vegetable brush under warm running water. Drain and dry. Place in a large deep kettle. Add water and salt included in A.

2—Bring **rapidly** to a boil, reduce heat to *low*, partially *cover* kettle, and *simmer* for 2 *hours*.

3—Remove tongue and plunge into cold water. Remove from water and allow to cool **slightly.** Trim off bone and gristle at thick end. Peel tongue.

4—With a knife, make a deep pocket from thick end towards tip of tongue.

5—Mix ingredients included in B and stuff tongue. Skewer or sew opening closed.

6—In a *caldero* or heavy kettle, heat fat included in C, and brown tongue **lightly.** Drain fat from *caldero*.

7—Add ingredients included in D and bring **rapidly** to a boil. Reduce heat to *low*, *cover*, and *simmer* until tongue is fork-tender. Taste and adjust seasoning.

8—Remove tongue. Boil sauce over *moderate* heat until sauce thickens to taste.

9—Cut tongue in slices, arrange on a serving platter, and garnish with potatoes. Serve sauce in a deep dish.

BARBECUED PIG
Lechón Asado
(Serves 12 to 15)

Barbecued pig is the customary dish for picnics and other open-air parties. It is cooked out-of-doors over an open fire of live charcoal built on layers of stone (see Jacket).

Green plantains are peeled and roasted over the stones, to be eaten with the pig.

Aji-li-mójili, (see Index) a sour garlic sauce, is the traditional dressing to be served with barbecued pig.

A—1 25-pound suckling pig, ready to cook

B—**Crush and mix in a mortar:**
    24 cloves garlic, peeled
    3 tablespoons whole dried *orégano*
    1 tablespoon peppercorns (whole black peppers)
    ¾ cup salt

C—½ cup *jugo de naranja agria* (sour orange juice) (see Glossary)

1—Mix *thoroughly* B and C ingredients.

2—Make deep gashes in pig on the neck, just under the lower jaw, on the loin, legs, shoulders, and over the ribs. Rub seasoning into the gashes, as well as inside and outside the pig.

3—Cover with a cheese cloth and set overnight in a cool place.

4—Barbecue the pig the traditional way, by passing a pole through its body. A slit is cut just under the tail and the pole goes through it and out the mouth opening (see Jacket). Tie front legs very tightly around the pole. Do the same with the hind legs, stretching them as far as possible. Place the pig over an open fire of live charcoal placed over layers of stone, resting both ends of the pole on Y-posts. Rotate pole **constantly** and **slowly** in order to roast pig evenly, and baste frequently with *Achiote Coloring.* (see Index)

5—Cook about 7 hours, or until meat reaches the **well-done** stage, when **all** pink color disappears and meat becomes gray.

6—Cut in serving pieces and serve with *Aji-li-mójili* sauce.

AJI-LI-MOJILI SAUCE
Ají-li-mójili

A—Crush and mix in a mortar:
8 large cloves garlic, peeled
8 peppercorns (whole black peppers)
12 sweet chili peppers, seeded

B—½ cup vinegar
½ cup lime juice
4 teaspoons salt
1 cup olive oil

1—Mix *A* and *B* ingredients *thoroughly*. Stir well when serving.

GANDINGA
(Serves 6 to 8)

A—4 pounds hog's *gandinga* (liver, kidney and heart)

B—2 ounces salt pork ⎫
 2 ounces lean cured ham ⎭ washed and diced
 1 onion, peeled ⎫
 1 green pepper, seeded ⎪
 2 sweet chili peppers, seeded ⎬ chopped
 1 clove garlic, peeled ⎪
 4 fresh *culantro* leaves ⎭
 ½ teaspoon whole dried *orégano*
 2 tablespoons vegetable oil or *Achiote Coloring* (see page xvi)

C—½ cup tomato sauce
 1 tomato, halved
 10 olives, stuffed with pimientos
 1 tablespoon capers
 1 tablespoon vinegar
 3½ teaspoons salt
 3 cups water
 1 pound potatoes, peeled and cubed

1—Wash and trim *gandinga*. In a pot, cover liver and heart with water, bring *rapidly* to a boil, and drain. In another pot, cover kidneys with water, bring *rapidly* to a boil, and drain. **Repeat.** Chop *gandinga* and **reserve.**

2—In a *caldero* or heavy kettle, brown salt pork and cured ham *rapidly*. Reduce heat to *low*, add rest of ingredients included in *B*, and sauté for *10 minutes*, stirring *occasionally*.

3—Add chopped *gandinga* and ingredients included in *C*. Bring *rapidly* to a boil, *cover*, and cook over *low* heat about 2 *hours*, or until fork-tender.

4—*Uncover*, and cook until sauce thickens to taste.

ROAST LEG OF PORK (FRESH HAM), LAMB OR VEAL A LA CRIOLLA

Pernil al Horno

I   Preparation of meat day before roasting:

1—Remove skin and excess fat.

2—Weigh meat and jot down its exact weight, since both quantity of seasoning and time required for roasting depends upon its weight.

3—Wash meat *rapidly* under running water, drain and wipe dry with absorbent paper.

4—Place meat in roasting pan, **fat side up.** Score top of roast in diamonds.

5—Prepare seasoning according to weight of trimmed roast, following recipe for seasoning given on next page. Season roast and set in refrigerator.

Seasoning for 4 to 5-pound trimmed roast

6 peppercorns (whole black peppers)
6 cloves garlic, peeled
1 teaspoon whole dried *orégano*
1½ tablespoons olive oil
1½ tablespoons vinegar
1 teaspoon salt for **each** pound of roast

} crush and mix in a mortar

Seasoning for 6 to 7-pound trimmed roast

8 peppercorns (whole black peppers)
8 cloves garlic, peeled
2 teaspoons whole dried *orégano*
2 tablespoons olive oil
2 tablespoons vinegar
1 teaspoon salt for **each** pound of roast

} crush and mix in a mortar

Seasoning for 8 to 10-pound trimmed roast

10 peppercorns (whole black peppers)
12 cloves garlic, peeled
1 tablespoon whole dried *orégano*
3 tablespoons olive oil
3 tablespoons vinegar
1 teaspoon salt for **each** pound of roast

} crush and mix in a mortar

II Roasting:

1—Remove roast from refrigerator ½ *hour* before cooking time.

2—Drain off any liquid that may have seeped from meat and pour liquid over meat before putting it in the oven.

3—Insert meat thermometer **carefully** into center of meat, **without** letting it rest against bone or fat.

4—Preheat oven and roast meat according to the following chart:

TIMETABLE FOR ROASTING

Roast	Oven Temperature	Approximate Minutes per Pound	Meat Thermometer Temperature
Leg of Veal	325°F	30	170°F
Leg of Lamb	325°F	35	180°F
Leg of Pork (Fresh Ham)	350°F	35 (see **Note**)	185°F

Note: Pork meat must be thoroughly cooked to the **well-done** stage.

III Gravy:

A—3 cups liquid

B—¼ cup fat | ¼ cup flour

1—Drain liquid from roasting pan into a glass measuring cup. Fat or drippings from the roast will rise to the surface.

2—Skim off fat, measure ¼ cup and **reserve.** (If drippings are scanty, use butter to complete the quantity of fat needed.)

3—Measure liquid. (If liquid does not yield the amount included in A, complete with water.) Pour liquid back into roasting pan and bring **rapidly** to a boil.

4—In a saucepan, stir together *slowly* the measured fat and flour included in B, *carefully* smoothing out lumps.

5—Turn heat to *moderate,* and *gradually* stir in the hot liquid, until it boils and thickens. Taste and adjust seasoning.

6—Remove from heat, strain, and serve hot.

POT ROAST WITH WINE

Pernil con Vino al Caldero

(Serves 6)

A—4-pound butt end of leg of pork (fresh ham) (see Note 1 on the use of **lamb** or **veal**)

B—4 peppercorns (whole black peppers)
4 large cloves garlic, peeled
1 teaspoon whole dried *orégano*   crush and mix
4 teaspoons salt   in a mortar
1 tablespoon olive oil
1 tablespoon vinegar

C—3 cups water
½ pound onions, peeled and sliced
2 bay leaves

D—1½ cups sweet or dry wine (see Note 2)
¼ cup sugar | 6 dry prunes, pitted
1 tablespoon seeded raisins | ½ teaspoon salt

E—2 pounds potatoes, peeled and quartered

1—Remove skin and excess fat from meat. Wash and dry. Score top of meat in diamonds.

2—Rub well into meat the crushed seasoning included in *B*. **Do not pierce meat.** Set in refrigerator **overnight.**

3—In a large *caldero* or heavy kettle, brown meat **lightly** over *high* heat.

4—Add ingredients included in *C* and bring **rapidly** to a boil. *Cover*, reduce heat to *moderate* and boil for *2 hours*. (**Halfway,** turn meat over.)

5—Add ingredients included in *D* and *E* and bring **rapidly** to a boil. Reduce heat to *moderate, cover,* and boil about *1 hour*, or until pork is **well-done** and thoroughly cooked.

6—*Uncover*, taste and adjust seasoning. Boil, *uncovered,* until sauce thickens to taste.

7—Set meat and potatoes on a serving platter. Drain sauce, skim off fat, and serve in a deep dish.

Note 1: Lamb or veal can substitute pork, adjusting cooking time accordingly.

Note 2: Sweet wine imparts a distinctive flavor to the recipe, but it can be replaced, according to taste, by any dry wine. Sugar included in D is optional.

POT ROAST WITH VEGETABLES
Pernil al Caldero
(Serves 6)

A—4-pound butt end of leg of pork (fresh ham) (see Note on the use of **lamb** or **veal**)

B—4 peppercorns (whole black peppers)
4 cloves garlic, peeled
1 teaspoon whole dried *orégano*   crush and mix
4 teaspoons salt   in a mortar
½ teaspoon olive oil
1 tablespoon vinegar

C—1½ quarts (6 cups) water
2 bay leaves
2 onions, peeled and halved

D—1 pound carrots, scraped and cut into ½-inch rounds
1 pound potatoes, peeled and quartered
½ teaspoon salt

1—Remove skin and excess fat from meat. Wash and dry. Score top of meat in diamonds.

2—Rub well into meat the crushed seasoning included in *B*. **Do not pierce meat.** Set in refrigerator **overnight.**

3—In a large *caldero* or heavy kettle, brown meat **lightly** over *high* heat.

4—Add ingredients included in *C* and bring **rapidly** to a boil. *Cover,* reduce heat to *moderate,* and boil for *2 hours.* (**Halfway,** turn meat over.)

5—Add ingredients included in *D*, and bring **rapidly** to a boil. Reduce heat to *moderate* and boil about *1 hour,* or until pork is **well-done** and thoroughly cooked.

6—*Uncover,* taste and adjust seasoning. Boil, *uncovered,* until sauce thickens to taste.

Note: Lamb or veal can substitute pork, adjusting cooking time accordingly.

STUFFED ROAST IN BLACK SAUCE

Pernil Mechado en Salsa Negra

(Serves 6)

A—4-pound butt end of leg of pork (fresh ham) (see Note on use of **lamb** or **veal**)

B—4 peppercorns (whole black pepper) ⎫
4 cloves garlic, peeled
1 teaspoon whole dried *orégano*   crush and mix
4 teaspoons salt   in a mortar
1 tablespoon olive oil
1 tablespoon vinegar ⎭

C—2 ounces lean cured ham, washed and diced
6 dry prunes, pitted and halved
12 olives, stuffed with pimientos

D—1½ cups brown sugar, firmly packed
3 bottles (12 ounces each) *malta* beverage (see Glossary)

1—Remove skin and excess fat from meat. Wash, dry and score top of meat in diamonds. Rub into meat the crushed seasoning included in *B*. Set in refrigerator **overnight.**

2—With a sharp knife, make deep incisions, about ½-inch wide, on different parts of the meat. Stuff each incision with alternate ingredients included in *C*.

3—In a large *caldero* or heavy kettle, add meat and ingredients included in *D*. Bring **rapidly** to a boil. Reduce heat to *moderate, cover,* and boil about 3 *hours,* or until meat is **well-done** and thoroughly cooked. (**Halfway,** turn meat over.)

4—Remove meat and allow to cool **slightly.** Pour sauce into a glass measuring cup and skim off fat.

5—Cut meat in slices and arrange on serving platter. Serve sauce in a separate dish.

Note: Lamb or veal can substitute pork, adjusting cooking time accordingly.

CHOPS A LA JARDINERA
Chuletas a la Jardinera

A—4 pounds ½-inch thick chops (pork, lamb, or veal)

B—1 clove garlic, peeled
½ teaspoon whole dried *orégano*
2 teaspoons salt   } crush and mix
1 teaspoon olive oil   } in a mortar
½ teaspoon vinegar

C—1 can (1 pound 12 ounces) whole tomatoes
1 cup onions, finely chopped
1 bay leaf
4 peppercorns (whole black peppers)
1 teaspoon salt
1 tablespoon sugar

D—1 can (1 pound 1 ounce) string beans
1 can (1 pound 1 ounce) whole kernel corn

1—Trim off **all** fat from chops. Wash chops, drain, dry and rub well with seasoning included in *B*.

2—In a large *caldero* or heavy kettle, brown chops *lightly*.

3—Add ingredients included in *C*, **including** liquid from can of whole tomatoes.

4—Bring to a boil over *moderate-high* heat. *Cover,* turn heat to *moderate,* and boil for *30 minutes*.

5—*Uncover,* remove peppercorns (whole black peppers) and boil for *30 minutes*.

6—Drain string beans and corn and add. Mix and boil for *10 minutes*.

7—Serve chops with vegetables and sauce.

BREADED CHOPS
Chuletas Empanadas
(Serves 6)

A—2 pounds lean pork chops, trimmed

B—4 peppercorns (whole black peppers) ⎤
  1 large clove garlic, peeled   ⎥
  1 teaspoon whole dried *orégano*   ⎬ crush and mix
  2 teaspoons salt   ⎥ in a mortar
  1 teaspoon vinegar or fresh lime juice ⎦

C—2 eggs
  ¼ teaspoon salt

D—1 cup bread or cracker crumbs

1—Wash chops, drain and dry. Rub well with seasoning included in *B*.

2—Beat eggs *lightly* with salt.

3—Dip chops in beaten eggs. Drain and coat with crumbs. Pound crumbs firmly over chops.

4—Grease a rectangular glass baking dish. Arrange chops in dish and bake in preheated oven to 350°F. for *1 hour*.

SMOTHERED YOUNG KID

Cabro Estofado

(Serves 12)

A—5 pounds tender kid meat, trimmed
½ cup *jugo de naranja agria* (sour orange juice) (see Glossary)

B—4 cloves garlic, peeled
1 tablespoon whole dried *orégano*
½ teaspoon ground pepper   crush and mix
2 tablespoons salt   in a mortar
1 tablespoon vinegar
1 tablespoon olive oil

C—24 olives, stuffed with pimientos
2 tablespoons capers
1 pound onions, peeled and sliced | 3 bay leaves
12 dry prunes, pitted | 2 cups water

D—2 cups sweet or dry wine
⅓ cup sugar (*optional*)
1½ pounds potatoes, peeled and cut in pieces

1—Wash meat and cut into 2-inch chunks. Soak in sour orange juice and set in refrigerator for several hours. Drain and rinse *rapidly* in cool water.

2—Place kid meat in a large *caldero* or heavy kettle and rub with seasoning included in *B*.

3—Add ingredients included in *C*, bring *rapidly* to a boil, *cover*, and boil over *moderate* heat for *2 hours*.

4—Add ingredients included in *D*, *cover*, and boil over *moderate* heat about *45 minutes*, or until meat is fork-tender.

5—*Uncover*, and boil over *moderate* heat until sauce thickens to taste.

KID FRICASSÉE

Cabro en Fricasé
(Serves 6 to 8)

A—4 pounds tender kid meat, trimmed
½ cup fresh *jugo de naranja agria* (sour orange juice) (see
Glossary)

B—3 cloves garlic, peeled
2 teaspoons whole dried *orégano*
¼ teaspoon ground pepper
4½ teaspoons salt
1 tablespoon vinegar
} crush and mix
in a mortar

C—1 ounce salt pork
2 ounces lean cured ham
} washed and diced

D—1 pound onions, peeled and sliced
2 bay leaves
½ cup tomato sauce
1 can (1 pound 12 ounces) whole tomatoes
1 can (1 pound) green peas (*Petit-Pois*)
12 olives, stuffed with pimientos
2 tablespoons capers

E—1 pound potatoes, peeled and quartered

1—Wash meat and cut into 2-inch chunks. Soak in the sour
orange juice and set in refrigerator for several hours. Drain
and rinse *rapidly* in cool water.

2—Rub well into pieces of meat the seasoning included in B.

3—In a *caldero* or heavy kettle, brown *rapidly* salt pork and ham.

4—Add ingredients included in D, **including** liquid from cans of
tomatoes and peas.

5—Add kid meat, mix, and bring *rapidly* to a boil. Turn heat to
moderate, cover, and boil for *2 hours.*

6—Add potatoes, *cover,* and boil about *30 minutes,* or until meat
is fork-tender.

7—*Uncover.* Taste and adjust seasoning. Boil over *moderate*
heat until sauce thickens to taste.

SMOTHERED RABBIT
Conejo Estofado

(Serves 6)

A—3 pounds cut-up ready-to-cook rabbit pieces

B—12 cloves garlic, peeled ⎱ minced
    1 onion, peeled ⎰
    1 can (8 ounces) tomato sauce
    1 tablespoon salt
    1 cup olive oil
    ¼ cup vinegar
    1 bay leaf
    12 olives, stuffed with pimientos
    2 tablespoons capers

C—2 pounds potatoes, peeled and cubed
    1 teaspoon salt
    3 cups white wine

1—Wash and dry rabbit pieces and place in a large *caldero* or heavy kettle.

2—Add ingredients included in B, mix, and bring **rapidly** to a boil. *Cover* and *simmer* over *low* heat about *1½ hours,* or until rabbit meat is **almost** fork-tender.

3—Add ingredients included in C, mix, and bring **rapidly** to a boil. Reduce heat to *low, cover,* and cook until potatoes are done and rabbit meat is tender.

4—*Uncover,* and boil over *moderate* heat until sauce thickens to taste.

CHAPTER III *Poultry*

Poultry

TABLE FOR SEASONING CHICKEN
(Adobo)

This seasoning gives a characteristic and distinctive Caribbean flavor to chicken.
Dressed-weight chicken means chicken plucked, singed and drawn, with head, neck and feet removed.
The first horizontal line indicates the dressed-weight of chicken in pounds, **either whole or in pieces.**
The vertical lines under each weight indicate the adequate seasoning.

To prepare seasoning — **Crush and mix in a mortar:** peppercorns (whole black peppers), peeled cloves garlic, whole dried *orégano* and salt. Add olive oil and vinegar or lime juice and mix well. Rub chicken with this seasoning.

Dressed-weight chicken, in pounds	1	1¼	1½	1¾	2	2¼	2½	2¾	3	3¼	3½
Peppercorns (whole black peppers)	1	1	2	2	2	3	3	3	4	4	4
Cloves garlic, peeled	1 small	1 small	1 medium	1 medium	1 large	1 large	2 small	2 small	2 medium	2 medium	2 large
Whole dried *orégano*, in teaspoons	½	½	¾	¾	1	1	1¼	1¼	1½	1½	1½
Salt, in teaspoons	1	1¼	1½	1¾	2	2¼	2½	2¾	3	3¼	3½
Olive oil, in teaspoons	¾	¾	1	1	1¼	1¼	1½	1½	1¾	1¾	2
Vinegar or lime juice, in teaspoons	¼	¼	¼	¼	½	½	½	½	¾	¾	1

CARIBBEAN CHICKEN DELIGHT
Pollo Delicioso

A—3 to 3½ pounds dressed-weight whole chicken, washed and dried

B—**Seasoning:**
Weigh chicken and season according to **Table for Seasoning Chicken** at beginning of chapter. Set in refrigerator **overnight.**

C—1 pound medium-sized onions, peeled and halved
2 bay leaves

D—1 can (8½ ounces) green peas (*Petit-Pois*), drained
2 ounces (4 tablespoons) butter
¼ cup dry sherry

E—1 can (4 ounces) pimientos (*for garnishing*)

1—Arrange onions in bottom of a pot with a **heavy lid.** Add bay leaves.

2—Place chicken, **breast down,** in pot, and *cover.*

3—Turn heat to *low, cover,* and cook about *1½ hours,* or until done (drumstick and thigh should move easily and fleshy part of drumstick feels soft when pressed. Drumstick, pierced with a cooking fork, renders no liquid.).

4—Remove chicken and bay leaves from pot. Cut chicken into pieces and separate meat from bones. Shred meat into large chunks and add to pot.

5—Add ingredients included in *D,* mix, and cook, *uncovered,* over *moderate* heat, until butter melts.

6—Serve in a deep dish. Heat pimientos in their juice, drain, cut in strips, and garnish.

CHICKEN IN WINE "A LA CRIOLLA"

Pollo en Vino Dulce
(Serves 6)

A—3½ pounds chicken pieces, washed and dried

B—**Seasoning:**
  4 peppercorns (whole black peppers)⎫
  3 cloves garlic, peeled   ⎪
  1½ teaspoons whole dried *orégano*   ⎬ crush and mix
  3½ teaspoons salt   ⎪ in a mortar
  2 teaspoons olive oil   ⎪
  1 teaspoon vinegar   ⎭

C—2 ounces (4 tablespoons) butter

D—1 cup water | 10 olives, stuffed with pimientos
  3 bay leaves | 1 pound tiny white onions, peeled
  1 teaspoon salt | 1½ pounds small potatoes, peeled
  1 teaspoon capers |

E—1½ cups sweet white wine ⎫
  ½ cup sugar   ⎬ (see Note)
  10 dry prunes, pitted   ⎭
  2 tablespoons seeded raisins

F—2 tablespoons cornstarch
  1 can (4 ounces) pimientos (*for garnishing*)

1—Rub chicken pieces with seasoning included in *B*.

2—Melt butter in a *caldero* or heavy kettle. Brown chicken **lightly** over *moderate-high* heat.

3—Add ingredients included in *D*, and bring **rapidly** to a boil. Reduce heat to *moderate, cover,* and boil for *30 minutes.*

4—Add ingredients included in *E*, and bring *rapidly* to a boil. Reduce heat to *moderate, cover,* and boil for *15 minutes.*

5—*Uncover,* and boil for *30 minutes.*

6—In a cup, dissolve cornstarch in part of sauce and pour back into *caldero*. Boil until sauce thickens to taste. Serve in a deep platter, garnished with pimientos slices.

Note: Sweet wine and sugar impart a distinctive flavor to the recipe, but wine can be replaced, according to taste, by any dry wine, and sugar is optional.

CHICKEN FRICASSÉE
Pollo en Fricasé
(Serves 6)

A—2½ pounds chicken pieces, washed and dried

B—1 tablespoon lard or vegetable oil
1 ounce salt pork   ⎫
2 ounces lean cured ham ⎬ washed and diced
1 teaspoon whole dried *orégano*
2 cloves garlic, peeled   ⎫
1 onion, peeled |
1 green pepper, seeded   ⎬ chopped
2 sweet chili peppers, seeded |
6 fresh *culantro* leaves   ⎭

C—12 olives, stuffed with pimientos
1 teaspoon capers | 8 dry prunes, pitted
1 tablespoon vinegar | ½ cup tomato sauce
2 bay leaves | 3½ teaspoons salt
¼ cup seeded raisins |
1 pound potatoes, peeled and cubed

D—1 can (1 pound) green peas (*Petit-Pois*)

E—1 ounce (2 tablespoons) butter

1—In a *caldero* or heavy kettle, heat fat and brown **rapidly** the salt pork and cured ham, stirring **occasionally.** Reduce heat to *low*, add rest of ingredients included in *B* and sauté for *10 minutes*, stirring **occasionally.**

2—Add chicken pieces, mix and cook for *2 or 3 minutes* over *moderate* heat. Add ingredients included in *C* and mix. Drain liquid from can of peas into a measuring cup, add enough water to measure 2½ cups and add to kettle. **Reserve** peas.

3—Bring **rapidly** to a boil. Reduce heat to *moderate, cover* and boil for *45 minutes*. Taste and adjust seasoning.

4—Add butter and drained peas and boil, *uncovered*, over *moderate* heat until sauce thickens to taste.

GOLDEN BRONZE CHICKENS

Pollos Bronceados

(Serves 12)

A—2 large whole chickens, about 3 to 3½ pounds dressed-weight
Seasoning: See **Table for Seasoning Chicken** at beginning of chapter.

B—¼ pound butter, clarified (see Instruction 2)

C—1½ pounds small potatoes, peeled
1 pound tiny white onions, peeled

D—1 can (1 pound 12 ounces) whole tomatoes, liquid included
1 teaspoon salt
12 olives, stuffed with pimientos
1 tablespoon tiny capers
3 bay leaves
1 cup sweet red wine

E—6 tablespoons cornstarch
1 cup sweet red wine

F—1 can (1 pound) green peas (*Petit-Pois*), drained
1 can (6 ounces) Broiled-in-Butter Mushrooms, drained

1—Wash chickens and season according to **Table for Seasoning Chicken** at beginning of chapter.

2—Simmer butter in a small saucepan until it melts. Remove and when the whey (milky) sediment has separated from the melted fat, pour off the clear fat (the *clarified butter*) into a large *caldero* or heavy kettle. Discard the sediment.

3—In this butter, brown *lightly* one chicken at a time. Remove from *caldero*.

4—Cover bottom of *caldero* with potatoes, surrounded with onions.

5—Place the chickens over them, **breast down.**

6—Distribute in the *caldero* the ingredients included in *D*. Bring *rapidly* to a boil. Reduce heat to *moderate, cover* and boil for *1½ hours.*

7—Dissolve cornstarch in wine included in *E* and pour into the *caldero*. Mix and cook, *uncovered*, over *moderate* heat, basting **occasionally,** about *30 minutes*, or until chickens are done. Add ingredients included in *F* and cook for *5 minutes.*

8—Remove chickens and cut into serving pieces. Slice white meat and arrange attractively on center of serving platter surrounded by drumsticks, thighs and wings, garnished with potatoes and onions. Serve sauce separately in a deep dish.

Note: Left-over sauce can be used with boiled spaghetti or linguine.

SMOTHERED CHICKEN

Pollo Estofado

(Serves 6 to 8)

A—4-pound dressed-weight whole chicken, cut into serving pieces or 4 pounds large chicken pieces

B—1 can (8 ounces) tomato sauce
5 teaspoons salt
1 cup olive oil
¼ cup vinegar
12 olives, stuffed with pimientos
1 teaspoon capers
12 cloves garlic, peeled and crushed
1 onion, peeled and sliced
2 pounds potatoes, peeled and cubed
1 cup sweet white wine or dry sherry

1—Wash chicken pieces and place in a *caldero* or heavy kettle, together with ingredients included in *B*.

2—Bring to a boil over *high* heat. Reduce heat to *moderate, cover,* and boil for *1 hour.*

3—*Uncover*, and boil about *30 minutes*, or until chicken is done and sauce thickens to taste.

CHICKEN IN SHERRY
Pollo al Jerez

(Serves 6)

A—3½ pounds large chicken pieces
3 cups sweet or dry sherry

B—¼ pound butter

C—1 pound tiny white onions, peeled
1 can (1 pound 12 ounces) whole tomatoes
2 bay leaves
4 teaspoons salt

D—8 olives, stuffed with pimientos

1—Wash and drain chicken pieces. Place in a deep glass vessel and add sherry. *Cover* and set **overnight** in refrigerator.

2—Remove from refrigerator, drain off wine, and **reserve.**

3—Melt half of the butter in a large *caldero* or heavy kettle over *moderate* heat. Add chicken pieces and brown **very lightly.**

4—Reduce heat to *low* and add remaining butter. Add ingredients included in C. Add reserved sherry. Bring **rapidly** to a boil. Reduce heat to *low, cover,* and cook for *1 hour.*

5—Add stuffed olives. Taste and adjust seasoning. Turn heat to *moderate* and cook, *uncovered,* about *1 hour,* or until chicken is done.

6—Serve in a deep dish with the sauce.

SWEET-AND-SOUR CHICKEN

Pollo en Agridulce

(Serves 6)

A — 3½-4 pounds dressed-weight whole chicken

B — **Seasoning:**

4 peppercorns (whole black peppers)
2 cloves garlic, peeled
1½ teaspoons whole dried *orégano*   crushed and mixed
3 to 4 teaspoons salt   in a mortar
2 teaspoons olive oil
1½ teaspoons vinegar

C — 1 can (5 ounces) *chorizos* (Spanish Sausages)

D — 2 ounces (4 tablespoons) butter

E — 1 cup brown sugar, firmly packed
¼ cup vinegar

1 — Wash and dry chicken. Rub seasoning inside and out *several hours* before cooking. Remove casings from *chorizos* and cut into ¼-inch slices. **Reserve.** Discard lard from can.

2 — In a heavy kettle, melt butter over *low* heat. Turn heat to *moderate high*, add chicken and cook for 4 minutes, turning chicken over on both sides.

3 — Reduce heat to *low* and set chicken **breast down.** Add sugar on sides of chicken and stir well, until **completely** dissolved. Add vinegar and *chorizos*, mix, *cover* and cook for *45 minutes.*

4 — Turn chicken **breast up,** *cover* and cook for *30 minutes,* or until chicken is done.

5 — Remove chicken from kettle. Strain sauce through a colander into a large glass measuring cup and **reserve** *chorizos.* As soon as fat rises to the top, skim off fat and discard. Add chicken, sauce and *chorizos* to kettle, heat and serve.

CHICKEN EN CASSEROLE
Pollo al Caldero
(Serves 6)

A—3-pound dressed-weight whole chicken or 3 pounds chicken pieces

B—**Seasoning:**
4 peppercorns (whole black peppers)
2 cloves garlic, peeled
1½ teaspoons whole dried *orégano*   crush and mix
1 tablespoon salt   in a mortar
1½ teaspoons olive oil
1 teaspoon vinegar

C—¼ pound butter

D—1 can (1 pound 12 ounces) whole tomatoes
1 pound tiny white onions, peeled
1½ teaspoons salt
1½ pounds potatoes, peeled and cubed

E—1 can (1 pound 1 ounce) green peas (*Petit-Pois*)

F—1 cup dry sherry

1—Wash and dry chicken. Rub seasoning into chicken **several hours** before cooking.

2—Melt butter over *moderate* heat in a **caldero** or casserole. Add chicken and brown **very lightly.**

3—Drain peas, add liquid and **reserve** peas. Add rest of ingredients included in *D.*

4—Cook over *high* heat until boiling. Reduce heat to *moderate, cover,* and cook for *45 minutes.*

5—Add peas and wine, *cover,* and cook about *30 minutes,* or until chicken is done. *Uncover,* and cook until sauce thickens to taste.

CHICKEN WITH ONIONS

Pollo Encebollado

(Serves 6)

A—1 stewing chicken, cut into serving pieces
Seasoning: See **Table for Seasoning Chicken** at beginning of chapter.

B—1½ pounds small potatoes, peeled
1 pound medium onions, peeled and sliced
½ cup *Consommé*
2 bay leaves

C—2 ounces (4 tablespoons) butter

1—Weigh chicken pieces. Wash and season according to **Table for Seasoning Chicken.**

2—Place chicken pieces in a *caldero* or heavy kettle. Add ingredients included in B. Bring **rapidly** to a boil. Reduce heat to *low, cover* and cook for *1 hour.*

3—*Uncover,* add butter included in C and cook about *30 minutes,* or until chicken is done.

CREAMED CHEESE CHICKEN

Pollo con Queso a la Crema

(Serves 8)

A—2 pounds chicken pieces
1 quart (4 cups) water
2 teaspoons salt

B—2 ounces (4 tablespoons) butter

C—**White Sauce:**
2 ounces (4 tablespoons) butter
¼ cup flour
½ teaspoon salt
2 cups milk

D—1 can (1 pound) cream style corn
  8 soda crackers
  ½ pound (8 ounces) *Velveeta* cheese

1—Bring to a boil water and salt included in A. Wash chicken, add, *cover*, and boil for *20 minutes*. Remove from heat, separate meat from bones of chicken and dice meat.

2—In a saucepan, melt butter included in B over *moderate* heat. Add chicken pieces and brown *lightly*. Remove from heat.

3—In another saucepan, melt butter included in C over *moderate* heat. Mix flour and salt and stir until blended. Add milk *gradually* and stir until mixture boils and thickens.

4—In a deep glass baking dish place in layers as follows:
  a—Contents of can of cream style corn
  b—Half of the soda crackers, crumbled
  c—The diced chicken
  d—The white sauce
  e—Remaining soda crackers, crumbled
  f—Sliced *Velveeta* cheese, covering surface

5—Preheat oven to 350°F. *Cover* dish and bake for *30 minutes*.

CHICKEN PIE

Pastelón de Pollo
(Serves 8)

A—1 tablespoon lard or vegetable oil
  1 ounce salt pork ⎫ washed and diced
  2 ounces lean cured ham ⎭
  1 small onion, peeled ⎫
  1 green pepper, seeded ⎪
  3 sweet chili peppers, seeded ⎬ chopped
  2 cloves garlic, peeled ⎭
  1 teaspoon whole dried *orégano*

B—2 pounds chicken pieces
  3¼ teaspoons salt
  2 teaspoons vinegar

C—1 can (4 ounces) pimientos, chopped in their juice
8 dry prunes, pitted and chopped
¼ cup seeded raisins
½ cup tomato sauce
8 olives, stuffed with pimientos
1 teaspoon capers

D—4 hard-cooked eggs, chopped
1 can (8 ounces) green peas (*Petit-Pois*), drained

1—In a *caldero* or skillet, heat fat. Brown *rapidly* salt pork and cured ham. Reduce heat to *low* and sauté rest of ingredients included in A until tender.

2—Wash chicken pieces and add, with rest of ingredients included in B. Mix over *moderate* heat about *3 minutes*.

3—Add ingredients included in C and bring **rapidly** to a boil. Reduce heat to *low, cover* and cook for *30 minutes*.

4—Add ingredients included in D, mix, and remove from heat.

5—Remove chicken pieces. Separate meat from bones and discard bones. Mince the meat and add to *caldero* or skillet.

Pastry:
A—3 cups flour
1½ teaspoons salt

B—1 cup vegetable shortening, chilled
½ cup milk, chilled

1—Sift together flour and salt included in A.

2—Add shortening and cut into flour with a dough blender or two knives.

3—Add milk and stir just enough to mix ingredients into a dough.

4—Place dough on a lightly-floured board and divide in half. Set aside **one half** and roll out other half, with a lightly floured rolling pin, into a circle large enough to cover a 9 to 10-inch pie plate. **Do not stretch dough.** Prick bottom and sides with a fork.

5—Prepare other half in same way and set aside for top covering.

6—Spoon filling into pie plate.

7—*Cover* top with other half of dough, being careful not to stretch it. Prick in several places with a fork. Fasten edges of dough by pressing together firmly with a fork dipped in milk. Brush top *lightly* with milk.

8—Bake in preheated oven to *350°F.* about *45 minutes,* or until golden brown.

CHICKEN CRACKLING
Pollo Frito
(Serves 4)

A—1 frying chicken, cut into serving pieces
  2 cups water | Juice of 1 lime

Seasoning: See **Table for Seasoning Chicken** at beginning of chapter.

B—1 cup flour
  Lard or vegetable oil (*for deep-frying*)

1—Weigh chicken to determine amount of seasoning required.

2—Wash chicken in water with lime juice included in *A.* Drain and dry well. Rub chicken pieces on both sides with the seasoning. (Rub seasoning well into skin of chicken. The breast has an open place on either side into which the seasoning should be introduced.) It will add to the taste if, after seasoning, the chicken is refrigerated for several hours.

3—Place flour included in *B* in a paper bag and shake pieces of chicken, *one at a time,* until well coated with flour.

4—Heat fat in a deep-fryer or heavy kettle and fry chicken *rapidly* until *lightly* browned. Reduce heat to *low, cover,* and cook for *1 hour.*

5—Turn heat to *high, uncover,* and cook, turning chicken *occasionally,* until crisp and golden.

6—Remove chicken from pan and drain on absorbent paper.

Note: Substitute lard or vegetable oil with butter and eliminate flour for frying chicken in butter in a frying pan.

PICKLED CHICKEN
Pollo en Salsa Perdiz (*Escabeche*)

(Serves 6)

A—2 pounds chicken pieces

B—1 cup olive oil
½ cup vinegar
1 pound onions, peeled and sliced
8 cloves garlic, peeled and crushed
1 green pepper, seeded and cut into thin strips
2 teaspoons salt

1—Wash and dry chicken pieces. Place in a *caldero* or heavy kettle, together with ingredients included in B.

2—Heat to boiling, *cover* and cook over *moderate* heat for *40 minutes.*

3—*Uncover,* and cook about *20 minutes,* or until chicken is done.

Note: The recipe yields abundant sauce. Use excess sauce as follows: Place sauce in a glass pie baking pan. Drop *carefully* six eggs, one next to the other, without breaking the yolks. *Cover* and bake in preheated oven at 325°F. about *20 minutes,* or until eggs set to taste.

GOLDEN CHICKEN
Pollo Dorado

(Serves 6)

A—2 pounds chicken pieces
2 cups water | Juice of 1 lime

B—**Seasoning:** See **Table for Seasoning Chicken** at beginning of chapter.

C—¼ teaspoon salt | ½ cup flour

D—½ cup vegetable | ¼ pound butter
oil

E—¼ cup hot water | ¼ cup dry white wine

1—Wash chicken in water with lime juice included in *A*. Drain and dry well.

2—Weigh chicken to determine amount of seasoning required. Rub seasoning into chicken pieces on both sides.

3—Place chicken in a glass dish, *cover*, and refrigerate for *1 hour*.

4—In a paper bag, mix ingredients included in *C* and shake pieces of chicken, *one at a time*, until well coated with flour. Place chicken on an aluminum sheet, ready to be fried.

5—In a frying pan, melt half the butter with half the vegetable oil included in *D*. When hot, brown **lightly** the chicken pieces, turning occasionally.

6—Add hot water and wine. *Cover*, and cook over *low* heat for *1 hour*.

7—In another frying pan, melt the rest of butter and vegetable oil included in *D*. Remove pieces of chicken from first frying pan to this pan and fry to crispness over *moderate* heat. Drain on absorbent paper.

BAKED BREADED CHICKEN

Pollo Empanado al Horno
(Serves 6)

A—1 frying chicken

Seasoning: See **Table for Seasoning Chicken** at beginning of chapter.

B—For **each pound** of dressed chicken: ¼ cup bread or cracker crumbs
2 eggs
⅛ teaspoon salt

1—After chicken is cleaned and drawn, wash well, cut into serving pieces, and weigh. **Remove chicken skin.** Season according to **Table for Seasoning Chicken** at the beginning of chapter. Rub seasonings well into chicken pieces on both sides.

2—Put bread or cracker crumbs on a sheet of waxed paper. Cover the chicken pieces thoroughly with the crumbs, then dip into the eggs beaten with salt.

3—Place chicken pieces in a greased baking dish. Dot surface with butter.

4—Preheat oven to *400°F.* and cook the chicken, *uncovered,* for *40 minutes.*

CHICKEN CARIBBEAN WITH POTATOES

Pollo con Papas al Horno
(Serves 6)

A—1 large chicken (3 to 3½ pounds, dressed-weight)
Seasoning: See **Table for Seasoning Chicken** at beginning of chapter.

B—¼ pound butter

C—2 pounds small potatoes
2 quarts (8 cups) boiling water | 2 tablespoons salt

1—Weigh dressed chicken to determine the amount of seasoning required. Wash and dry chicken. Rub inside and out with the seasoning.

2—Place chicken, **breast down,** in a baking dish. Put half of butter *inside* chicken. Dot surface with rest of butter.

3—Preheat oven to *350°F.* and bake about *1½ hours,* or until drumstick and thigh move easily and fleshy part of drumstick feels soft when pressed.

4—As soon as chicken is placed in the oven, prepare potatoes as follows:
Wash potatoes, without peeling, and cook, whole, in the boiling water and salt included in *C* over *moderate* heat for *30 minutes.* Remove, peel and place surrounding chicken in the pan. Baste *occasionally* until chicken is done.

5—Remove chicken and cut into serving pieces. Arrange breast slices attractively on center of a serving platter, surrounded by rest of serving pieces and potatoes. Serve sauce separately in a deep dish.

BROILED CHICKENS
Pollitos Asados a la Parrilla

A—Broiler-fryer chickens (1½ to 2½ pounds, dressed-weight)

Seasoning: See **Table for Seasoning Chicken** at beginning of chapter III

B—**For each chicken use:**
2 ounces (4 tablespoons) butter
2 strips bacon

1—Wash chickens and cut in halves. Weigh chickens to determine amount of seasoning required. Rub chickens on both sides with seasoning.

2—Set oven rack, where broiler pan will be placed, *10 inches* from heat. Preheat broiler *10 minutes* before using. In a saucepan, melt butter over *low* heat.

3—Remove rack from broiler pan, line bottom of pan with aluminum foil and place rack back on broiler pan.

4—Grease the broiler rack with a brush. Place chicken halves on rack, **skin side down.** Brush chickens all over with part of the melted butter and place a strip of bacon over each half. **Reserve** remaining butter to baste chickens while broiling.

5—Broil chickens for *30 minutes,* basting *occasionally.*

6—Turn chickens and broil about *15 to 30 minutes,* or until fork-tender and crisp. Baste *occasionally* while broiling. (Drumstick, thigh and wings should move easily when done.)

CHICKEN IN THE NEST

Pollo al Nido

(Serves 6)

A—2 pounds chicken pieces
1 onion, peeled and halved
1 cup water
1 sweet chili pepper, seeded
2 teaspoons salt

B—3 ounces (6 tablespoons) butter
4 tablespoons flour
2 cups milk
2 canned pimientos, chopped
1 teaspoon salt
½ teaspoon Worcestershire sauce
2 tablespoons muscatel or dry wine
¼ teaspoon prepared mustard

C—½ cup bread or cracker crumbs
1 ounce (2 tablespoons) butter

1—Wash chicken, dry and place in a pot with rest of ingredients included in A. Bring *rapidly* to a boil. *Cover* pot and cook over *low* heat for *1 hour.*

2—Remove chicken. Separate meat from bones and mince the meat.

3—Melt butter in a saucepan, add flour, and stir for *1 minute.* *Gradually* stir in milk. Add rest of ingredients included in B.

4—Add minced chicken and stir *constantly* over *moderate* heat, until sauce boils and thickens *slightly.*

5—Spoon sauce into individual oven-proof glass dishes. Sprinkle tops *lightly* with crumbs and dot with butter included in C.

6—Preheat oven to 400°F. and bake just long enough to brown crumbs.

STUFFED ROAST CHICKEN
Pollo Relleno al Horno

Chicken:

A—5-pound dressed-weight roasting chicken

1—Wash chicken, dry and season according to **Table for Seasoning Chicken** at beginning of chapter.

Stuffing:

A—Chicken giblets (heart, liver and gizzard)
 1 cup water
 ¼ teaspoon salt

B—4 slices sandwich bread, crusts trimmed
 1 cup milk

C—1 apple
 1 cup water
 1 teaspoon salt

D—1 tablespoon lard or vegetable oil
 2 ounces lean cured ham, washed and diced

E—2 hard-cooked eggs ⎤
 1 stalk celery   ⎥
 10 dry prunes, pitted ⎬ chopped
 10 olives, stuffed with pimientos ⎦
 1¼ cups tomato sauce
 ¼ cup seeded raisins
 1 teaspoon salt

1—Boil chicken giblets for *15 minutes* over *moderate* heat, *covered*, in water and salt included in A. Drain and **reserve** liquid. Chop giblets.

2—Crumble bread and soak in the milk. Mash thoroughly with a fork.

3—Peel and dice apple. Rinse in water and salt included in C. Drain.

4—Heat fat included in *D* and brown cured ham *rapidly*. Reduce heat to *low*, add chopped ingredients included in *E*, and mix. Add remaining ingredients, mix, and cook for *10 minutes*, stirring *occasionally*. **Cool thoroughly.**

5—Stuff chicken **three-quarters full.** Sew or skewer opening closed, using neck skin for a "patch."

Roasting:

1—Heat oven to *325°F.*

2—Place chicken in roasting pan, **breast down.**

3—Brush surface of chicken with 4 tablespoons of melted butter.

4—Add to pan reserved liquid from boiled giblets.

5—Fold a loose piece of aluminum foil in the shape of a tent and place over chicken, **not** touching ends of pan. Lift foil *occasionally* and baste chicken.

6—Roast chicken about *3½ hours*, or until drumstick and thigh move easily and fleshy part of drumstick feels soft when pressed.

Gravy:

A—3 cups liquid

B—¼ cup fat | ¼ cup flour

1—Drain drippings from roasting pan into a glass container.

2—The fat will soon rise to surface. Skim off fat with a spoon. Measure ¼ cup of this fat. (In case drippings do not yield ¼ cup, make up deficiency by adding melted butter.)

3—Measure liquid from drippings and add enough water to measure 3 cups liquid.

4—Pour liquid into pan in which chicken was roasted. Bring to a boil over *high* heat while scraping the bottom of the pan.

5—Put fat and flour included in *B* into a saucepan. Stir over *low* heat until well blended.

6—Turn heat to *moderate* and add liquid from pan *slowly*, stirring *constantly*, until gravy boils and thickens. Taste and adjust seasoning.

7—Remove from heat, strain, and serve hot.

SMOTHERED TURKEY

Pavo Estofado

(Serves 8 to 10)

A—8½ pound dressed-weight turkey

B—12 peppercorns (whole black peppers) ⎫
    7 cloves garlic, peeled   ⎪ crush and mix
    5 teaspoons whole dried *orégano*   ⎬ in a mortar
    10 teaspoons salt   ⎪
    2 tablespoons vinegar   ⎭

C—12 dry prunes, pitted
    12 cloves garlic, peeled and crushed
    1 pound small whole onions, peeled
    12 olives, stuffed with pimientos
    2 tablespoons capers
    4 bay leaves
    2 tablespoons water

D—½ cup white sweet or dry wine
    ¾ cup sugar (*optional*)

1—Cut turkey into serving pieces. Wash, dry and season with ingredients included in *B*.

2—Place turkey pieces in a glass baking dish. Add giblets and ingredients included in *C*. Set in refrigerator overnight.

3—Next day, place in a large *caldero* or heavy kettle and bring *rapidly* to a boil. *Cover*, reduce heat to *moderate* and cook for 2 *hours*. **Halfway,** turn turkey pieces.

4—Add wine and sugar. Reduce heat to *low* and cook 1 *hour*, or until turkey is done.

STUFFED ROAST TURKEY

Pavo Relleno al Horno

Turkey:

10 to 12 pounds dressed-weight turkey

1—Wash turkey inside and out. Wipe dry and cut off neck and tip of wings. **Reserve** skin of neck to be used later as a "patch" to cover opening after turkey is stuffed. Wash giblets (heart, liver and gizzard), drain and wipe dry.

Seasoning:

Basic seasoning for **one pound** of **dressed-weight** turkey: (**Multiply** the following seasoning by the weight **in pounds** of the dressed-weight turkey.)

1 small clove garlic, peeled ⎫
1 peppercorn (whole black pepper) ⎪
¼ teaspoon whole dried *orégano* ⎬ crush and mix
1 teaspoon salt ⎪ in a mortar
1 teaspoon olive oil ⎪
½ teaspoon vinegar ⎭

1—Rub seasoning inside and out of turkey. Set overnight in refrigerator.

Stuffing:

A—1½ pounds lean ground beef
Turkey giblets (*optional*) ⎱ ground or finely chopped
⅓ cup onions ⎰
18 dried prunes, pitted and chopped
1 can (7 ounces) pimientos, chopped in their juice
8 olives, stuffed with pimientos
1 teaspoon capers
½ cup seeded raisins
1 tablespoon salt

B—2 tablespoons lard or vegetable oil

C—4 hard-cooked eggs, coarsely chopped
1 tablespoon sugar
1 can (1 pound) applesauce

1—In a bowl, mix ingredients included in *A*.

2—Heat fat in a *caldero* or heavy kettle. Add meat mixture and stir *rapidly* over *high* heat, until meat loses its red color. *Immediately* reduce heat to *low* and cook for *10 minutes*, stirring *occasionally*.

3—Add ingredients included in *C*, mix and cook for *5 minutes*.

4—Remove from heat and cool *thoroughly*.

5—Sew together neck end of turkey. Stuff turkey **three-quarters full** through the end. Patch opening with reserved skin from neck. Tie legs together.

Note: This recipe for stuffing renders an abundant amount. Use **only** enough to fill the turkey **three-quarters full,** to allow for expansion. If there is any stuffing left, place in a covered glass baking dish and bake at *350°F.* for *30 minutes.*

Roasting:

1—Place turkey in a pan, **breast down.**

2—Brush surface of turkey with either melted butter, oleomargarine or *Achiote Coloring*. (see Index)

3—Fold a loose piece of aluminum foil in the shape of a tent and place over turkey, **not** touching ends of pan. While roasting, lift foil and baste turkey *occasionally*.

4—Roast turkey according to the following time chart:

TIME CHART FOR ROASTING STUFFED TURKEY

Weight of Ready-to-cook Turkey	Oven Temperature	Approximate Cooking Time
4–8 pounds	325°F.	3–4½ hours
8–12 pounds	325°F.	4½–5 hours
12–16 pounds	325°F.	5–5½ hours
16–20 pounds	325°F.	5½–6 hours
20–24 pounds	325°F.	6–7 hours

(See **Note** on page 82)

Note: Turkey is done when drumstick and thigh move easily and thickest part of drumstick feels very soft when pressed.

5—Remove turkey from pan and use drippings for making gravy.

Gravy:

A—3 cups liquid

B—¼ cup fat
   ¼ cup flour

1—Drain drippings from roasting pan into a glass container.

2—The fat will soon rise to surface. Skim off fat with a spoon. Measure ¼ cup of this fat. (In case drippings do not yield ¼ cup, make up deficiency by adding melted butter.)

3—Measure liquid from drippings and add enough water to measure 3 cups liquid.

4—Pour liquid into pan in which turkey was roasted. Bring to a boil over *high* heat while scraping bottom of the pan.

5—Put fat and flour included in *B* into a saucepan. Stir over *low* heat until well blended.

6—Turn heat to *moderate* and add liquid from pan *slowly*, stirring *constantly*, until gravy boils and thickens. Taste and adjust seasoning.

7—Remove from heat, strain, and serve hot.

TURKEY STUFFING WITH WINE
Relleno con Vino para Pavo

A—2 pounds lean ground beef
1 tablespoon salt
½ teaspoon ground pepper

B—Turkey giblets (*optional*) ⎫
1 onion, peeled   ⎬ ground or finely chopped
¼ pound lean cured ham ⎭

C—3 hard-cooked eggs, chopped
12 dried prunes, pitted and chopped
2 tablespoons sugar
⅓ cup bread or cracker crumbs
1½ cup seeded raisins
1 cup sweet wine
1 can (1 pound) applesauce

1—Mix in a bowl *A* and *B* ingredients. Put in a *caldero* or heavy kettle and stir over *high* heat, until meat loses its red color.

2—Reduce heat to *low* and stir *occasionally* for *10 minutes.*

3—Add *C* ingredients and cook for *5 minutes* longer, stirring *occasionally.*

4—Remove from heat and when **thoroughly cool,** stuff turkey **three-quarters full.** If there is any stuffing left, place in a *covered* glass baking dish and bake at *350°F.* for *30 minutes.*

BONED TURKEY STUFFED WITH TRUFFLES
Pavo Trufado

(A full-grown turkey should be used for this recipe, since a young turkey is too tender.)

A—1 10 to 12-pound dressed-weight turkey

B—1 tablespoon salt

C—3 pounds lean pork meat
½ pound lean cured ham

D—¼ pound butter
5 eggs

E—2 medium onions ⎱ peeled and
4 cloves garlic ⎰ finely chopped

F—½ cup tomato sauce
¼ cup olive oil
4½ teaspoons salt
1 tablespoon vinegar
¼ teaspoon ground pepper

G—½ pound liverwurst
2 cans (1¼ ounce each) truffles

H—2 cups bread or cracker crumbs

1—Make a deep cut along the backbone of the turkey. **Reserve** heart, liver, and gizzard.

2—Loosen and remove the skin *carefully* from the turkey, beginning with the part where the first cut was made. **Be careful not to tear the skin.** Use a small and very sharp knife. Cut the legs and wings at the joints, being careful not to splinter the bones, and pull the legs and wings out of the skin.

3—Wash and dry the skin and **reserve,** to be stuffed later. If the skin happens to be torn during the process, mend it so that it may be used as a closed bag with an opening at the place where it was originally cut.

4—Separate the meat from the bones. Keep the breast meat whole, but cut the rest of the meat into small pieces.

5—Sprinkle salt listed in *B* over the breasts and **reserve.**

6—Boil the turkey bones in 5 quarts (20 cups) water with 5 tablespoons salt for *40 minutes.*

7—Remove skin and cartilage from gizzard and trim the heart. Wash heart and gizzard.

8—Grind turkey meat (except breast meat), the pork, ham, heart, and gizzard. Add butter and eggs included in *D* and mix well.

9—Add garlic and onions and mix.

10—Mash liverwurst with a fork and add together with ingredients included in *F.*

11—Add liquid from truffles. Cut truffles into small pieces and **reserve.**

12—Add crumbs and mix well.

13—Stuff the turkey skin in the following way:
For a pouch with the skin. Place the turkey breasts in the bottom to serve as a base. Cover with half the stuffing, then add the turkey liver, cut in small pieces and mixed with the truffles. Cover with rest of the stuffing. (Do not fill completely to allow for expansion.) Sew the skin together at the top and wrap the stuffed skin loosely in a cloth bag. Tie the bag closed at the top.

14—Discard the bones from the boiling water. Place the stuffed turkey skin in the boiling liquid, *cover,* and cook over *high* heat for *1 hour.* Turn the bag, add boiling water, if necessary, to cover the bag, and cook for *1 hour* longer.

15—Remove turkey from liquid, drain, and put under a heavy weight. When cool, set in the refrigerator overnight.

16—To serve, remove the cloth and cut in half, so that each portion has breast of turkey at bottom. Cut into thin slices and serve cold, with salad and marmalade.

CHAPTER IV *Fish and Shellfish*

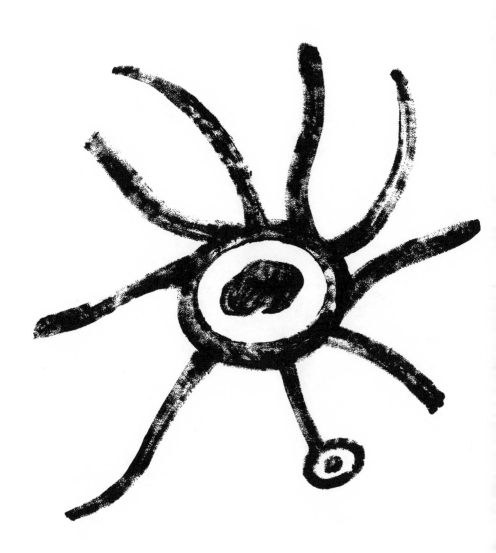

Fish and Shellfish

FRIED FISH WITH PUERTO RICAN SAUCE

Mojo Isleño

(Serves 12)

A—½ cup olive oil
2½ pounds onions, peeled, sliced and halved
1½ cups water
24 olives, stuffed with pimientos
2 tablespoons capers
1 can (4 ounces) pimientos, cut in tiny slices, in their juice
2 cans (8 ounces each) tomato sauce
2 tablespoons vinegar
1 tablespoon salt
2 bay leaves

B—4 pounds fish slices, 1 inch thick
4 teaspoons salt
1 cup olive oil
1 large clove garlic, peeled and crushed

1—Prepare sauce by mixing ingredients included in A, *cover* and cook over *moderate* heat for *30 minutes*. Then uncover and continue cooking for *30 minutes* more.

2—When sauce is nearly done, season fish with salt included in B and fry as follows:

Put oil and garlic included in B into a frying pan. Brown garlic over *moderate* heat. Remove garlic and place in the pan as many slices of fish as will fit. Cook at *moderate* heat for *3 minutes* on each side, reduce heat to *low* and cook about *15 minutes*, or until fish flakes easily when tested with a fork. Fry remaining slices in same way. Cover with the sauce and serve.

89

PICKLED FISH

Pescado en Escabeche

(Serves 8)

A—2 cups olive oil
  1 cup vinegar
  12 peppercorns (whole black peppers)
  ½ teaspoon salt
  2 bay leaves
  1½ pounds onions, peeled and sliced

B—3 pounds firm-fleshed fish slices, 1 inch thick
  Juice of 1 large lime
  4½ teaspoons salt
  ¼ cup flour
  1 cup olive oil
  2 large cloves garlic, peeled and crushed

1—In a large kettle, mix sauce ingredients included in A and cook over *low* heat for *1 hour.* Allow to cool.

2—Rinse fish in running water and dry. Sprinkle lime juice over the fish slices and season with the salt included in B. Flour both sides of the slices lightly *when ready to fry.*

3—In a frying pan, heat olive oil with crushed cloves garlic. Remove garlic as soon as it is brown.

4—Add as many fish slices as will fit in the pan and brown over *moderate* heat on both sides.

5—Reduce heat to *low*, and cook the slices for *15 minutes,* or until fish flakes easily when tested with a fork. Fry remaining slices in the same way.

6—In a deep glass dish, arrange alternate layers of sauce and fish, beginning and finishing with sauce.

7—Cover and place in refrigerator for at least *24 hours* before serving. Serve cold.

FISH A LA JARDINERA
Pescado a la Jardinera
(Serves 6 to 8)

A—4-pound cleaned and scaled fish, with head and tail intact

B—4 quarts (16 cups) water   1 onion, peeled and halved
4 tablespoons salt   2 bay leaves

C—2 large tomatoes, sliced

D—¼ cup olive oil   ¼ teaspoons salt
2 tablespoons vinegar   ½ teaspoon fresh lime juice

E—4 hard-cooked eggs
Parsley sprigs

1—Wash fish in 2 cups of water, to which juice of 1 lime has been added. Drain and dry.

2—In a deep rectangular kettle, bring to a boil ingredients included in B. Turn heat to *low*, keeping the water just below the boiling point. Add fish, *cover*, and cook about *40 minutes*, or until fish flakes easily when tested with a fork.

3—Cover bottom of a large, rectangular glass baking dish with tomato slices.

4—Remove fish **carefully** from kettle. Drain and place over tomato slices.

5—Strain into a saucepan ¼ cup broth in which fish was cooked and stir in ingredients included in D. Bring to a boil and remove from heat.

6—Mash with a fork 4 egg yolks and 2 egg whites and add. (Use remaining egg whites for garnishing.) Pour sauce over fish.

7—Serve fish in the baking dish, garnished with remaining egg whites and parsley sprigs.

FISH AU GRATIN

Pescado au Gratin

(Serves 6)

A—2 pounds fish fillets, skinned and boned

B—3 peppercorns (whole black peppers) ⎤
   2 large cloves garlic, peeled   ⎥
   1 small onion, peeled and chopped   ⎬ crush and mix
   2 teaspoons salt   ⎥ in a mortar
   2 teaspoons fresh lime juice   ⎦

C—1 tomato, thinly sliced

D—2 ounces (4 tablespoons) butter
   ½ cup flour
   ¾ teaspoon salt
   3 cups milk
   ½ pound Cheddar cheese, shredded

E—2 tablespoons cracker or bread crumbs

F—¼ cup freshly grated Parmesan cheese

1—Wash and dry fish fillets. Season with ingredients included in *B*.

2—Arrange tomato slices in bottom of a 13 x 9 x 2-inch glass baking dish. Place fish fillets over tomato slices.

3—In a saucepan, melt butter *slowly*. Blend in flour and salt. Add milk *gradually* and stir over *moderate* heat until sauce boils and thickens. Add shredded cheese and stir until it melts. Pour sauce over fish fillets.

4—Sprinkle with crumbs and bake in a preheated oven to *350°F.* about *30 minutes,* or until fish flakes easily when tested with a fork.

5—Remove from oven, sprinkle with grated Parmesan cheese, and serve *immediately.*

GOLDEN "DORADO" (MAHIMAHI) FISH

Pescado Dorado

A—2 pounds "Dorado" (mahimahi) fish fillets, skinned and boned
2 teaspoons fresh lime juice
2 teaspoons salt
1 pinch ground pepper (optional)

B—1 can (1 pound 12 ounces) whole tomatoes
2 small onions, peeled, sliced and cut in halves
2 garlic cloves, peeled and crushed
12 olives, stuffed with pimientos
1 tablespoon small capers
2 tablespoons extravirgin olive oil
1 teaspoon salt
2 bay leaves
¼ cup dry white wine

1—Wash and dry fish fillets. Cut fillets into 6 portions and place in a 13 x 9 x 2-inch glass baking dish. Pour lime juice over surface of fillets and sprinkle with salt and pepper.

2—Mix ingredients included in *B* and pour over top and sides of fillets.

3—Preheat oven to 350°F. and bake fillets about *30 minutes* or until fillets flake easily when tested with a fork.

CODFISH A LA VIZCAINA
Bacalao a la Vizcaína

(Serves 4 to 6)

A—1 pound dried, salted codfish fillets

B—1 pound potatoes, peeled and **very thinly** sliced
2 onions, peeled and **thinly** sliced

C—½ cup tomato sauce
½ cup water
½ cup olive oil
2 canned pimientos, chopped
¼ cup olives, stuffed with pimientos
1 tablespoon capers
½ cup seeded raisins
2 cloves garlic, peeled and crushed
1 bay leaf

1—Soak codfish in water to cover for *4 hours.* Drain well and boil **rapidly** in 2 quarts (8 cups) water for *15 minutes.* Drain, discard skin and bones, and shred flesh.

2—Mix ingredients included in *C.*

3—In a large frying pan, arrange alternate layers of codfish, sliced potatoes, sliced onions and ingredients mixed in *C.*

4—Bring to a boil. Cook over *low* heat, *covered,* for *30 minutes,* or until potatoes are fork-tender.

CODFISH SALAD

Serenata
(Serves 4 to 6)

A—1 pound dried, salted codfish fillets

B—1 pound onions
   1 pound tomatoes } peeled and sliced

C—1 cup olive oil | ½ teaspoon salt
   ½ cup vinegar | ¼ teaspoon ground pepper

1—Soak codfish in water to cover for *4 hours*. Drain well. Boil codfish in enough water to cover for *15 minutes*. Drain and rinse in fresh water. Discard skin and bones, and shred flesh.

2—Arrange codfish on a platter. Garnish with onions and tomato slices.

3—Combine ingredients included in *C* to make a sauce. Pour sauce over fish, chill, and serve cold.

CODFISH WITH SCRAMBLED EGGS

Bacalao Revuelto con Huevos
(Serves 4)

A—¼ pound dried, salted codfish fillets

B—2 tablespoons lard or vegetable oil
   3 onions, finely chopped | ⅓ cup tomato sauce
   2 tablespoons fat or *Achiote Coloring* (see Index)

C—8 eggs

1—Soak codfish in water to cover for *4 hours*. Drain well and boil in 4 cups water for *15 minutes*. Drain and rinse in fresh water. Discard skin and bones, and shred flesh.

2—Heat fat in a frying pan. Add onions and brown *slowly*. Add the shredded codfish. Add tomato sauce and fat or *Achiote Coloring*.

3—Beat eggs and add. Stir over *low* heat until eggs are cooked to taste.

SARDINE PIE

Coca de Sardinas

(Serves 8)

Pastry:

A—1½ cups flour

¼ teaspoon salt | 1 tablespoon baking powder

1½ ounces (3 tablespoons) butter, chilled

B—1 egg

½ cup cold milk

1—Into a bowl, sift flour **3 times** with salt and baking powder.

2—*Rapidly* cut in butter, using a dough blender or two knives, until mixture resembles coarse meal.

3—Break egg into measuring cup. Mix well egg yolk and white, *without beating.* Add enough of milk included in B to total ½ **cup** liquid. Stir and pour into flour-butter mixture. Mix *rapidly* with a fork until no loose flour remains on bottom of bowl.

4—Turn dough onto a floured board. Roll out a circle large enough to cover a 9 to 10-inch pie pan.

5—Place waxed paper over the dough. Roll up paper and dough together and unroll to fit loosely into pan. Discard paper.

6—Prick dough in several places and press around the edges with a fork moistened in milk.

7—Bake in preheated oven to *350°F.* about *30 minutes,* or until golden.

Filling:

8 tablespoons olive oil

¾ pound onions, peeled, halved and sliced

1 can (1 pound) sardines in tomato sauce (see Note)

1 can (4 ounces) pimientos, chopped in their juice

⅓ cup finely chopped fresh parsley

1 teaspoon salt

6 tablespoons tomato sauce

1—In a skillet, heat olive oil and sauté onions over *low* heat for *15 minutes*, stirring *occasionally*.

2—Slit the sardines, remove the backbone and add sardines, together with their sauce, to the skillet.

3—Add rest of ingredients, mix and bring to a boil over *moderate* heat.

4—Spoon filling into baked pastry and serve hot.

Note: Sardines can be substituted by 3 cans (5½ ounces each) Boned Chicken or Boned Turkey. Substitute olive oil by ¼ pound butter and add ½ teaspoon curry powder.

TUNA FISH PUDDING

Budín de Atún

(Serves 6)

A—2 ounces (4 tablespoons) butter

B—1 can (9¼ ounces) tuna fish (see Note)
¼ teaspoon ground nutmeg
2 teaspoons sugar
½ teaspoon salt

C—1 cup milk
8 soda crackers

D—4 eggs

1—Preheat oven to 350°F. Grease a 2-quart round glass baking dish.

2—Place butter in a bowl and mix with ingredients included in B.

3—Crumble soda crackers over milk and add.

4—Beat eggs, **fold into mixture,** and pour into baking dish. Bake about *30 minutes*, or until set.

Note: Tuna fish can be substituted by 2 cans (5½ ounces each) Boned Chicken or Boned Turkey, omitting sugar. For a different taste, nutmeg can be substituted by curry powder.

BOILED LOBSTER
Langosta Hervida

1—Lobster should be alive when plunged into boiling water.

2—In a large kettle, heat enough water to *cover* lobster. For **each quart** of water add **1 tablespoon** salt.

3—When boiling briskly, plunge the lobster in, **head first.** Bring **rapidly** to a boil, *cover,* and simmer for 5 *minutes* for the **first pound** and 3 *minutes* more for each **additional pound.** If lobster meat is going to be cooked again in a recipe **boil slowly** for 5 *minutes.*)

4—Remove the lobster and slit the undershell, **lengthwise.** Discard small intestinal canal, which runs its entire length; the stomach, which is a small sac in back of the head; and the gills, which are spongy and are found between the shell and the meat. If the lobster has coral, (red roe) use it, as it is very tasty.

5—Remove lobster meat from tail and crack claws to remove meat too.

LOBSTER A LA ROYAL
Langosta a la Royal

(Serves 4)

A—2 finely chopped pimientos
1 teaspoon salt
½ teaspoon Worcestershire sauce
2 tablespoons *muscatel* or dry wine
¼ teaspoon prepared mustard

B—1 pound boiled lobster meat

C—3 ounces (6 tablespoons) butter
6 tablespoons flour | 2 cups diluted evaporated milk

D—1 tablespoon cracker or bread crumbs
1 ounce (2 tablespoons) butter

1—Mix together ingredients included in *A*.

2—Cut lobster meat into ½-inch chunks.

3—In a saucepan, melt *slowly* butter included in *C*. Add flour and stir **constantly** for a few seconds.

4—*Gradually*, stir in milk and continue *stirring* with heat increased to *moderate*. Add the mixed *A* ingredients and the lobster meat. Cook, *stirring*, until mixture boils and thickens.

5—Pour mixture into a glass baking dish, cover *lightly* with crumbs and dot with butter included in *D*.

6—Preheat oven at *350°F.* and bake for *10 minutes*.

Note: Freshly cooked fish or poached shrimp tails, shelled and deveined, may be substituted for the lobster meat.

LOBSTER VINAIGRETTE

Langosta a la Vinagreta

(Serves 3)

A—1 pound boiled lobster meat
2 cups water
1½ teaspoons salt

B—½ cup olive oil
⅓ cup vinegar
1 teaspoon salt

C—1 onion, peeled
1 green pepper, seeded ⎤
1 sprig parsley ⎬ chopped
4 hard-cooked eggs ⎦

1—Bring to a boil the water with salt included in *A*. Add boiled lobster meat and cook for *5 minutes* over *low* heat. Allow to cool and cut lobster meat into 1-inch chunks.

2—Combine ingredients included in *B* and *C* to make a sauce. Pour sauce over lobster. Chill in refrigerator and serve cold.

Note: 2 pounds poached shrimp tails, shelled and deveined, may substitute lobster meat.

POACHED SHRIMPS

Camarones Hervidos

(Serves 4)

A—2 pounds fresh or frozen shrimp *tails* in the shell

B—2 quarts (8 cups) water
  4 tablespoons salt | 2 bay leaves
  4 peppercorns (whole black peppers)

1—Wash shrimps well. (If frozen, allow to defrost.)

2—Bring to a brisk boil over *high* heat ingredients included in B. Add shrimps and turn heat to *low*. *Cover* and cook for 5 *minutes*, or until shrimps are done, according to their size. (When done, the shell turns pink and the meat loses its translucence and becomes dull.)

3—Drain shrimps, remove shells and devein.

Note: 2 pounds of fresh or frozen shrimp **tails** in the shell will yield about 1 **pound** shelled, cooked shrimps.

STEWED SHRIMPS

Camarones Guisados

(Serves 6)

A—2 pounds poached shrimps, shelled and deveined
  1 teaspoon fresh lime juice

B—1 ounce salt pork | 2 ounces lean cured ham, diced

C—1 onion, peeled
  1 green pepper, seeded
  3 sweet chili peppers, seeded } chopped
  2 cloves garlic, peeled
  6 fresh *culantro* leaves

D—1 pound potatoes, peeled and cubed
  1 can (1 pound 12 ounces) whole tomatoes
  ¼ cup ketchup
  6 olives, stuffed with pimientos | 2 teaspoons salt
  1 teaspoon capers | 2 bay leaves

1—Score the salt pork, keeping the rind together. In a *caldero* or heavy kettle, brown **rapidly** salt pork and ham. Remove salt pork.

2—Reduce heat to *low,* add ingredients included in *C,* and sauté for *10 minutes,* stirring **occasionally.**

3—Add ingredients included in *D* and bring **rapidly** to a boil. Reduce heat to *moderate, cover,* and cook about *30 minutes,* or until potatoes are fork-tender.

4—Add shrimps and lime juice, mix, and cook, *uncovered,* until sauce thickens to taste.

SHRIMPS IN BEER

Camarones en Cerveza

(Serves 6)

A—2 pounds fresh or frozen shrimp *tails* in the shell
   2 cans (10 ounces each) beer
   2 teaspoons salt

B—1 tablespoon lard or vegetable oil
   1 ounce salt pork ⎫
   2 ounces lean cured ham ⎭ washed and diced

C—1 onion, peeled ⎫
   1 green pepper, seeded
   3 sweet chili peppers, seeded ⎬ chopped
   2 cloves garlic, peeled
   8 fresh *culantro* leaves ⎭

D—8 olives, stuffed with pimientos
   1 teaspoon tiny capers
   2 bay leaves
   ½ cup ketchup
   1 pound potatoes, peeled and quartered

1—Wash well and drain shrimps. In a kettle, bring to a brisk boil over *high* heat beer and salt included in *A.* Add shrimps. Reduce heat to *low, cover,* and cook for *5 minutes.* Drain shrimps and **reserve** beer. Remove shell and devein shrimps.

2—In a *caldero* or heavy kettle, heat fat included in *B*. Brown **rapidly** salt pork and cured ham. Reduce heat to *low* and sauté ingredients included in *C* for *10 minutes,* stirring **occasionally.**

3—Add ingredients included in *D* and reserved beer. Bring **rapidly** to a boil. Reduce heat to *moderate, cover,* and cook about *30 minutes,* or until potatoes are fork-tender. Add shrimps, mix, and cook, *uncovered,* over *moderate* heat, until sauce thickens to taste.

BOILED CRABS

Jueyes Hervidos

Fill a very large kettle with abundant water to cover the crabs, when added. Bring to a brisk boil over *high heat.* Plunge crabs alive and boil until they stop kicking. **Immediately** drain and wash under cold running water.

Rinse kettle and fill again with abundant **over-salted** water. Add peeled onions, halved, green peppers, seeded, sweet chili peppers, seeded, cloves garlic and fresh *"culantro"* leaves. Bring to a brisk boil over *high heat.* Drop in crabs and boil for *20 minutes.* Drain.

When cool enough to handle, grab crabs, one at a time, and place on back. Remove and discard "apron" or tail facing. Twist off claws and legs. Crack the claws and pull or pick out meat. Scoop meat from leg sockets, keeping free from bones. **Reserve** meat from claws and legs.

Pull apart and separate body from shell. Scrape away spongy gills at sides of body and remove loose matter in center of body. Break body in half, down center, and remove meat between sections, discarding all body spines. **Reserve** meat.

Carefully, remove and discard gall and stomach bag from shell. Spoon out into a bowl, liver, corals and rest of contents inside shell and **reserve.** The reserved meat and shell contents can be readily eaten or used in recipes calling for crab meat.

Note: When crabs are to be cooked again in the preparation of a recipe, boil the second time for *5 minutes* **only.**

CRABS AL SALMOREJO

Jueyes al Salmorejo
(Serves 3)

A—1 pound boiled crab meat (see page 102)

B—**Mix well:**
  2 tablespoons olive oil
  2 teaspoons fresh lime juice
  3 sweet chili peppers, seeded ⎱
  1 green pepper, seeded   ⎰ minced
  1 onion, peeled
  1 can (4 ounces) pimiento ⎰
  2 peppercorns (whole black peppers) ⎱ crushed and mixed
  ¼ teaspoon whole dried *orégano*   ⎰ in a mortar
  4 large cloves garlic, peeled
  1 teaspoon salt

1—In a *caldero* or heavy kettle, sauté ingredients included in B over *low* heat for *10 minutes,* stirring **occasionally.**

2—Add boiled crab meat, mix, *cover,* and cook over *moderate* heat for *10 minutes.*

CRABS ON THE SHELL

Jueyes al Carapacho
(Serves 3)

A—1 pound boiled crab meat (see page 102)
  Crab shells

B—2 tablespoons olive oil
  1 teaspoon fresh lime juice
  1¼ teaspoons salt
  3 fresh *culantro* leaves ⎱
  1 green pepper, seeded
  1 tablespoon capers
  1 onion, peeled   ⎰ minced
  2 canned pimientos
  6 olives, stuffed with pimientos
  2 sweet chili peppers, seeded ⎰

C—8 peppercorns (whole black peppers) } crushed in
2 large cloves garlic, peeled   } a mortar

D—2 teaspoons flour ⎫
¼ teaspoon salt   ⎬ *optional*
½ teaspoon water   ⎭
2 eggs

1—In a small *caldero* or heavy kettle, mix ingredients included in *B* and *C*. Sauté over *low* heat for *10 minutes*.

2—Add boiled crab meat and mix. *Cover* and cook for *10 minutes* over *moderate* heat.

3—Spoon filling into crab shells.

4—In a cup, blend flour and salt with water. Add eggs and mix well. Cover filling with mixture and brown **rapidly** by placing shells, **face down,** in a skillet with hot lard or vegetable oil.

Note: Instruction 4 is optional.

CRABS ROYALE

Empanadas de Jueyes

(Makes 20)

Casabe Paste:

A—1 pound *casabe* cakes (see Glossary)
3 cups milk

B—1 tablespoon salt
½ cup *Achiote Coloring* (see Index)
2 cups milk

1—In a bowl, crumble *casabe* cakes over milk included in *A*. Soak for *3 hours*.

2—Add ingredients included in *B* and stir until a soft, smooth paste is formed.

Filling:

A—1 pound boiled crab meat (see page 102)

B—1 tablespoon lard or vegetable oil
½ green pepper, seeded
1 sweet chili pepper, seeded
2 cloves garlic, peeled
1 onion, peeled
1 canned pimiento
1 teaspoon capers
6 olives, stuffed with pimientos
    } ground or very finely minced
6 peppercorns (whole black peppers), crushed
1 teaspoon salt
1 teaspoon fresh lime juice
1 tablespoon *Achiote Coloring* (see Index)

1—In a small *caldero* or heavy kettle, heat fat included in *B*. Sauté rest of ingredients included in *B* over *low* heat for *10 minutes,* stirring **occasionally.**

2—Add crab meat, mix, *cover* and cook for *10 minutes* over *low* heat.

Procedure for Combining *Casabe* Paste and Filling

1—Wash several plantain leaves and cut into 12-inch squares. Remove central vein of leaves with scissors. (Squares of aluminum foil may be used instead of plantain leaves.) Grease each square with *Achiote Coloring.*

2—Place 4 tablespoons of *casabe* paste in center of each square and spoon it out, toward sides of leaf.

3—Spoon 3 tablespoons of the filling in the center and spread out.

4—Fold the square over **twice** and fold opposite ends toward center to resemble a package.

5—Place packages on baking sheet in oven preheated to 350°F. and bake for *20 minutes.* Turn *empanadas* over and bake for *25 minutes* longer. Serve in leaves.

Note: Beef or pork may substitute crab meat in above recipe using recipe for Basic Meat Filling. (See Index)

CHAPTER V *Eggs and Vegetables*

Eggs and Vegetables

SPANISH OMELET
(*Tortilla Española*)
(Serves 6)

A—¼ cup olive oil
½ pound onions, peeled and finely chopped
¼ teaspoon salt | ⅛ teaspoon ground pepper

B—½ pound potatoes, peeled and cubed or thinly sliced
¼ teaspoon salt

C—6 large eggs | ¾ teaspoon salt

1—In a 10-inch *Teflon* frying pan, combine ingredients included in A and sauté for *10 minutes* over *low* heat, stirring *occasionally*.

2—Strain in a colander. **Reserve** onions and pour oil back into the frying pan.

3—Add potatoes and salt included in B, mix, *cover*, and cook over *low* heat for *25 minutes*, or until potatoes are fork-tender.

4—Remove potatoes and **reserve.**

5—Beat eggs and salt included in C *thoroughly*, and mix with the reserved onions and potatoes.

6—Turn heat to *moderate-high*, add egg mixture so that the oil in the frying pan browns the eggs *rapidly. Immediately*, reduce heat to *low* and cook until upper part is dry. *Occasionally*, move the frying pan back and forth and release borders. When dry, put plate over and turn *tortilla*, slip again into frying pan and cook for *10 minutes* on other side.

Note: Vary by adding chopped *chorizos* (Spanish Sausages), boiled shrimps, etc. Taste and adjust seasoning.

CREAMED EGGS WITH ASPARAGUS
Huevos a la Crema con Espárragos
(Serves 6)

A—1 can (10½ ounces) asparagus tips | ¼ cup flour

B—1 can (13 ounces) evaporated milk, **undiluted**
½ teaspoon salt | 1 ounce (2 tablespoons) butter

C—6 hard-cooked eggs, sliced

D—1 tablespoon cracker or bread crumbs

1—Preheat oven to *350°F*. Grease a round 2-quart glass baking dish. Drain liquid from asparagus can, and **reserve.** Cut asparagus into 1-inch pieces and **reserve.**

2—Place flour in a saucepan and dissolve with reserved liquid from asparagus. Add ingredients included in *B*, mix, and stir over *moderate* heat until boiling.

3—Add cut asparagus and remove from heat.

4—Arrange in pan alternate layers of sauce and egg slices, beginning and ending with sauce. Sprinkle with crumbs.

5—Bake about *10 to 15 minutes,* or until crumbs brown attractively.

EGGS WITH GREEN PEAS
Huevos con Salsa de Guisantes
6 poached or fried eggs

Sauce:
2 tablespoons lard or vegetable oil
1 onion, peeled and finely chopped
½ cup tomato sauce
1 can (1 pound) green peas (*Petit-Pois*), drained

1—Sauté onion in fat for *5 minutes*. Add tomato sauce and green peas.

2—Cook over *moderate* heat for *10 minutes*. Serve hot, over poached or fried eggs.

TASTY EGGS

Pisto

(Serves 6)

A—2 pounds potatoes, peeled and cubed
1 quart (4 cups) water
2 tablespoons salt

B—2 cups lard or vegetable oil

C—2 medium onions, peeled and finely chopped
1 can (8 ounces) tomato sauce

D—6 eggs, separated
½ teaspoon salt

1—Soak potatoes for *10 minutes* in water and salt included in *A*.

2—Heat fat in a deep pan. Drain potatoes and add. *Cover,* and cook over *moderate* heat for *30 minutes,* stirring *occasionally.*

3—Remove potatoes from fat and drain on absorbent paper.

4—Measure 6 tablespoons of the fat into a large frying pan.

5—Add chopped onions and sauté for *10 minutes* over *low* heat, stirring *occasionally.*

6—Add tomato sauce and potatoes.

7—Beat egg whites until stiff. Fold in yolks, beaten with the salt included in *D*. Add to frying pan and stir *constantly* over *low* heat, until eggs set to taste.

EGGS VINAIGRETTE

Huevos a la Vinagreta

(Serves 3)

A—6 eggs
   2 large onions | 2 large tomatoes

B—¼ cup olive oil
   3 tablespoons vinegar | ½ teaspoon salt

1—Preheat oven to 325°F.

2—Wash and trim tomatoes and cut each into 3 slices. Place slices in bottom of glass baking dish.

3—Peel and wash onions. Cut each into 3 slices, removing center of each onion slice to form a nest in which to place an egg. Arrange onion slices over tomato slices.

4—Break an egg **carefully** into each nest, without breaking the yolk.

5—Mix ingredients included in *B* and pour over the eggs.

6—*Cover* baking dish and bake about *30 minutes,* or until eggs set to taste.

SCRAMBLED EGGS WITH CHAYOTE

Huevos Revueltos con Chayote

(Serves 4)

A—2 large or 3 medium *chayotes* (see Glossary), cut in two, **lengthwise**
   2 quarts (8 cups) water
   4 teaspoons salt

B—4 eggs
   ½ teaspoon salt
   1 pinch ground pepper
   ¼ cup milk

C—2 tablespoons lard or vegetable oil

1—Wash *chayotes* and bring to a boil in water and salt included in A. Turn heat to *moderate, cover,* and boil about *1 hour,* or until fork-tender.

2—Drain, remove cores and fibrous part under cores. Peel and allow to cool. Cut pulp into small cubes.

3—Separate yolks and egg whites. Combine yolks with remaining ingredients included in B.

4—Beat egg whites until very stiff. Add yolk mixture and *chayotes.*

5—Heat fat lightly in a frying pan. Add mixture and cook over *low* heat, stirring **occasionally,** until eggs set to taste.

EGGS IN THE NEST

Huevos al Nido

(Serves 6)

A—1 pound potatoes, peeled and quartered
  1 quart (4 cups) water | 1 tablespoon salt

B—1 ounce (2 tablespoons) butter | ⅛ teaspoon salt
  3 ounces (6 tablespoons) lukewarm milk

C—6 eggs | ¾ teaspoon salt
  6 teaspoons freshly grated Parmesan cheese

1—Wash potatoes and bring to a boil in water and salt included in A. Reduce heat to *moderate, cover* and boil about *30 minutes,* or until fork-tender. Drain and mash or put **immediately** through a potato ricer.

2—Add ingredients included in B, and mix.

3—Preheat oven to *300°F.* Grease 6 individual baking cups.

4—Fill half of each cup with mashed potato. **Carefully** break an egg over potato. Sprinkle each with ⅛ teaspoon salt and 1 teaspoon grated cheese.

5—*Cover* with remaining mashed potato.

6—Bake about *45 minutes,* or until eggs set to taste.

TART

Torta

(Makes 2 tarts)

A—2 cups flour
  2 teaspoons baking powder
  1½ teaspoons salt

B—2 cups milk

C—2 ounces (4 tablespoons) butter
  1 cup freshly grated Parmesan cheese

D—4 eggs, beaten

1—Sift together ingredients included in A into a bowl.

2—Add milk and mix well.

3—Beat butter until creamy and add to the flour mixture with the grated cheese.

4—Add well-beaten eggs and mix.

5—Butter a half-moon-shaped omelet pan with top.

6—Turn half the mixture into pan and cook over *moderate* heat about *7 minutes* on each side. Remove from pan and cook rest of the mixture in the same way.

7—Serve hot, with butter and pancake syrup.

FINGER BANANAS IN WINE

Guineitos Niños en Vino

A—2 ounces (4 tablespoons) butter
18 finger bananas (*guineitos niños*) (select **ripe** bananas with *yellow* skin and firm to the touch)

B—1 cup sugar

C—½ cup water
1 teaspoon vanilla extract

D—½ cup muscatel wine or Grand Marnier (Orange Liqueur)

1—In a large frying pan, melt butter *slowly*. Peel finger bananas, add and brown to a golden color over *moderate* heat.

2—Sprinkle finger bananas with sugar included in *B*.

3—Mix water and vanilla extract included in *C* and pour over finger bananas.

4—Turn heat to *moderate-high* and bring to a boil. Reduce heat to *moderate* and boil for *5 minutes*.

5—Pour wine **over finger bananas** and boil until syrup thickens to taste.

FINGER BANANAS WITH CHEESE

Guineitos Niños con Queso

A—12 ripe finger bananas (*guineitos niños*) (select **ripe** bananas with *yellow* skin and firm to the touch)

B—Lard, vegetable oil, or butter (*for frying*)

C—2 tablespoons freshly grated Parmesan cheese

1—Peel finger bananas and brown to a golden color in a frying pan over *moderate* heat, in fat included in *B*.

2—Drain on absorbent paper. Set on a platter and sprinkle with cheese.

GREEN BANANAS IN AJI-LI-MOJILI SAUCE

Guineitos Verdes en Salsa Aji-li-mójili

A—10 green bananas

B—8 cups water
2 tablespoons salt

C—**Aji-li-mójili sauce:**
2 cloves garlic, peeled
3 sweet chili peppers, seeded
2 peppercorns (whole black
   peppers)   crush and mix
1 teaspoon salt   in a mortar
¼ cup olive oil
2 tablespoons vinegar
2 tablespoons fresh lime juice

D—1 cup water

1—Trim ends of bananas and slit **just** the peel, **lengthwise,** on both sides. In a deep kettle, bring to a boil water to cover green bananas. Add bananas, *cover,* and boil over *low* heat for *15 minutes.* Drain and peel.

2—Fill kettle with ingredients included in *B* and bring **rapidly** to a boil. Add peeled bananas, *cover,* and boil over *low* heat for *10 minutes.* Add *1 cup of water* and boil for *5 minutes.* Drain and allow to cool.

3—Cut bananas into 1-inch rounds. Place in a deep glass or porcelain dish, *alternating* with *Aji-li-mójili* sauce. Marinate for *24 hours.*

4—Serve as an appetizer.

PICKLED GREEN BANANAS
Guineitos Verdes en Escabeche

A—**Escabeche sauce:**
  2 cups olive oil
  1 cup vinegar
  12 peppercorns (whole black peppers)
  ½ teaspoon salt
  2 bay leaves
  1½ pounds onions, peeled and sliced
  2 cloves garlic, minced

B—10 green bananas

C—8 cups water
  2 tablespoons salt

1—In a *caldero* or heavy kettle, mix ingredients included in A, and cook over *low* heat for *1 hour*. Allow to cool.

2—Trim ends of bananas and slit **just** the peel, **lengthwise,** on both sides. In a deep pot, bring to a boil water to cover bananas. Add bananas, *cover,* and boil over *low* heat for *15 minutes*. Drain and peel.

3—Fill the pot with ingredients included in C and bring **rapidly** to a boil. Add peeled bananas, *cover,* and boil over *low* heat for *10 minutes*. Add *1 cup of water* and boil for *5 minutes*. Drain and allow to cool.

4—Cut bananas into 1-inch rounds. Place in a deep glass or porcelain dish, alternating with the *Escabeche* sauce. Marinate for *24 hours*.

5—Serve as an appetizer.

PLANTAINS IN SYRUP
Plátanos Maduros (Amarillos) *en Almíbar*

A—4 large, 5 medium or 6 small **ripe** plantains (*amarillos*)
2 quarts (8 cups) water
2 tablespoons salt

B—2 ounces (4 tablespoons) butter
2 cups sugar
1½ cups water
1 teaspoon vanilla extract

C—½ cup muscatel wine

1—Peel plantains, make 3 diagonal superficial gashes on each side and soak in water and salt included in A for *½ hour*. Remove and drain.

2—Melt butter *slowly* in a frying pan. Add drained plantains and brown *lightly* over *moderate-high* heat.

3—Cover plantains with sugar. Combine vanilla extract with water and pour over plantains. Bring to a boil. *Cover* and boil for *20 minutes*.

4—*Uncover*, pour wine **over plantains,** reduce heat to *moderate* and boil until syrup thickens to taste.

Note: Select ripe plantains with *yellow* skin and black patches. If skin is totally black, the plantains are too ripe and will break while cooking.

PLANTAINS IN MILK
Plátanos Maduros (Amarillos) *en Leche*

A—3 large **ripe** plantains (*amarillos*)

B—2 ounces (4 tablespoons) butter
1 cup sugar
3 cups milk
1 small cinnamon stick
Cheddar cheese, cut in thin slices

1—Peel plantains. Make a deep gash, *lengthwise,* to allow for stuffing.

2—Melt butter *slowly.* Add plantains and brown *lightly* over *moderate-high* heat.

3—Fill gashes with slices of cheese. Top with sugar, cover with milk and add cinnamon stick. *Cover* and *cook* over *moderate* heat for *10 minutes.*

4—*Uncover,* turn heat to *low,* and cook about *1 hour,* or until fork-tender.

Note: Cooking time might vary according to ripeness of plantains.

CANDIED PLANTAINS

Plátanos Maduros (Amarillos) *al Horno*

1—Select **ripe** plantains with skin **partially** black. Peel, make 3 diagonal gashes on each side, and soak for *30 minutes* in water to cover, using 1 tablespoon salt for **each** quart (4 cups) of water. Remove and drain well.

2—Rub plantains *generously* with oleomargarine and place in a greased shallow baking dish. Sprinkle with sugar and dot with butter.

3—Cook in preheated oven to 350°F. for *30 minutes.*

4—Turn, sprinkle again with sugar and dot with butter, and bake about *30 minutes,* or until fork-tender.

Note: Cooking time might vary according to ripeness of plantains.

BAKED PLANTAINS

Plátanos Maduros (Amarillos) *Asados en su Cáscara*

1—Select very **ripe** plantains, with the skin **totally** black. Wash and dry. **Do not peel.** Trim ends of plantains and slit **just** the peel, **lengthwise.** Arrange on an aluminum baking sheet, lined with aluminum foil.

2—Preheat oven to 350°F. and bake the plantains about 45 *minutes* or until fork-tender. Turn over **halfway** through cooking period.

PLANTAINS CONES

Piononos

(12 cones)

A—3 large **ripe** plantains (*amarillos*)

B—Lard or vegetable oil (*for pan-frying*)

C—2 eggs | 1 tablespoon flour
¼ teaspoon salt | 1 tablespoon water

D—⅔ cup Cheddar cheese, shredded

1—Peel plantains and cut each into 4 slices, *lengthwise.*

2—Heat fat in a frying pan and brown slices *rapidly.* Drain on absorbent paper and cool *slightly.*

3—Roll each slice into a cone and secure with wooden picks.

4—Beat eggs and salt *lightly.* Blend flour and water and mix with beaten eggs.

5—Stuff the cones with the shredded cheese and cover stuffing with the egg batter.

6—Fry in hot fat, with stuffing **downward,** until egg is golden brown. Remove and drain on absorbent paper. Remove picks before serving.

Note: Cheese can be substituted by any cooked meat filling.

PLANTAINS WITH PORK CRACKLING

Mofongo

(10 balls)

A—3 green plantains
1 quart (4 cups) water | 1 tablespoon salt

B—3 large cloves garlic, peeled | 1 tablespoon olive oil

C—½ pound **very crisp** pork crackling (*chicharrón*)

D—Lard or vegetable oil (*for deep-frying*)

1—Peel plantains, cut into 1-inch diagonal slices and soak for *15 minutes* in water and salt included in *A*. Drain well.

2—Heat fat to *350°F*. Add plantain slices and allow to fry at *300°F*. about *15 minutes*, or until done, but not browned. Drain on absorbent paper and **reserve.**

3—In a mortar, crush cloves garlic well, add olive oil and mix. Remove from mortar and **reserve.**

4—Crush in the mortar part of the fried plantain slices together with part of the pork crackling. Add some of the mixture of crushed cloves garlic and olive oil and mix *thoroughly.*

5—Spoon the mixture and shape into 2-inch balls. Repeat with the rest. Serve hot.

CHEESE-PLANTAIN PIE

Pastelón de Plátanos Maduros (Amarillos) *con Queso*

(Serves 8)

A—6 large **ripe,** partially ripe plantains (*amarillos*)
2 quarts (8 cups) water | 4½ teaspoons salt

B—¼ pound butter | ¾ cup flour

C—½ pound Cheddar cheese, shredded

1—Cut plantains in two and **without** peeling, bring to a boil in water and salt, included in *A*. Reduce heat to *moderate, cover* and boil for *20 minutes*. Drain, peel, and mash.

2—Add ingredients included in *B*, and mix.

3—Heat oven to 350°F. Grease a 10-inch pie glass baking plate and spread half of the plantain mixture.

4—Top with shredded cheese.

5—Cover with the remaining plantain mixture.

6—Bake about *30 minutes.*

MEAT-PLANTAIN PIE

Pastelón de Plátanos Maduros (Amarillos) *con Carne*

Filling:

A—½ ounce salt pork } washed and diced
  1 ounce lean cured ham }

1 tablespoon fat or *Achiote Coloring* (see Index)

¼ green pepper, seeded ⎫
1 sweet chili pepper, seeded ⎬ finely chopped
1 onion, peeled ⎪
1 tomato ⎭

B—½ teaspoon whole dried *orégano* } crushed
  1 clove garlic, peeled }

3 olives, stuffed with pimientos } chopped
2 dry prunes, pitted }

1 teaspoon seeded raisins   ½ teaspoon salt
½ teaspoon capers   ¼ teaspoon vinegar
¼ cup tomato sauce   ½ pound lean ground beef

Plantain mixture:

A—4 or 5 large **ripe** plantains (*amarillos*)
  1½ quarts (6 cups) water | 1 tablespoon salt

B—2 ounces (4 tablespoons) butter or oleomargarine
  ½ cup flour

1—Prepare filling as follows: Brown salt pork and cured ham **rapidly.** Reduce heat to low, add rest of ingredients included in A, and sauté for *5 minutes.* Add ingredients included in B, mix well, cover and cook over *moderate* heat for *10 minutes.* *Uncover* and cook for *10 minutes,* stirring **occasionally.**

2—Prepare plantain mixture as follows: In a pot, mix water and salt included in A. Add **unpeeled** *plantains,* halved. Boil over *high* heat for *15 minutes.* Drain, peel, mash, and mix with butter. Add flour and mix.

3—Grease a 10-inch pie glass baking plate and spread half of the plantain mixture. Top with the filling and *cover* with remaining of plantain mixture.

4—Preheat oven to *350°F.,* and bake for *30 minutes.*

PLANTAIN AND MEAT SURPRISE

Piñón

(Serves 8)

A—1 ounce salt pork
   2 ounces lean cured ham } washed and diced
   1 tablespoon lard or vegetable oil
   1 green pepper, seeded
   3 sweet chili peppers, seeded
   1 onion, peeled } chopped
   2 cloves garlic, peeled

B—1 pound lean ground beef

C—2 hard-cooked eggs
   6 olives, stuffed with pimientos } chopped
   6 dry prunes, pitted
   2 tablespoons seeded raisins
   1 teaspoon capers
   1 teaspoon salt
   1 teaspoon whole dried *orégano*
   ¼ teaspoon vinegar
   ¾ cup tomato sauce

D—½ pound fresh string beans, trimmed   or 1 can (1 pound) string beans, drained
   3 cups water   or 1 package (1 pound) frozen string beans, prepared
   1 teaspoon salt   according to instructions

E—6 large, **ripe** plantains (*amarillos*)

F—Lard or vegetable oil (*for deep frying*)

G—6 eggs
   ¾ teaspoon salt

1—In a *caldero* or heavy kettle, brown *rapidly* salt pork and ham. Reduce heat to *low* and sauté rest of ingredients included in A for *10 minutes,* stirring *occasionally.*

2—Add meat and stir *constantly* over *high* heat until meat loses its red color. Reduce heat to *low* and add ingredients included in C. *Cover* and cook for *15 minutes.*

3—Wash the beans and bring to a boil in water and salt included in D. Reduce heat to *moderate, cover,* and boil for *20 minutes.* Drain, add to *caldero* and mix.

4—Peel plantains and cut each into 4 *lengthwise* slices.

5—In a *caldero* or heavy kettle, heat fat included in F. Brown plantain slices on both sides. Remove and drain on absorbent paper.

6—Beat eggs until stiff. Add salt and beat again.

7—Heat 2 tablespoons fat in a 9-inch *Teflon* frying pan and assemble the *Piñón* by arranging layers as follows: (see Note)

    a—Half of the beaten eggs
    b—⅓ of the plantain slices
    c—Half of the meat mixture
    d—⅓ of the plantain slices
    e—Remainder of the meat mixture
    f—⅓ of the plantain slices
    g—Remainder of the beaten eggs

8—Cook over *moderate* heat for *15 minutes.* Remove from heat, place a big platter over frying pan and turn over **carefully.**

9—Add 1 tablespoon of fat to the frying pan. Heat fat and **slowly** slip *Piñón* back into the frying pan. Cook over *low* heat for *15 minutes.* **Unmold** on a round serving platter.

Note: Pinóñ can also be assembled and baked in a 13 x 9 x 2-inch glass baking dish, in a preheated oven to 350°F., about *30 minutes,* or until egg is set and golden brown. *Do not unmold.* Serve in baking dish.

STUFFED PLANTAINS

Rellenos de Plátanos Maduros (Amarillos)

(16 Stuffings)

Plantain:

A—6 **ripe** plantains (*amarillos*), unpeeled and halved
2 quarts (8 cups) water
1½ tablespoons salt

B—2 ounces (4 tablespoons) butter
½ teaspoon salt
2 tablespoons cornstarch

Filling:

A—½ pound Cheddar cheese, shredded
  or ½ recipe of Basic Meat Filling (see Index)

B—Lard or vegetable oil (*for deep-frying*)

1—Bring to a boil water and salt included in A. Add plantains, *cover*, and boil *rapidly* for *20 minutes*. Drain, peel, and mash together with ingredients in B. Allow to cool *slightly*.

2—Coat hand palm with cornstarch. Spread some of the plantain mixture and make a nest in center. Stuff center with filling. Cover with plantain mixture and shape into balls. Repeat to make 16 stuffings.

3—Deep-fry at 375°F. until golden. Remove and drain on absorbent paper.

PASTELES

(Makes 36)

Filling:

A—2 pounds lean pork meat, without bone
6 tablespoons *jugo de naranja agria* (sour orange juice) (see Glossary)

B—**Crush and mix in a mortar:**
4 sweet chili peppers, seeded | 4 fresh *culantro* leaves
2 large cloves garlic, peeled
2 tablespoons whole dried *orégano* | 1 tablespoon salt

C—**Cube finely:**
1 pound lean cured ham
1 green pepper, seeded | 1 onion, peeled

D—1½ cups seeded raisins

E—1 can (1 pound) *garbanzos* (Chick-Peas), liquid **included**
1 cup water

F—24 olives, stuffed with pimientos, finely chopped
1½ tablespoons capers
6 tablespoons *Achiote Coloring* (see Glossary)

1—Wash and dry pork meat **rapidly** and cut into very small cubes. Mix meat cubes with the sour orange juice.

2—Add ingredients included in *B* to meat.

3—Add ingredients included in *C* and the seeded raisins. Mix together well.

4—In a saucepan, bring to a boil ingredients included in *E*. Drain the liquid over the meat mixture. Remove skins from chick-peas and add chick-peas to the meat mixture.

5—Add olives and capers.

6—Add ingredients included in *F*, mix well, *cover,* and set in refrigerator until the **masa** is ready.

Masa (Paste)

A—4 pounds white *yautía*, peeled } (see Glossary)
    4 pounds yellow *yautía*, peeled }
    15 green bananas, peeled and rinsed in salted water
    2 cups lukewarm milk

B—1¼ cups (10 ounces) *Achiote Coloring* (see Index)
    2½ tablespoons salt

Diagram of method used to shape the "pastel"

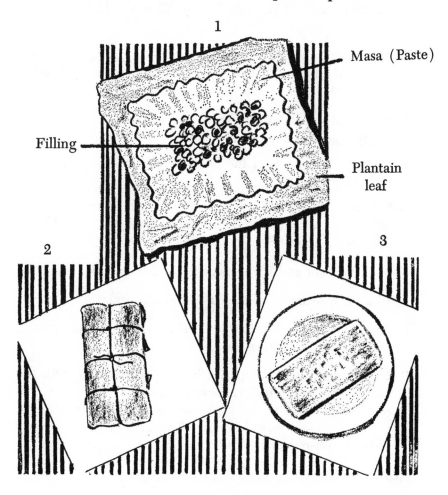

Masa (Paste)

Filling

Plantain leaf

1—Wash, drain, and grate the *yautías* and bananas. Crush *gradually* in a mortar *yautías* and bananas. Mix in a bowl with lukewarm milk to make a smooth paste. (If using an electric blender, crush *gradually yautías* and bananas with lukewarm milk. Set in a bowl.)

2—Add the *Achiote Coloring* and salt, mix well, *cover*, and set aside to make the *pasteles*.

To Shape and Cook the Pasteles

1—Use 20 bundles of plantain leaves. They should be long and wide.

2—With a knife, remove the central ridge to give greater flexibility to the leaves. Divide leaves into pieces, about 12 inches square. Wash and clean leaves with a damp cloth.

3—Place 3 tablespoons of the *masa* on a leaf and spread it out so **thinly,** that it is almost transparent.

4—Place 3 tablespoons of the filling in the center of the *masa*. (see diagram)

5—Fold the leaf one half over the other to make a top and bottom layer of plantain leaf and enclose the contents in it. Fold it over once more.

6—Fold the right and left ends of the leaf toward the center.

7—Wrap in a second leaf placed on the diagonal.

8—Tie the *pasteles* together, in pairs, with a string, placing folded edges facing each other.

9—In a large vessel, bring to a boil 5 quarts water with 3½ tablespoons salt. Add 12 *pasteles* and boil, *covered*, for *1 hour*. **Halfway,** turn over *pasteles*. When cooking period is finished, remove *pasteles* from the water **at once.** Repeat process with rest of *pasteles*.

Note: Parchment cooking paper may be used in place of plantain leaves.

PLANTAIN GUANIMES
Guanimes de Plátano
(Serves 6)

A—3 green plantains
2 quarts (8 cups) water
2 tablespoons salt

B—½ cup coconut milk, **undiluted** (see Index)
¾ cup sugar
1 teaspoon salt
1 teaspoon aniseeds

C—Plantain leaves or squares of parchment paper
3 quarts (12 cups) boiling water
3 tablespoons salt

1—Peel plantains and soak for *30 minutes* in water with salt included in A. Remove from water, drain well, and grate.

2—Combine grated plantains with ingredients included in B.

3—Wash plantain leaves and cut into pieces large enough to wrap mixture as follows:
Place 2 tablespoons of the plantain mixture in the center of each piece of leaf, spreading with a spoon to an oblong shape. Fold up sides and ends and tie with a string.

4—Put the *guanimes* into the boiling water with salt included in C. Cook, *covered,* over *moderate* heat for *30 minutes.*

5—Drain and serve in the leaves.

CORNMEAL GUANIMES

Guanimes de Maíz

(Makes 18)

A—1 pound yellow cornmeal
2 cups coconut milk, **undiluted** (see Index)
1 cup molasses
½ teaspoon aniseeds | 1 teaspoon salt

B—Plantain leaves or squares of parchment paper
3 quarts (12 cups) boiling water
3 tablespoons salt

1—Mix thoroughly ingredients included in A.

2—Wash plantain leaves and cut into pieces large enough to enfold portions of the mixture as follows:
Put 2 tablespoons of the mixture in center of each piece of leaf and spread with a spoon to an oblong shape. Fold up sides and ends and tie securely.

3—Cook the *guanimes* in the boiling water with salt included in B over *moderate* heat for *45 minutes* in *covered* pot. Drain and serve in the leaves.

CORNMEAL FUNGI

Funche de Maíz Filo

1 cup yellow cornmeal, sifted
¾ teaspoon salt
½ cup sugar
¼ teaspoon ground cinnamon
1 quart (4 cups) milk
1 ounce (2 tablespoons) butter

1—In a large saucepan, combine all ingredients and bring *rapidly* to a boil, stirring *constantly*.

2—Reduce heat to *low* and stir *occasionally* for *15 minutes*. Serve immediately.

POTATO CHEESE SOUFFLÉ

Soufflé de Papa y Queso

(Serves 8)

A—2 ounces (4 tablespoons) butter | 1½ cups water
2 cups milk | 1¼ teaspoons salt

B—1 box (5½ ounces) *Whipped* or *Mashed Potatoes*

C—4 eggs, separated | ¾ cup shredded Swiss cheese

1—Preheat oven to *350°F*. Grease a 2-quart round glass baking dish.

2—In a large kettle, combine ingredients included in *A* and bring *rapidly* to a boil.

3—Remove from heat and add, **all at once,** contents of box of *Whipped* or *Mashed Potatoes*. With a wooden spoon, mix **vigorously** to consistency of mashed potatoes.

4—Add egg yolks and mix. Add shredded cheese and mix.

5—Beat egg whites until stiff and fold into the mixture.

6—Turn into baking dish and bake about *40 minutes,* or until golden brown and set.

POTATO BUNS

Buñuelos de Papas

(Serves 6)

A—1 pound potatoes, peeled and halved

B—½ ounce (1 tablespoon) butter | ½ teaspoon sugar
Dash ground pepper | 1 teaspoon salt
2 tablespoons cornstarch | 2 egg yolks

C—Cornstarch (*to coat buns*)

D—Lard or vegetable oil (*for deep-frying*)

1—Wash potatoes and bring *rapidly* to a boil in water to *cover,* **without salt.** Turn heat to *moderate* and boil for *30 minutes.* Drain and mash or put through a potato ricer.

2—Add ingredients included in *B* and mix.

3—Allow mixture to cool **slightly.** Take mixture by teaspoonfuls, form into small balls, and coat with cornstarch.

4—Deep-fry at *375°F.*, until golden brown. Remove and drain on absorbent paper.

GRANDMA'S POTATO PUDDING

Papa Empanada al Horno

(Serves 6)

A—2 pounds potatoes
2 quarts (8 cups) water
1½ tablespoons salt

B—2 ounces (4 tablespoons) butter
¾ teaspoon salt
2 tablespoons sugar
1½ cups lukewarm milk
1 egg
2 tablespoons bread or cracker crumbs

1—Peel and halve potatoes. Bring **rapidly** to a boil in water with salt included in *A*. *Cover* and boil over *moderate* heat about *30 minutes,* or until fork-tender.

2—Drain and **immediately** mash or put through a potato ricer.

3—Add butter, salt, sugar, and milk and mix well with a wooden spoon.

4—Beat egg until stiff and fold into potato mixture.

5—Grease a 2-quart round glass baking dish and sprinkle bottom with half of the crumbs.

6—Turn potato mixture into the dish, sprinkle with remaining crumbs, and bake in oven, preheated to *375°F.*, about *30 minutes,* or until golden brown and set.

BAKED POTATOES AND CARROTS
Papas y Zanahorias al Horno
(Serves 6)

A—1 pound potatoes
1 pound carrots
6 cups water
2 tablespoons salt

B—2 tablespoons bread or cracker crumbs

C—2 hard-cooked eggs, chopped
½ cup lukewarm milk
¼ teaspoon salt
1 ounce (2 tablespoons) butter

1—Peel and halve potatoes. Scrape carrots and halve. In a pot, bring vegetables to a boil in water with salt included in A. *Cover*, and boil about *40 minutes* or until fork-tender.

2—Grease a 2-quart round glass baking dish and sprinkle half the crumbs over the bottom.

3—Preheat oven to *375°F.*

4—Drain potatoes and carrots and *immediately* mash or put through a potato ricer.

5—Add ingredients included in *C* and mix well.

6—Turn mixture into baking dish. Sprinkle with remaining crumbs and bake, *uncovered*, for *10 minutes*.

BAKED POTATOES WITH MILK AND CHEESE

Papas con Leche y Queso al Horno

(Serves 8)

A—2 pounds potatoes, washed, peeled and thinly sliced
¾ cup flour   ¾ ounce (1½ tablespoons) butter
3 teaspoons salt   1 quart (4 cups) milk
3 tablespoons freshly grated Parmesan cheese

1—Preheat oven to 350°F.

2—Grease a 3-quart round glass baking dish.

3—In baking dish, arrange ingredients included in A, in *alternate* layers, as follows:

⅓ of potato slices   1⅓ cups milk
¼ cup flour   ½ tablespoon butter
1 teaspoon salt   1 tablespoon grated cheese

4—Repeat layers **twice.**

5—*Cover* pan and bake in preheated oven for *1 hour.*

6—*Uncover,* and bake for *30 minutes.* Allow to rest for *5 minutes* before serving.

BUFFET POTATO

Papa Ilusión

(Serves 10)

A—1 quart (4 cups) milk
3 cups water
1 tablespoon salt
¼ pound butter
½ cup sugar (*optional*)

B—5 cups of *Potato Flakes* from a large box of *Whipped* or *Mashed Potatoes*

C—4 eggs, large

D—1 tablespoon bread or cracker crumbs
Paprika (*for dusting potatoes*)

1—Preheat oven to *350°F.* Grease a 13 x 9 x 2-inch glass baking dish.

2—In a deep large pot, heat to boiling ingredients included in *A.* Remove from heat and add, **all at once,** *Potato Flakes.* With a wooden spoon, mix **vigorously** to consistency of mashed potatoes.

3—Beat eggs and fold into mixture. Spoon into baking dish. Sprinkle crumbs and dust with paprika.

4—Bake about *30 minutes* and serve.

POTATOES ROYALE
Papas Reales

A—8 large Idaho potatoes

B—¼ pound butter
1 teaspoon salt
3 eggs
¼ cup freshly grated Parmesan cheese
1 jar (6 ounces) *Avoset Cream* (Blue Label) or heavy cream

C—Paprika (*for dusting potatoes*)

1—Preheat oven to *425°F.* Scrub and wash potatoes carefully. Remove and discard sprouts. Wipe, dry, and wrap potatoes, individually, with heavy aluminum foil. Bake about *1½ hours,* or until tender.

2—Remove from oven, discard foil, and **immediately** cut slice off bottom of each potato. Scoop out pulp, without breaking shells. Place empty shells on an aluminum sheet.

3—Mash pulp **immediately** and mix **thoroughly** with ingredients included in *B.* Fill potato shells and dust with paprika.

4—Reduce oven heat to *375°F.,* and bake about *20 minutes.*

Note: If there is any left-over filling, place in a small baking dish and bake together with potato shells.

CANDIED SWEET POTATOES
Batatas en Almíbar

A—1 quart (4 cups) water
1 tablespoon salt
2 pounds small sweet potatoes, scrubbed and washed

B—2 cups sugar
1½ cups water

C—1 teaspoon vanilla extract
2 ounces (4 tablespoons) butter

1—In a pot, bring to a boil sweet potatoes in water and salt included in *A. Cover,* and boil at *moderate* heat for *30 minutes.*

2—Drain, peel, and cut sweet potatoes into *¼-inch* slices.

3—Set slices in a frying pan. Add ingredients included in *B,* mix, and cook over *high* heat until it reaches consistency of light syrup (Candy Thermometer — *222°F.*).

4—Add ingredients included in *C* and cook until butter melts. Remove from heat and serve.

ASPARAGUS SOUFFLÉ
Soufflé de Espárragos

A—2 ounces (4 tablespoons) butter
6 tablespoons flour
1 teaspoon salt
1½ cups lukewarm milk

B—2 cans (10½ ounces each) asparagus tips

C—6 eggs
1 tablespoon fresh lime juice

1—Preheat oven to *350°F.* Grease a 2-quart round glass baking dish.

2—In a saucepan, melt butter over *low heat*. Blend in flour and salt. Stir in milk **gradually.** Turn heat to *moderate* and stir **constantly** until mixture boils and thickens **slightly.**

3—Remove from heat and add asparagus tips, drained and finely cut.

4—Separate white and yolks of eggs. Beat yolks **lightly** and add to mixture. Add lime juice and mix.

5—Beat egg whites until stiff and fold into mixture. Pour **immediately** into the greased dish.

6—Bake about *50 minutes,* or until golden brown and set.

7—Serve **immediately.**

BREAD-FRUIT SEEDS
Semillas de Panas

A—2 pounds breadfruit seeds (see Glossary)
2 quarts (8 cups) boiling water

B—3 tablespoons salt

1—Wash breadfruit seeds well. Cook in boiling water, *covered,* for *30 minutes.*

2—Add salt, and boil for *15 minutes,* or until tender. Remove and serve. Peel and eat **immediately.**

Note: Follow above recipe for cooking *Lerenes* (see Glossary), but boil for *1 hour,* or until tender.

CAULIFLOWER SOUFFLÉ

Soufflé de Coliflor

(Serves 8)

A—1 large cauliflower (after removing outer leaves, flowerets should weigh about 2 pounds)
2 quarts (8 cups) water | 2 teaspoons salt

B—2 quarts (8 cups) water | 2 tablespoons salt

C—1 tablespoon bread or cracker crumbs

D—2 ounces (4 tablespoons) butter
¼ cup flour | ⅛ teaspoon ground pepper
1 teaspoon salt | 2 cups lukewarm milk

E—3 eggs, separated
1 cup freshly grated Parmesan cheese

1—Remove outer cauliflower leaves. Separate the flowerets. Wash and soak in water and salt included in *A* for *20 minutes.* Drain. Heat to boiling water and salt included in *B*. Add drained flowerets, *cover,* and boil for *20 minutes.* Drain *thoroughly.*

2—Grease a 2-quart round glass baking dish and sprinkle bottom with crumbs.

3—Preheat oven to *350°F.*

4—Prepare the following white sauce: Melt butter **slowly** in a saucepan. Add flour and blend until smooth. Add salt, pepper, and lukewarm milk. Stir over *moderate* heat until sauce boils and is lightly thick.

5—Add flowerets to the sauce, heat to boiling and remove from heat.

6—Beat egg whites until stiff. Add yolks to the whites and beat well together.

7—Arrange ingredients in baking dish as follows:
    Cover bottom with ⅓ of the beaten eggs
    Sprinkle with ¼ cup grated cheese
    Cover with ⅓ of the beaten eggs
    Sprinkle with ¼ cup grated cheese
    Cover with ⅓ of the beaten eggs
    Sprinkle with ¼ cup grated cheese
    Spoon mixture of sauce and flowerets
    Sprinkle with ¼ cup grated cheese

8—Bake about *30 minutes* or until golden brown and set.

9—Serve **immediately.**

CREAMED CHAYOTES

Chayotes a la Crema

(12 *chayote* shells)

A—6 large *chayotes*, cut in two, lengthwise (see Glossary)
    3 quarts (12 cups) water | 3 tablespoons salt

B—⅓ cup sugar | 2 tablespoons seeded raisins
    ½ teaspoon salt | 2 egg yolks

C—6 tablespoons cornstarch | ¾ cup milk
    1 teaspoon vanilla extract or peel of 1 small fresh lime

D—2 egg whites }
    ⅓ cup sugar } *for meringue*

1—Wash *chayotes*, bring to a boil in water and salt included in A. Reduce heat to *moderate, cover,* and boil about *1 hour,* or until fork-tender. Drain well, remove cores and fibrous part under cores. Scoop out the pulp, being careful not to break the shells. Place *chayote* shells on an aluminum sheet. Mash pulp **immediately** (or use an electric blender) and combine with ingredients included in *B*.

2—In a saucepan, dissolve cornstarch in part of milk. Apart, bring to a boil rest of milk, together with vanilla extract or lime peel. Remove peel. Add milk to dissolved cornstarch and mix. Add to the mashed *chayotes* and mix well.

3—Cook mixture to boiling over *moderate* heat, stirring *constantly*. Remove from heat and fill *chayote* shells with the mixture.

4—Preheat oven to *350°F.* and bake about *20 minutes*.

5—Beat egg whites stiff, add sugar **gradually,** and beat until well blended. Garnish shells with meringue. Bake for *10 minutes*.

Note: If preferred, turn mixture into a 3-quart glass baking dish, omit meringue, and bake for 30 minutes.

CHAYOTES STUFFED WITH CHEESE

Chayotes Rellenos con Queso

(Serves 6)

A—3 large *chayotes,* cut in two, lengthwise (see Glossary)
2 quarts (8 cups) water
2 tablespoons salt

B—1 cup Cheddar cheese, shredded
1 teaspoon salt
½ ounce (1 tablespoon) butter

1—Wash *chayotes* and bring to a boil in water and salt included in A. Reduce heat to *moderate, cover,* and boil about *1 hour,* or until fork-tender. Drain, remove cores and fibrous part under cores. Scoop out pulp, being careful not to break shells. Place shells on an aluminum sheet. **Immediately,** mash pulps and mix with ingredients included in B.

2—Stuff shells with the mixture. Sprinkle with crumbs and bake in preheated oven to *350°F.,* for *30 minutes*.

CHAYOTES STUFFED WITH BEEF OR PORK

Chayotes Rellenos con Carne de Res o Cerdo

(Serves 6)

A—3 large *chayotes,* cut in two, lengthwise (see Glossary)
2 quarts (8 cups) water | 2 tablespoons salt

B—1 teaspoon lard or vegetable oil
½ pound ground lean beef or pork
2 ounces lean cured ham, washed and minced
1 teaspoon salt

C—¼ cup minced onion
5 dry prunes, pitted } minced
1 clove garlic, peeled }
½ teaspoon whole dried *orégano*
½ teaspoon capers | ¼ cup tomato sauce
2 tablespoons seeded raisins | ¼ teaspoon vinegar

D—2 tablespoons bread or cracker crumbs
1 ounce (2 tablespoons) butter

1—Wash *chayotes* and bring to a boil in water and salt included
in A. Reduce heat to *moderate, cover,* and boil about *1 hour,*
or until fork-tender.

2—In a *caldero* or heavy kettle, heat fat included in B. Add rest
of ingredients included in B, and stir **constantly** over *high*
heat until meat loses its red color.

3—Reduce heat to *moderate.* Add ingredients included in C,
mix, *cover,* and cook for *45 minutes,* stirring **occasionally.**

4—Drain *chayotes,* remove cores and fibrous part under cores.
Scoop out the pulp, being careful not to break the shells. Place
shells on an aluminum sheet. Mash the pulp **immediately,** and
add to *caldero.* Mix and cook at *low* heat for *15 minutes.*

5—Fill *chayote* shells with the mixture. Sprinkle with crumbs
and dot with butter. Preheat oven to *375°F.,* and bake until
crumbs are golden brown.

SCRAMBLED CHAYOTES

Boronia de Chayote

(Serves 6)

A—3 large *chayotes,* cut in two, lengthwise (see Glossary)
2 quarts (8 cups) water
2 tablespoons salt

B—2 tablespoons lard or vegetable oil
¼ pound lean cured ham, washed and diced

C—1 onion, peeled
1 green pepper, seeded
3 sweet chili peppers, seeded
1 tomato   } minced
1 clove garlic, peeled
3 fresh *culantro* leaves
3 tablespoons tomato sauce

D—3 eggs
½ teaspoon salt

1—Wash *chayotes* and bring to a boil in water and salt included
in A. Reduce heat to *moderate, cover,* and boil about *1 hour,*
or until fork-tender. Drain, remove cores and fibrous part under cores. Peel and allow to cool.

2—In a *caldero* or heavy kettle, heat fat or *Achiote Coloring* and
brown *rapidly* diced ham. Add ingredients included in *C,*
reduce heat to *low* and sauté for *10 minutes,* stirring **occasionally.**

3—Dice *chayotes,* add, and mix.

4—Beat eggs and salt. Add and stir mixture over *low* heat until
eggs cook to taste.

EGGPLANT WITH CHEESE

Berenjena con Queso

(Serves 6)

A — 2 pounds eggplants   1½ teaspoons salt
1½ quarts (6 cups) water

B — 1 cup freshly grated Parmesan cheese   1 egg
2 ounces (4 tablespoons) butter

C — 1 tablespoon bread or cracker crumbs
1 ounce (2 tablespoons) butter

1 — Peel eggplants, wash and cut in half, **lengthwise.**
Bring to a boil over *high heat* in water and salt
included in *A*. Reduce heat to *moderate, cover* and
boil for *30 minutes.*

2 — Preheat oven to 375°F. Grease a 2-quart glass baking dish.

3 — Remove eggplants from pot, drain thoroughly and
mash. Add ingredients included in *B*, mix, and
spoon into baking dish. Sprinkle with crumbs, dot
with butter and bake about *40 minutes.*

PLANTAIN ARAÑITAS

Arañitas

(Makes about 12 *Arañitas*)

A — 3 large green plantains, peeled and grated into shreds

B — Vegetable oil (for deep frying)

Mojito sauce:

C — 2 tablespoons *Sofrito* (see page xvii)
½ cup ketchup
2 tablespoons dry red wine
1 tablespoon fresh lime juice
1 teaspoon whole dried *orégano*
Tabasco (optional)

1 — Preheat oil to 350°F. Divide plantain shreds into 12 portions.

2 — Take one portion of the plantain shreds, place in the palm of
one hand and pound with the palm of the other hand. Drop

over a tabletop and press again to flatten *arañitas* irregularly. Scoop with a spatula and drop **carefully** into heated oil. Repeat procedure and deep fry 3 or 4 at a time, turning **occasionally,** for *3 or 4 minutes,* until crisp and golden. (Discard from oil scattered pieces of plantain.)

3 — Remove *arañitas,* drain on absorbent paper and set on a platter.

4 — Mix ingredients in *C* and serve *Mojito* sauce as a dip for *arañitas.*

OKRA STEW
Guingambós Guisados
(Serves 4)

A—1 pound okra, ends cut off and pods halved
1 quart (4 cups) water
1 teaspoon salt

B—1 ounce salt pork
2 ounces lean cured ham } washed and diced

C—1 tablespoon fat or *Achiote Coloring* (see Index)
1 onion, peeled
1 tomato
1 green pepper, seeded
2 sweet chili peppers, seeded } finely chopped
1 clove garlic, peeled
6 fresh *culantro* leaves

D—3 cups water
¼ cup tomato sauce
1 teaspoon salt
½ pound potatoes, peeled and quartered

1—Soak okra in water and salt included in *A*, for *1 hour*.

2—In a *caldero* or heavy kettle, combine ingredients included in *B*, and brown salt pork and ham *rapidly*.

3—Turn heat to *low* and sauté ingredients included in *C* for *10 minutes*, stirring *occasionally*.

4—Drain okra, rinse in clear water, and add to kettle, together with ingredients included in *D*.

5—Heat to boiling, reduce heat to *moderate, cover*, and cook for *30 minutes*.

6—*Uncover* and cook about *30 minutes*, or until sauce thickens to taste.

PUMPKIN PUDDING

Budín de Calabaza

(Serves 6)

A—2 pounds pumpkin, peeled and cut into pieces
1 quart (4 cups) water
1 tablespoon salt

B—3 eggs
1 ounce (2 tablespoons) butter
½ teaspoon ground cinnamon
⅓ cup flour
⅓ cup sugar
⅓ cup milk

1—Preheat oven to 400°F. Grease a 2-quart glass baking dish.

2—Cook pumpkin *rapidly* in water and salt included in *A, covered*, for *20 minutes*. Drain and put pumpkin through a potato ricer.

3—Add ingredients included in *B*, and mix. Turn mixture into baking dish and bake about *40 minutes*.

GOLDEN CABBAGE
Chou au Lait

(Serves 6)

A—2½ pounds cabbage, quartered, cored and shredded
2 quarts (8 cups) water
1½ tablespoons salt
1 tablespoon sugar

B—¼ cup cornstarch
2 cups milk
¾ teaspoon salt
2 ounces (4 tablespoons) butter

C—¼ pound Swiss cheese, shredded

1—Combine shredded cabbage with rest of ingredients included in *A*. Bring to a boil, *cover,* reduce heat to *moderate,* and cook for *1 hour.* Remove from heat and **drain thoroughly.**

2—In a saucepan, dissolve cornstarch in part of the milk. Add rest of milk, salt and butter. Stir over *moderate* heat until sauce boils. Add drained cabbage.

3—Set aside 4 tablespoons of the shredded cheese. Add the rest to the saucepan and mix well.

4—Turn mixture into a 12 x 7½ x 2-inch broiler-proof dish. Sprinkle with the reserved cheese and brown **lightly** for a **few seconds** under broiler heat.

CABBAGE PASTELES

Pasteles de Col

(Makes 12)

Cabbage:

1 cabbage, weighing about 4 pounds
4 quarts (16 cups) water
3 tablespoons salt

1—To make leaves pliable, place cabbage, *stem down,* in water and salt, *cover,* and boil at *moderate* heat for 25 *minutes.*

2—Drain, and **reserve** the water to boil the *pasteles.* Thrust a knife through center of cabbage, and remove leaves, *one at a time.*

3—Turn cabbage leaves over and carefully scrape down central ridge of each leaf to level it, **without** breaking the leaf.

Masa (Paste):

A—1 pound white *yautía,* scrubbed and peeled (see Glossary)
½ pound green plantains, peeled
1 pound green bananas, peeled
1 quart (4 cups) water
1 tablespoon salt

B—2 tablespoons fat or *Achiote Coloring* (see Index)
1½ teaspoons salt

1—Cut vegetables into large pieces and soak in water and salt included in A, for 15 *minutes.* Drain and grate. Mash *thoroughly* in a mortar or blend in an electric blender to make a smooth paste. Set in a bowl.

2—Add ingredients included in B, mix well, and **reserve.**

Filling:

A—½ ounce salt pork ⎱ washed and diced
½ ounce lean cured ham ⎰

B—1 tablespoon fat or *Achiote Coloring* (see Index)
   1 clove garlic, peeled
   1 tomato
   1 sweet chili pepper, seeded   chop and crush
   ¼ green pepper, seeded   in a mortar
   1 onion, peeled
   6 fresh *culantro* leaves

C—¾ teaspoon salt
   ½ teaspoon vinegar
   ⅓ cup tomato sauce
   ¼ cup seeded raisins
   ¼ teaspoon whole dried *orégano*, crushed
   4 olives, stuffed with pimiento, chopped

D—½ pound lean ground beef

1—In a frying pan, brown *rapidly* salt pork and cured ham. Reduce heat to *low*, add ingredients included in *B*, and sauté until tender, stirring *occasionally.*

2—Add ingredients included in *C* and *D*, mix, and stir over *moderate* heat for 5 *minutes.* Remove from heat and **reserve** to fill the *pasteles.*

To shape and cook the *pasteles:*

1—Place a large cabbage leaf on the table with a smaller size leaf on top. Spread **very thinly** over inner leaf 2 tablespoons of the *masa,* partially covering the leaf. Spoon 1½ tablespoons of the filling in the center of the *masa.* Fold the leaves, enclosing the contents in it. Secure with wooden picks. Repeat to make *12 pasteles.*

2—Bring to a boil the water in which the cabbage was cooked. Add the *pasteles, cover,* and boil for *45 minutes.* Drain, remove picks and serve hot.

CABBAGE PASTELITOS WITH RICE

Pastelitos Arabes

(Makes 12)

Cabbage:

Prepare cabbage, following instructions from the preceding recipe, using **only** 2 tablespoons salt, and **reserve only** 6 cups of the water in which cabbage boiled.

Filling:

A—½ pound lean ground beef
  ¾ teaspoon salt
  ½ teaspoon vinegar
  1 teaspoon capers
  4 olives, stuffed with pimientos
  1 tomato, chopped
  ⅓ cup tomato sauce
  ¼ cup seeded raisins
  1 tablespoon fat or *Achiote Coloring* (see Index)

B—¼ teaspoon whole dried *orégano* } crush in a mortar
  1 clove garlic, peeled
  1 sweet chili pepper, seeded
  ¼ green pepper, seeded
  1 onion, peeled } chopped
  6 *culantro* leaves

C—1 tablespoon lard or vegetable oil
  ½ ounce salt pork
  1 ounce lean cured ham } washed and diced

D—1 cup rice

1—Combine ingredients included in A.

2—Add ingredients included in B and mix.

3—In a frying pan, heat fat included in C and brown **rapidly** salt pork and ham. Reduce heat to *low* and add mixed ingredients. Mix well.

4—Place rice in a colander and wash under running water. Drain well and add to frying pan. Stir *thoroughly* and remove from heat *immediately*.

5—Proceed to make the *pastelitos* as follows:
Place a large cabbage leaf on the table with a smaller leaf on top. Spread over middle of leaf 2 tablespoons of filling. Fold the leaves, enclosing the contents. Secure with wooden picks. Prepare other *pastelitos* in the same way.

To Cook the Pastelitos:
1 tomato, halved	¼ cup tomato sauce
1 onion, peeled and halved	6 cups (water reserved)

1—Mix ingredients in a large deep vessel.

2—Add water reserved when boiling the cabbage. Bring *rapidly* to a boil, add *pastelitos, cover,* and boil over *moderate* heat for *40 minutes.*

3—*Uncover* and boil for *20 minutes.*

4—Remove picks before serving. Serve *pastelitos* together with the sauce.

FRESH CORN TART

Torta de Maiz Tierno
(Serves 6)

A—1½ cups corn, grated from fresh corn kernels
¼ pound butter

1 teaspoon salt	¾ cup sugar

B—3 eggs

1¼ cups milk	1 teaspoon vanilla extract

1—Melt butter and mix with ingredients included in A.

2—Break eggs with a fork, without beating, Add milk *gradually* and add vanilla. Mix and combine with A mixture.

3—Turn mixture into a greased 8 x 8 x 3-inch glass baking dish.

4—Preheat oven to 375°F. and bake about *1 hour,* or until golden brown and set.

TAMALES
(Makes 16)

A—Corn husks

B—2½ cups corn, grated from fresh corn kernels
1 tablespoon salt
¼ cup milk
2 ounces (4 tablespoons) melted butter

C—1 clove garlic, peeled
½ teaspoon whole dried *orégano*
2 peppercorns (whole black peppers) ⎫ crush and mix
1 teaspoon salt ⎬ in a mortar
1½ teaspoons olive oil
1 teaspoon vinegar ⎭

D—1 pound ground lean beef or pork
½ teaspoon lard or vegetable oil

E—½ green pepper, seeded ⎫
½ tomato ⎬ chopped
1 onion, peeled ⎭

F—10 olives, stuffed with pimientos ⎫
6 dry prunes, pitted ⎬ chopped
2 hard-cooked eggs ⎭
2 tablespoons seeded raisins
¼ cup tomato sauce
2 teaspoons capers
1 tablespoon fat or *Achiote Coloring* (see Index)

1—Mix ingredients included in B to form a smooth paste and **reserve.**

2—Mix crushed ingredients included in C with the ground meat included in D.

3—In a kettle, heat the fat included in D and add E ingredients. Cook over *low* heat, stirring *occasionally*, for *10 minutes.*

4—Add the seasoned meat and stir *rapidly* over *high* heat until meat loses its red color.

5—Add ingredients included in *F* and cook at *low* heat for 5 *minutes.* Set aside to be used as filling.

6—Grease the inside of a corn husk with 1 teaspoon fat or *Achiote Coloring.*

7—Spread **very thinly** one heaping tablespoon of the corn paste on husk.

8—Place in the center of the corn paste 1 tablespoon of the meat filling. Fold over leaf to cover filling and wrap in a second leaf to form the *tamales.* Tie both ends with a string.

9—Heat to boiling 5 quarts water and 3 tablespoons salt. Add *tamales.* Bring liquid again to a boil, reduce heat to *moderate* and cook for *1 hour.* Drain, *unwrap,* and serve in the husk.

HALLACAS

(Makes 40)

Hominy Paste:

A—2¼ pounds pearl hominy
8 quarts (32 cups) water
6 tablespoons salt

B—½ cup *Achiote Coloring* (see Index)

1—Combine ingredients included in A and boil *rapidly, covered,* for *2 hours.* Soak **overnight.**

2—Drain and **reserve only** 2½ cups liquid. (Liquid will be thick and white.)

3—Put drained hominy in an electric blender with the reserved liquid and blend *thoroughly.*

4—Add *Achiote Coloring* included in B to the hominy mixture. Mix well together and **reserve** until filling is ready.

Filling:

A—2¼ pounds chicken breasts
4 pounds lean beef or pork, without bone

B—¼ cup fat or *Achiote Coloring* (see Index)

C—24 cloves garlic, peeled ⎫
    10 sweet chili peppers, seeded ⎬ ground
    1 pound green peppers, seeded ⎭
    2 cans (8 ounces each) tomato sauce
    3 tablespoons salt

1—Skin chicken and separate meat from bones. Cut up chicken into pieces. Cut beef or pork into very small pieces.

2—In a *caldero* or heavy kettle, heat fat or *Achiote Coloring* included in *B*. Add the chopped chicken and beef or pork and cook *rapidly* for *10 minutes*.

3—Reduce heat to *moderate* and add ingredients included in *C*. Mix well and cook, *uncovered*, for *30 minutes*, stirring *occasionally*. Set aside to fill hominy paste.

Garnishing:

A—15 bundles plantain leaves or 40 pieces parchment paper (10 x 12-inches)

B—1 pound lean cured ham ⎫ washed and chopped together
    ¼ pound salt pork ⎭
    8 olives, stuffed with pimientos ⎫
    ½ pound small onion, peeled ⎪
    1 can (4 ounces) pimientos, drained ⎬ sliced
    2 hard-cooked eggs ⎭
    ¼ pound blanched almonds
    ⅔ cup seeded raisins
    2 tablespoons capers

To shape and cook the hallacas:

1—Place on work table:
    The hominy paste
    The filling
    The plantain leaves or parchment paper
    The garnishing (chopped cured ham and salt pork, and the remaining ingredients, set in individual bowls)

2—Grease a piece of plantain leaf or parchment paper with *Achiote Coloring.*

3—Put 3 tablespoons hominy paste in center of leaf and spread **very thinly,** almost to edges of leaf.

4—Place 2 tablespoons meat filling in center and spread out to the sides.

5—Place on top of the filling some pieces of chopped cured ham and salt pork, a slice each of olive, hard-cooked egg, onion, and pimiento. Add 2 almonds, 3 raisins, and 3 capers.

6—Fold the *hallacas* sides and ends toward the center, so that the filling is completely covered with hominy paste. Wrap in a second plantain leaf or piece of parchment paper placed on the diagonal. Tie *hallacas* by pairs, with folded sides facing each other.

7—Heat to boiling 10 quarts water with 7 tablespoons salt. Add the *hallacas, cover,* and boil for *1 hour.* Remove from kettle, **unwrap,** and serve in the leaf or paper.

CAMILLE'S CORN PUDDING

Torta de Maíz Camille

(Serves 6)

4 eggs, lightly beaten
¼ teaspoon salt
⅓ cup sugar
½ cup milk
1 teaspoon vanilla
2 ounces (4 tablespoons) butter
1 can (1 pound 1 ounce) cream-style corn

Mix ingredients. Pour into an 8 x 8 x 2-inch greased baking dish. Bake in preheated over at *350° F.* for *1 hour* or until golden. Serve hot.

CHAPTER VI

Fritters and Croquettes

Fritters and Croquettes

PLANTAIN TOSTONES

Tostones de Plátano
(Makes 12 to 18)

A—3 green plantains
   4 cups water
   2 cloves garlic, peeled and crushed (*optional*)
   2 tablespoons salt

B—Lard or vegetable oil (*for deep-frying*)

1—Peel plantains and cut into diagonal slices 1-inch thick.

2—Add cloves garlic and salt to water included in A. Soak plantain slices for *15 minutes.*

3—Drain well and deep-fry in fat, heated to *350°F.*, about *7 minutes.*

4—Remove from pan and place on absorbent paper.

5—Fold the paper over slices and pound flat with the palm of the hand.

6—Dip in the salted water again and remove *immediately.* Drain *thoroughly* on absorbent paper.

7—Deep-fry in fat, heated to *375°F.*, until crisp and golden. Remove and drain on absorbent paper. Sprinkle *lightly* with salt or dip in *Mojito* sauce (see page 143).

FINGER BANANAS IN DISGUISE
Jibaritos Envueltos
(Makes 36)

A—18 *guineitos niños* (finger bananas), ripe (see Glossary)

B—1 cup flour | ½ teaspoon baking powder
½ teaspoon salt | 1 cup water

C—Lard or vegetable oil (*for deep-frying*)

1—Peel *guineitos niños* and cut in two slices, *lengthwise.*

2—In a bowl, blend ingredients included in B. Dip *guineitos* slices *gradually* and remove with a slotted spoon.

3—Deep-fry in fat, heated to 375°F., until golden brown. Remove and drain on absorbent paper.

CORNMEAL STICKS
Surullitos de Maíz
(Makes 50)

A—2 cups water | 1½ cups yellow cornmeal
1¼ teaspoons salt |

B—1 cup grated Edam cheese

C—Lard or vegetable oil (*for deep-frying*)

1—Combine water and salt in a saucepan. Heat to boiling. Remove from heat. Add cornmeal and mix *thoroughly.*

2—Cook over *moderate* heat until mixture separates from bottom and sides of pan.

3—Remove from heat. Add grated cheese and mix well.

4—Take mixture by teaspoonfuls and shape into balls. In the palm of the hands roll balls to ½-inch thickness, in the shape of small cigars.

5—Deep-fry in fat, heated to 375°F., until golden brown. Remove and drain on absorbent paper.

Note: Serve as an appetizer or with main dish.

FRIED BISCUITS

Yani-Clecas

(Makes about 30)

A—4 cups flour
  1 tablespoon baking powder
  3 tablespoons vegetable lard, chilled
  1 ounce (2 tablespoons) butter, chilled

B—1 egg, beaten

C—1 tablespoon sugar
  1½ teaspoons salt
  1 cup milk

D—Lard or vegetable oil (*for deep-frying*)

1—Sift flour and baking powder into a mixing bowl. With a dough blender or 2 knives cut in lard and butter.

2—Add egg and continue mixing.

3—Dissolve sugar and salt in the milk included in C. Add liquid by spoonsfuls to the flour mixture and stir until a soft dough is formed. Turn out on floured board and knead *gently*.

4—Shape dough into a roll, about 2 inches thick, and cut into narrow slices.

5—Press each slice to form a bun about ¼ inch thick.

6—Deep-fry buns, in fat heated to 365°F., until golden brown. Remove and drain on absorbent paper. Serve with butter and preserves.

STUFFED POTATO BALLS

Rellenos de Papa

(Makes 12)

A—2 pounds potatoes, peeled and quartered
2 quarts (8 cups) water
1½ tablespoons salt

B—2 ounces (4 tablespoons) butter
1 egg, slightly beaten
½ teaspoon salt
1 tablespoon cornstarch

C—¼ of recipe for **Basic Meat Filling** (see Index)

D—Cornstarch (*to coat balls*)
Lard or vegetable oil (*for deep-frying*)

1—In a pot, combine ingredients included in *A. Cover* and boil at *moderate* heat for *30 minutes,* or until potatoes are fork-tender.

2—Drain and **immediately** mash or put through a potato ricer.

3—Add and mix ingredients included in *B.*

4—Cool to room temperature.

5—Divide mixture in 12 parts. Cover palm of hand with corn-starch and spread over hand one part of the mixture. Spoon the center with part of the filling and bring mixture over to cover filling. Coat **lightly** with cornstarch and proceed with remaining mixture until 12 balls are ready.

6—Deep fry in fat, heated to 375°F., until golden brown. Remove and drain on absorbent paper.

Note: Potato balls can also be filled with shredded cheese.

OLD MAMA'S BELLIES

Barrigas de Vieja

A—1¾ cups flour | 1 teaspoon salt
2 cups water
1 egg yolk and egg white, blended
Vegetable oil or vegetable lard (for frying)

1—In a large bowl, combine flour and salt. Add water **slowly,** while mixing **vigorously** with a wooden spoon, until all lumps disappear. Strain mixture through a sieve, **completely.** Add blended egg and mix into a very thin batter.

2—In a large frying pan, heat abundant fat. Fill a cooking spoon with batter and drop into pan. (It will spread into a flat, irregular shape.) Turn **occasionally** until golden brown. Remove and drain on absorbent paper. Continue frying rest of batter. Sprinkle with sugar and serve **immediately.**

Note: To serve as appetizer, fry by spoonfuls and omit sugar.

RICEMEAL BALLS

Bolitas de Harina de Arroz

(Makes 24)

A—1½ cups milk
½ teaspoon salt
2 ounces (4 tablespoons) butter

B—¾ cup ricemeal
¼ pound (1 cup) freshly grated Parmesan cheese

C—Lard or vegetable oil *(for deep-frying)*

1—In a saucepan, bring to a boil ingredients included in A. When boiling, remove from heat and add ingredients included in B. Stir *constantly* over *moderate* heat until mixture separates from sides and bottom of saucepan.

2—Remove from heat and pour onto a shallow platter. Cool **slightly** and shape into small balls, about the size of walnuts.

3—Deep-fry in fat, heated to 375°F., until golden brown. Remove and drain on absorbent paper.

Note: Serve as an appetizer or with main dish.

APIO BUNS

Buñuelos de Apio

(Makes about 12)

A—1 pound *apio*, peeled and cut into pieces (see Glossary)
1 quart (4 cups) water | 1 tablespoon salt

B—3 eggs, beaten | 2 teaspoons baking powder
½ teaspoon salt |

C—Lard or vegetable oil (*for deep-frying*)

1—Bring water with salt included in A to a boil. Wash *apio* and boil, *covered*, for *40 minutes* at *moderate* heat. Drain and mash until smooth.

2—Add ingredients included in B and mix well.

3—Deep-fry mixture by spoonfuls in fat, heated to 365°F., until golden brown. Remove and drain on absorbent paper.

CHEESE BUNS

Buñuelitos de Queso

(Makes 24)

A—2 eggs, beaten | 1 cup milk

B—2 cups flour | 2 teaspoons baking powder
1¼ teaspoons salt |

C—3 tablespoons sugar
1 cup shredded Cheddar cheese

D—Lard or vegetable oil (*for deep-frying*)

1—Combine eggs and milk.

2—Sift together flour, salt, and baking powder and add to the milk-egg mixture.

3—Add sugar and shredded cheese and mix well.

4—Drop batter by spoonfuls in fat, heated to 365°F., until golden brown. Remove and drain on absorbent paper.

GREEN CORN BUNS

Buñuelitos de Maíz Tierno Fresco
(Makes 24)

A—1¼ cups grated fresh corn | 1 teaspoon melted butter

B—1 egg | 1 teaspoon baking powder
1 cup flour | 2 tablespoons sugar
1 teaspoon salt |

C—½ cup milk

D—Lard or vegetable oil (*for deep-frying*)

1—Combine corn and melted butter.

2—Mix ingredients included in *B*, and add to the corn, **alternately,** with the milk included in *C*.

3—Drop batter by spoonfuls in fat, heated to 365°F., until golden brown. Remove and drain on absorbent paper.

FRANCISCA'S CORNMEAL BUNS

Buñuelitos de Maíz Francisca

A—2 ounces (4 tablespoons) butter | ½ cup sugar
1¼ teaspoons salt | 2 cups water

B—1½ cups yellow cornmeal

C—3 eggs | 1 teaspoon vanilla extract

D—Lard or vegetable oil (*for deep-frying*)

1—In a saucepan, heat to boiling ingredients included in *A*.

2—Reduce heat to *moderate*, add cornmeal, **all at once,** and stir **constantly** with a wooden spoon, until mixture separates from bottom and sides of saucepan.

3—Remove from heat, blend eggs **one at a time.** Add vanilla and mix.

4—Deep-fry mixture by spoonfuls in fat, heated to 365°F., until golden brown. Remove and drain on absorbent paper.

CHEESE BALLS

Bolitas de Queso

A—½ pound cheese, shredded (Gouda, Cheddar, or Swiss cheese)
1 egg
2 tablespoons cornstarch

B—Bread or cracker crumbs (*to coat balls*)

C—Lard or vegetable oil (*for deep-frying*)

1—In the small bowl of electric mixer, blend ingredients included in A at *high* speed.

2—Take mixture by teaspoons, turn into balls, coat with crumbs and deep-fry until golden brown in fat heated to 350°F.

3—Remove and drain on absorbent paper. Serve immediately.

Note: Serve as an appetizer or with main dish.

FLOUR BUNS

Buñuelitos de Harina

(Makes 20)

A—1⅓ cups flour
1 teaspoon salt
2 teaspoons baking powder
2 tablespoons sugar
1 egg, beaten
1 cup milk

B—Lard or vegetable oil (*for deep-frying*)

1—Mix all ingredients included in A together.

2—Drop batter by spoonfuls in fat, heated to 375°F., until golden brown. Remove and drain on absorbent paper.

PUERTO RICAN RICEMEAL BUNS
Almojábanas

(Makes 24)

A—2 cups milk
2 ounces (4 tablespoons) butter
¾ teaspoon salt

B—2 cups very fine ricemeal
2 teaspoons baking powder
3 eggs

C—½ pound mild white cheese (preferably, native cheese called *queso de la tierra*)

D—Lard or vegetable oil (*for deep-frying*)

1—In a saucepan, heat to boiling ingredients included in A. Remove from heat.

2—Combine ricemeal and baking powder and mix with contents in saucepan. Add eggs, *one at a time,* and mix.

3—Cook over *moderate* heat, stirring *constantly* with a wooden spoon, until mixture separates from sides and bottom of saucepan.

4—Remove from heat. Mash cheese with a fork and add. Mix *thoroughly.*

5—Drop mixture by spoonfuls in fat, heated to 375°F., until golden brown. Remove and drain on absorbent paper.

Note: Serve as an appetizer or with main dish.

TANIER BUNS

Buñuelos de Yautía

(Makes 24)

A—1 pound white *yautía* (see Glossary)
1½ quarts (6 cups) water | 1 tablespoon salt

B—¼ pound Cheddar cheese, shredded
2 eggs | ¼ teaspoon salt

C—Lard or vegetable oil (*for deep-frying*)

1—Peel and wash the *yautías.* Cut into pieces and place in a pot with water and salt included in A. Bring to a boil over *high* heat. Reduce heat to *moderate* and boil for *45 minutes.*

2—Drain the *yautías* and mash **immediately.** Add shredded cheese and mix. Beat eggs and salt, add and mix.

3—Drop mixture by spoonfuls in fat, heated to 375°F., until golden brown. Remove and drain on absorbent paper.

Note: Serve as an appetizer or with main dish.

YAM BUNS

Buñuelos de Ñame

(Makes 12)

A—1 pound *ñame*, peeled (see Glossary)
1½ quarts (6 cups) boiling water | 1 tablespoon salt

B—1 ounce (2 tablespoons) butter | 6 tablespoons flour
2 tablespoons lard or vegetable oil | 1 egg, beaten
2 tablespoons milk | ½ teaspoon salt

C—Lard or vegetable oil (*for deep-frying*)

1—Cook *ñame* in boiling water with salt included in A for *40 minutes, covered.* Drain and mash well while still hot.

2—Add ingredients included in B and mix **thoroughly.**

3—Drop mixture by spoonfuls in fat, heated to 375°F., until golden brown. Remove and drain on absorbent paper.

4—Serve sprinkled with sifted confectioners' sugar, syrup or jelly.

BRAIN FRITTERS

Frituras de Seso

(Serves 4)

A—1 pound of fresh calf brain | 1½ teaspoons salt
1 quart (4 cups) water | 1 tablespoon fresh lime juice

B—1 cup flour
½ teaspoon salt
1 cup water

C—Butter, lard or vegetable oil (*for pan-frying*)

1—Wash brain and place in a saucepan, together with rest of ingredients included in A. Bring to a boil over *high* heat, *cover*, reduce heat to *low* and simmer for *20 minutes*. Drain and plunge into cold water. Drain again, remove outer membrane and cut brain into thin slices.

2—Combine flour, salt and water to make a batter. Pat dry each slice of brain and dip into batter.

3—In a frying pan, heat fat and fry the brain slices over *moderate* heat until golden brown on both sides. Remove and drain on absorbent paper.

CODFISH FRITTERS

Bacalaitos Fritos

(Makes 30)

A—½ pound dried salted fillet of codfish

B—1½ cups flour | 1 teaspoon baking powder
¾ teaspoon salt | 1½ cups water

C—4 peppercorns (whole black peppers) ⎤
2 cloves garlic, peeled ⎬ crush and mix
3 fresh *culantro* leaves (optional) ⎦ in a mortar

D—Lard or vegetable oil (*for deep-frying*)

1—Cut codfish into 2-inch pieces. Cover with water in a large pot and boil **rapidly** for *15 minutes*. (If preferred, do not boil codfish but soak in water to cover for *3 hours*.)

2—Drain, remove skin and bones from codfish. Rinse in fresh water **two or three times.**

3—Squeeze codfish with the hands and shred, making sure all bones have been removed.

4—In a bowl, make a batter by blending ingredients included in *B*. Add ingredients included in *C* and mix.

5—Add shredded codfish and mix **thoroughly.**

6—Drop mixture by spoonfuls in fat, heated to *365°F.*, until golden brown. (Discard from fat scattered pieces of batter.) Remove and drain on absorbent paper.

Note: Serve as an appetizer or with main dish.

CREAMED CORN FRITTERS

Frituras de Maíz a la Crema
(12 fritters)

A—½ cup flour
1 teaspoon baking powder

3 tablespoons sugar
½ teaspoon salt

B—1 can (8½ ounces) cream style corn
1 egg

C—Lard or vegetable oil (*for pan-frying*)

1—In a bowl, combine ingredients included in *A*. Add ingredients included in *B* and mix well.

2—In a frying pan, heat fat and drop mixture by spoonfuls to fry in shape of thin fritters. Fry until golden brown. Remove and drain on absorbent paper.

Note: For smaller fritters, fry by teaspoonfuls.

HAM AND POTATO FRITTERS

Frituras de Papa y Jamón
(Makes 14)

A—1½ pounds medium potatoes, peeled and halved
2 quarts (8 cups) boiling water   1½ tablespoons salt

B—½ pound sliced boiled ham   ½ teaspoon salt
4 eggs, separated

C—Lard or vegetable oil (*for pan-frying*)

1—Place ingredients included in A in a deep kettle, *cover* and boil over *moderate* heat for *30 minutes*. Drain.

2—Cool potatoes and cut into thin slices.

3—Put a piece of ham between each two slices of potatoes. Fasten with wooden picks.

4—Beat whites of eggs until stiff. Add egg yolks and salt and beat well together.

5—Coat the potato and ham "sandwiches" with the egg mixture.

6—In a frying pan, heat fat and fry the potato "sandwiches" until golden brown. Remove and drain on absorbent paper. Remove picks before serving.

PUMPKIN FRITTERS
Frituras de Calabaza
(Makes about 24)

A—1½ pounds sound, dry pumpkin, weighed after peeled, seeded and cut into pieces
2 quarts (8 cups) water │ 2 tablespoons salt

B—1 cup sugar │ ¾ teaspoon vanilla extract
1 cup flour │

C—Lard or vegetable oil (*for pan-frying*)

1—Place ingredients included in A in a deep kettle. Bring **rapidly** to a boil, *cover,* reduce heat to *moderate* and cook for *30 minutes*. Drain **thoroughly** and mash.

2—Stir in ingredients included in B, mixing well after each addition.

3—In a frying pan, heat fat and drop mixture by spoonfuls to fry in shape of thin fritters. Fry until golden brown. Remove and drain on absorbent paper.

RICE FRITTERS

Frituras de Arroz

(Makes 16)

A—1 cup left-over cooked rice   1 tablespoon milk
  1 egg, beaten   1 tablespoon sugar
  ¼ teaspoon salt

B—⅔ cup flour   ½ cup milk
  ¼ teaspoon salt   1½ tablespoons sugar
  1 teaspoon baking powder   1 teaspoon vanilla extract
  1 egg, beaten

C—Lard or vegetable oil (*for pan-frying*)

1—Mix together ingredients included in A.

2—Mix together ingredients included in B and combine both mixtures.

3—In a frying pan, heat fat and drop mixture by spoonfuls to fry in shape of thin fritters. Fry until golden brown. Remove and drain on absorbent paper.

TANIER FRITTERS

Frituras de Yautía

(Makes 24)

A—2 pounds white *yautía* (see Glossary)
  1 teaspoon salt | 1 teaspoon baking powder

B—Lard or vegetable oil (*for deep-frying*)

1—Wash and peel the *yautías*. Wash again and grate.

2—Add salt and baking powder and mix.

3—Drop mixture by spoonfuls in fat, heated to 365°F., until golden brown. Remove and drain on absorbent paper.

Note: Serve as an appetizer or with main dish.

STUFFED GREEN BANANA CROQUETTES

Alcapurrias

(Makes 16)

Paste (*Masa*):

A—5 green bananas | 1 tablespoon salt
1 quart (4 cups) water | 1 pound *yautía* (see Glossary)

B—1 teaspoon vinegar | 2 teaspoons salt
1 tablespoon fat or *Achiote Coloring* (see Index)

1—Peel green bananas. Rinse in water and salt included in *A*. Drain. Wash and peel *yautías*.

2—Grate green bananas and *yautías*. Mix with ingredients included in *B*.

Filling:

A—½ pound ground lean beef or pork
    1 ounce cured ham
    ½ ounce salt pork
    1 clove garlic, peeled
    ½ small green pepper, seeded   } ground or finely chopped
    1 sweet chili pepper, seeded
    ½ small onion, peeled
    ½ small tomato

B—½ teaspoon whole dried *orégano* | ½ teaspoon olive oil
½ teaspoon salt | ¼ teaspoon vinegar

C—2 teaspoons lard or vegetable oil (**if beef is used**)
½ teaspoon lard or vegetable oil (**if pork is used**)

D—3 olives, stuffed with pimientos   } chopped
    3 dry prunes, pitted
    2 teaspoons seeded raisins
    ½ teaspoon capers
    1 tablespoon fat or *Achiote Coloring* (see Index)

E—Lard or vegetable oil (*for deep-frying*)

1—Put ingredients included in *A* in a bowl. Add ingredients included in *B* and mix **thoroughly.**

2—In a small *caldero* or heavy kettle, heat fat included in *C*. Add contents of bowl and mix *constantly* over *high* heat until meat loses its red color.

3—Reduce heat to *low*, add ingredients included in *D*, mix, cover, and cook for 15 *minutes*. (**For pork,** cook an additional 15 *minutes*.)

4—*Uncover*, mix and cook for 15 *minutes* longer.

To shape and cook *alcapurrias:*

1—Spread some of the *masa* in a dessert dish.

2—Place a teaspoon of the filling in the center, cover well with the *masa*, and shape into a cylinder or croquette. Fry in deep fat, heated to 365°F., until cooked and golden brown. Remove and drain on absorbent paper.

EGG CROQUETTES

Croquetas de Huevo
(Makes 12 croquettes)

A—1½ ounces (3 tablespoons) butter
⅓ cup flour | ¼ teaspoon ground nutmeg
½ teaspoon salt | 1 cup milk

B—4 hard-cooked eggs, chopped

C—½ cup bread or cracker crumbs | ¼ teaspoon salt
1 egg, lightly beaten | 2 tablespoons water

D—Lard or vegetable oil (*for deep-frying*)

1—Prepare white sauce as follows: Melt butter over *low* heat, blend in flour, salt and nutmeg. Add milk **gradually** and stir over *moderate* heat, until it boils and thickens.

2—Add chopped eggs, mix, and allow to cool.

3—Form into croquettes and coat with crumbs. Break egg into cup, add salt and water. Beat with fork until blended. Dip croquettes into egg mixture, and coat again with crumbs.

4—Deep-fry in fat, heated to 375°F., until golden brown. Remove and drain on absorbent paper.

EGGPLANT CROQUETTES

Croquetas de Berenjena

(Makes 12 croquettes)

A—1 pound eggplants
1 quart (4 cups) water
2 teaspoons salt

B—½ cup flour
½ teaspoon salt
¼ teaspoon ground nutmeg
¼ cup freshly-grated Parmesan cheese

C—½ ounce (1 tablespoon) butter

D—⅔ cup bread or cracker crumbs

E—1 egg, lightly beaten
¼ teaspoon salt
2 tablespoons water

F—Lard or vegetable oil (*for deep-frying*)

1—Peel eggplants with vegetable peeler. Wash and cut in half, **lengthwise.** Bring to a boil over *high* heat in water and salt included in A. Reduce heat to *moderate, cover* and boil for *30 minutes.*

2—Remove eggplants from pot, drain and mash. Add ingredients included in *B* and mix well.

3—Melt butter in a saucepan. Add eggplant mixture and stir at *low* heat about 5 *minutes.* Remove from heat and allow to cool.

4—**Gradually,** take mixture by spoonfuls and form into croquettes. Coat with crumbs.

5—In a cup, mix ingredients included in E. Dip croquettes and remove with a slotted spoon. Coat again with crumbs.

6—Deep-fry in fat, heated to *375° F.,* until golden brown. Remove and drain on absorbent paper.

CRISPY FRIED WHOLE POTATOES

Papitas Enteras Fritas

(Serves 6)

A—2 pounds very small potatoes
1½ quarts (6 cups) boiling water
3 tablespoons salt

B—Lard or vegetable oil (*for deep-frying*)

1—Scrub and wash potatoes. Cook, without peeling, in water with salt included in A for 25 *minutes, covered.* Drain and peel **at once.**

2—Deep-fry in fat, heated to 350°F., about 5 *minutes.*

3—Remove potatoes from fat and place on absorbent paper. Cover with absorbent paper and pound with the palm of the hand to flatten each potato.

4—Deep-fry in fat, heated to 375°F., until crisp and golden brown. Remove and drain on absorbent paper.

CHAPTER VII *Pasta Dishes*

Pasta Dishes

DELICIOUS TURNOVERS

Pastelillos al Aire

(Makes about 12)

A—2 cups flour
1 teaspoon salt
2 teaspoons baking powder

B—6 tablespoons vegetable lard, chilled
½ cup water, chilled

C—¼ pound cheese (preferably Cheddar), shredded

D—Lard or vegetable oil (*for deep-frying*)

1—Sift together flour with salt and baking powder into a large bowl.

2—Using a dough blender or 2 knives, cut lard included in *B* **rapidly** into the flour.

3—Add water **gradually** and mix into a dough.

4—Turn dough onto a lightly floured board and knead **gently,** flouring the board whenever necessary, to prevent sticking. Shape dough into a ball, place in a bowl and cover with a cloth. Allow to rest for *30 minutes.*

5—Shape ball into a roll, about 2-inches thick.

6—Cut roll into slices about 1-inch wide, as needed.

7—With a lightly floured rolling pin, roll out each slice into a **very thin circle.**

8—Place about 1 tablespoon of shredded cheese on half the circle, fold over the other half, and cut into a half-moon shape with the edge of a sauce dish. (The *pastelillo* should be from 2½ to 3 inches from bottom to top, to allow for expansion while frying.)

9—Press the edges of the *pastelillo* together, first with the fingertips and then, with a lightly floured fork.

10—Place *pastelillos* on a lightly floured aluminum sheet, ready to be fried. (If not fried *immediately*, set in refrigerator and remove ½ *hour* before frying.)

11—Deep-fry *gradually*, in fat heated to 375°F., until golden brown.

12—Baste with the hot fat while frying, to make the *pastelillos* swell. Remove and drain on absorbent paper.

Note: Basic Meat Filling may be used instead of cheese (see Index).

GALLICIAN TURNOVERS

Pastelillos Gallegos

(Makes about 30)

A—2 cups flour

B—1 cup water
1 ounce (2 tablespoons) butter
1½ teaspoons salt

C—¼ pound cheese (preferably Cheddar), shredded

D—Lard or vegetable oil (*for deep-frying*)

1—Measure and sift flour.

2—Heat to boiling the water, butter, and salt included in B. *Immediately* add flour **all at once.** Cook for *1 minute*, stirring to avoid lumps. Remove from heat and continue to stir until mixture is smooth.

3—Turn mixture onto a lightly floured board while still hot. Knead **rapidly** for about 2 *minutes*. Shape dough into a ball. Place ball in a bowl and cover with a cloth. Allow to rest for *1 hour*.

4—Shape ball into a roll about 2 inches thick. Cut the roll, **gradually**, into slices about ½-inch wide. Roll out slices **thinly, one at a time,** with lightly floured rolling pin.

5—Cut each slice into a circle the size of a doughnut. Two circles will make a *pastelillo*. Place one circle on top of the other, with shredded cheese in between. Press the edges together, first with the fingertips and then, with a lightly floured fork.

6—Place *pastelillos* on a lightly floured aluminum sheet, ready to be fried. (If not fried **immediately,** set in refrigerator.)

7—Deep-fry **gradually,** in fat heated to 375°F., until golden brown. Remove and drain on absorbent paper.

GOLDEN TURNOVERS

Pastelillos Volados
(Makes about 20)

A—3⅓ cups flour
2½ teaspoons salt | 2 teaspoons baking powder

B—3½ tablespoons vegetable lard, chilled
1 large egg, lightly beaten | ¾ cup water

C—½ pound cheese (preferably Cheddar), shredded
3 tablespoons sugar (*optional*)

D—Lard or vegetable oil (*for deep-frying*)

1—Sift together flour with salt and baking powder into a large bowl.

2—Using a dough blender or 2 knives, cut lard included in *B* **rapidly** into the flour. Add eggs and mix.

3—Add water **gradually** and mix.

4—Turn dough onto a lightly floured board and knead *gently* until dough is soft and light, adding flour *occasionally,* to prevent it from sticking.

5—Shape dough into a ball, place in a bowl and cover with a cloth. Allow to rest for *30 minutes.*

6—Shape dough into a roll, about 2 inches thick.

7—Cut roll into slices about 1 inch wide, as needed.

8—With a lightly floured rolling pin, roll out each slice into a very thin circle.

9—Place about 1 tablespoon of shredded cheese on half the circle, fold over the other half, and cut into a half-moon shape with the edge of a sauce dish. (The *pastelillo* should be around 2½ to 3 inches from bottom to top, to allow for expansion while frying.)

10—Press the edges of the *pastelillo* together, first with the fingertips and then, with a lightly floured fork.

11—Place *pastelillos* on a lightly floured aluminum sheet, ready to be fried. (If not fried *immediately,* set in refrigerator and remove ½ *hour* before frying.)

12—Deep-fry *gradually,* in fat heated to 375°F., until golden brown.

13—Baste with the hot fat while frying, to make the *pastelillos* swell. Remove and drain on absorbent paper.

Note: Basic Meat Filling may be used instead of cheese (see Index).

DOUGHNUTS A LA CARIBE

Rosquillas a la Caribe

A—¼ cup vegetable oil
2 eggs
1 cup sugar

B—½ cup milk
2 tablespoons fresh lime juice

C—4 cups flour
4 teaspoons baking powder
¼ teaspoon baking soda
¼ teaspoon ground nutmeg
1 teaspoon salt

D—Lard or vegetable oil (*for deep-frying*)

E—Confectioners' powdered sugar, sifted (*for garnishing*)

1—In a bowl, pour vegetable oil included in A. Add eggs, mix, and blend in sugar.

2—Combine milk and lime juice, add to bowl, and mix.

3—Sift together ingredients included in C and mix until all flour is moistened.

4—Turn dough onto a lightly floured board and knead *gently*, flouring the board whenever necessary, to prevent it from sticking.

5—With a lightly floured rolling pin, roll out dough into a circle around ½ inch thick.

6—Cut doughnuts with a doughnut cutter and deep fry in fat, heated to 375°F., until golden brown.

7—Remove with a slotted spoon and drain on absorbent paper.

8—Sprinkle *lightly* with confectioners' sugar. Serve *immediately*.

Note: These doughnuts have a crispy consistency, different from the regular doughnuts.

LASAGNE A LA SAN JUAN

Lasagna a la San Juan

(Serves 12)

A—2 tablespoons olive oil
   2 ounces salt pork
   6 cloves garlic, peeled } washed and diced

B—1 ounce (2 tablespoons) butter
   ¾ cup chopped onions
   ¼ cup chopped green peppers, seeded

C—1½ pounds lean ground beef
   1 egg
   ¼ cup bread or cracker crumbs

D—1 can (14½ ounces) whole tomatoes, liquid **included**
   1½ teaspoons salt
   1 tablespoon sugar
   ¼ teaspoon ground pepper
   1½ teaspoons whole dried *orégano*
   1 teaspoon basil leaves
   ⅓ cup fresh parsley sprigs, minced
   ¼ cup seeded raisins
   3 tablespoons tomato paste
   ¼ cup white wine

E—6 quarts water
   3 tablespoons salt
   1 tablespoon olive oil
   1 pound packaged ribbed lasagne noodles

F—**Cream:**
   ¼ pound butter
   1 teaspoon salt
   ½ cup flour
   1 quart (4 cups) milk

G—Cheeses:
3 packages (4 ounces each) Mozzarella cheese, shredded
12 ounces Ricotta or Pot Cottage cheese
1½ cups freshly grated Parmesan cheese

1—Preheat oven to *350°F.* Grease a 16 x 10 x 3-inch lasagne pan.

2—In a large frying pan, heat olive oil included in *A.* Brown **rapidly** salt pork and garlic and discard.

3—Reduce heat to *low,* add ingredients included in *B,* and sauté for *10 minutes,* stirring **occasionally.**

4—Meanwhile, place meat in a bowl and mix *thoroughly* with rest of ingredients included in *C.*

5—Add to frying pan and mix **constantly** over *moderate-high* heat, until meat loses its red color.

6—Reduce heat to *low* and add ingredients included in *D.* Break tomatoes into pieces. Cook for *15 minutes,* stirring **occasionally.**

7—In a big pot, combine water, salt and olive oil included in *E,* and bring **rapidly** to a boil. Add lasagne noodles and boil over *high* heat for *20 minutes.* Drain thoroughly. Arrange lasagne noodles, **one next to the other,** on an aluminum sheet and **reserve.**

8—Meanwhile, prepare **cream** as follows:
In a saucepan, melt butter **slowly.** Blend in salt and flour. Add milk. Stir with a wooden spoon, over *moderate* heat, until it boils and thickens. Remove from heat.

9—In lasagne pan, arrange alternate layers as follows:
a—Cover bottom of pan **lightly** with cream
b—Arrange a layer of 3 lasagne noodles
c—Cover with one-third of the cream sauce
d—Spread with one-half of meat mixture
e—Top with:
1 package Mozzarella cheese, shredded
4 ounces Ricotta or Pot Cottage cheese
½ cup freshly grated Parmesan cheese

f—Repeat instructions **9b** to **9e** once more
g—Arrange a layer of 3 lasagne noodles
h—Cover with balance of cream sauce
i—Top with balance of cheeses

10—Bake for *30 minutes.*

11—Remove from oven, place over wire rack, and allow to rest for *15 minutes* before serving.

MACARONI WITH CHICKEN

Macarrones con Pollo
(Serves 8)

A—2 tablespoons olive oil
  2 ounces salt pork
  2 ounces lean cured ham } washed and diced

B—1 green pepper, seeded
  2 sweet chili peppers, seeded } chopped
  1 onion, peeled

C—2 pounds chicken pieces
  8 olives, stuffed with pimientos
  1 teaspoon capers
  2 teaspoons salt
  1 teaspoon whole dried *orégano*
  1 can (8 ounces) tomato sauce

D—1 can (1 pound 12 ounces) whole tomatoes

E—3½ quarts (14 cups) water
  4½ teaspoons salt
  1 tablespoon olive oil
  1 pound macaroni

F—½ cup freshly grated Parmesan cheese

1—In a large *caldero* or heavy kettle, heat oil included in *A* and brown **rapidly** salt pork and ham. Reduce heat to *low,* add ingredients included in *B*, and sauté for *10 minutes,* stirring **occasionally.**

2—Divide each chicken piece in two, wash, dry and add to kettle, together with rest of ingredients included in *C*. Mix and cook for 5 *minutes*.

3—Add ingredients included in *D*, bring *rapidly* to a boil, reduce heat to *moderate, cover,* and boil for *30 minutes*.

4—Meanwhile, in a large pot, heat to boiling water, salt and olive oil included in *E*. Add macaroni and boil *rapidly* for *20 minutes*.

5—Drain and add to kettle, *cover,* and cook for *30 minutes*.

6—Remove from heat, sprinkle with grated cheese and serve immediately.

MACARONI WITH CHEESE

Macarrones con Queso

(Serves 6)

A—3 quarts (12 cups) water | 1 teaspoon olive oil
4½ teaspoons salt | ½ pound macaroni

B—¼ pound (4 ounces) butter | 2 teaspoons salt
½ cup flour | 1 quart (4 cups) milk

C—½ pound Cheddar cheese, shredded

1—In a large pot, heat to boiling water, salt and olive oil included in *A*. Add macaroni and boil *rapidly* for *20 minutes*.

2—Meanwhile, prepare sauce as follows:

In a saucepan, melt butter *slowly,* blend in flour and salt. Add milk *gradually* and stir with a wooden spoon over *moderate* heat, until mixture boils and thickens. Remove from heat.

3—Drain macaroni and mix with the sauce. Spoon, alternating with part of the cheese, into a 3-quart round glass baking dish. Top with remaining cheese. *Cover* and bake in preheated oven to *350°F.* for *30 minutes*.

MACARONI WITH SPARERIBS

Macarrones con Costillitas de Cerdo
(Serves 8)

A—1 ounce salt pork
   2 ounces lean cured ham   } washed and diced

B—1 tablespoon fat or *Achiote Coloring* (see Index)
   1 green pepper, seeded
   2 sweet chili peppers, seeded } chopped
   1 onion, peeled

C—½ cup tomato sauce
   1 pound spareribs, cut into serving pieces
   1 teaspoon salt
   8 olives, stuffed with pimientos
   1 tablespoon capers
   1¾ cups water

D—3½ quarts (14 cups) water
   4½ teaspoons salt
   1 tablespoon olive oil
   1 pound macaroni

E—1 can (1 pound 12 ounces) whole tomatoes

F—½ cup freshly grated Parmesan cheese

1—In a *caldero* or heavy kettle, brown *rapidly* ingredients included in A. Add ingredients included in B, reduce heat to *low*, and sauté for *10 minutes*, stirring *occasionally*.

2—Add ingredients included in C and bring *rapidly* to a boil. Reduce heat to *moderate, cover,* and boil for *1 hour*.

3—In a large pot, bring to a boil water, salt and olive oil included in D. Add macaroni and cook *rapidly* for *20 minutes*.

4—Drain and add to kettle.

5—Add tomatoes, **including** liquid, *cover,* and cook over *low* heat for *15 minutes*.

6—Add grated cheese, mix and serve immediately.

MACARONI WITH CREAMED CORN

Macarrones con Maíz a la Crema
(Serves 4)

A—1½ quarts (6 cups) water
  2 teaspoons salt
  1 teaspoon olive oil

B—¼ pound macaroni

C—2 ounces (4 tablespoons) butter
  ¼ cup flour
  1¼ teaspoons salt
  2 cups lukewarm milk

D—1 tablespoon sugar
  1 can (1 pound 1 ounce) cream style corn   } mix together

E—¼ pound Cheddar cheese, shredded

1—Preheat oven to 375°F.

2—Grease a 2-quart round glass baking dish.

3—Bring to a boil ingredients included in A. Add macaroni and boil over *high* heat, for *20 minutes*. Remove and drain.

4—In a saucepan, melt butter *slowly*. Blend in flour and salt. Add milk and stir *constantly* over *moderate* heat, until mixture boils and thickens.

5—Pour ingredients into pan, in *alternate* layers, as follows:
  a—sauce
  b—macaroni
  c—creamed corn
  d—shredded cheese

6—Repeat in the same order, until all ingredients are used.

7—Cover dish and bake about *20 minutes*.

SPAGHETTI ROYALE

Espagueti a la Reina

(Serves 6)

A—3 quarts (12 cups) water
4½ teaspoons salt
1 tablespoon olive oil
½ pound spaghetti

B—⅓ cup olive oil
2 ounces lean cured ham, washed and diced
¼ pound onions, peeled and chopped

C—1 can (1 pound 12 ounces) whole tomatoes
⅓ cup tomato sauce
½ teaspoon salt
½ cup freshly grated Parmesan cheese
1 can (12 ounces) corned beef

D—½ cup freshly grated Parmesan cheese

1—In a large pot, heat to boiling water, salt and olive oil included in A. Add spaghetti and boil *rapidly* for *13 minutes.*

2—Meanwhile, in a *caldero* or heavy kettle, heat olive oil and brown ham *rapidly.* Reduce heat to *low,* add chopped onions, and sauté for *10 minutes,* stirring *occasionally.*

3—Add ingredients included in *C* and mix.

4—Drain spaghetti, add and mix. *Cover,* and cook over *moderate* heat for *15 minutes.*

5—*Uncover,* reduce heat to *low,* and cook for *15 minutes.*

6—Serve immediately, sprinkled with Parmesan cheese included in *E.*

SPAGHETTI WITH VIENNA SAUSAGES

Espagueti con Salchichas

(Serves 6)

A—3 quarts (12 cups) water
4½ teaspoons salt
1 tablespoon olive oil
½ pound spaghetti

B—1 tablespoon lard or vegetable oil
2 ounces lean cured ham, washed and diced

C—1 tablespoon fat or *Achiote Coloring* (see Index)
1 onion, peeled ⎫
1 tomato ⎪
1 green pepper, seeded ⎬ chopped
2 sweet chili peppers, seeded ⎭

D—1 can (8 ounces) tomato sauce
8 olives, stuffed with pimientos
1 teaspoon capers
2 cans (4 ounces each) Vienna sausages, chopped in their juice

E—⅓ cup freshly grated Parmesan cheese

1—In a large pot, bring *rapidly* to a boil water, salt, and olive oil included in A. Add spaghetti and boil *rapidly* for *13 minutes*.

2—While spaghetti cooks, prepare the sauce as follows:
   In a *caldero* or heavy kettle, heat fat included in *B* and brown ham *rapidly*. Reduce heat to *low*, add ingredients included in *C*, and sauté for *10 minutes*, stirring *occasionally* Add ingredients included in *D* and mix.

3—As soon as spaghetti is done, drain and add to kettle. Stir well. *Cover* kettle and cook over *moderate* heat for *10 minutes*. Turn into a deep dish.

4—Sprinkle with grated cheese and serve immediately.

CANNELLONI A LA CARIBE
Canelones con Queso
(Serves 8)

A—Filling:
Make half recipe for **Basic Meat Filling** (see Index)

B—Cannelloni:
3 quarts (12 cups) water
1 tablespoon salt
1 tablespoon olive oil
½ pound cannelloni

C—Sauce:
1 can (10½ ounces) tomato soup
1 can (8 ounces) spaghetti sauce or tomato sauce

D—½ pound (4 ounces) Velveeta cheese, sliced

1—In a large pot, bring to a boil water, salt, and olive oil included in A. Add cannelloni and boil *rapidly* for *15 minutes.* Drain, arrange cannelloni one next to the other on an aluminum sheet.

2—Stuff each cannelloni with the filling included in A.

3—Grease a 13 x 9 x 2-inch glass baking dish and line bottom of dish with cannelloni. Mix ingredients included in C and pour over cannelloni. Top with Velveeta slices.

4—*Cover* dish with aluminum foil and bake, in preheated oven to *350°F.,* for *30 minutes.*

CARIBBEAN PIZZA
Pizza

Dough:

A—3 cups flour
  1 teaspoon salt
  2 tablespoons baking powder
  ¼ pound butter, chilled

B—2 eggs
  ½ cup milk

1—Measure flour and sift together with salt and baking powder included in *A* into a bowl.

2—Add butter and cut **rapidly** with a dough blender or 2 knives, until mixture resembles coarse meal.

3—Break eggs into a measuring cup and add enough of the milk included in *B* to make ¾ cup liquid.

4—Add egg-milk mixture to flour-butter mixture. Stir together well to form a soft dough. Turn dough onto a lightly floured board.

5—Knead lightly, **10 to 12 strokes,** and roll out in a circle large enough to cover a 12-inch pizza pan.

6—Place a piece of waxed paper over the dough. Roll up paper with dough like a jelly roll.

7—Grease *pizza* pan.

8—Place rolled dough on one side of pan and unroll, removing waxed paper.

9—Prick bottom and sides of dough with a fork.

10—Form a border, using a fork to press edge of dough against edge of pan. Set in refrigerator until filling is ready.

Note: This dough has a bread-like consistency.

Filling:

A—¼ pound onions, peeled ⎫
   ¼ pound green peppers, seeded ⎬ chopped

B—2 tablespoons olive oil
   1 teaspoon whole dried *orégano*
   9 ounces tomato paste, diluted with an equal amount of water
   1½ teaspoons salt
   2 tablespoons freshly grated Parmesan cheese
   ¼ pound Mozzarella cheese, shredded

C—2 cans (7 ounces each) sardines (*preferably with skins*)
   2 *chorizos* (Spanish sausages) (casings removed and *chorizos* crumbled)

D—¼ pound Mozzarella cheese, *thinly sliced*
   ½ cup Parmesan cheese, freshly grated

1—In a large frying pan, sauté onions and peppers at *low* heat in olive oil for *10 minutes,* stirring *occasionally.*

2—Add rest of B ingredients, mix, and cook at *low* heat for *30 minutes,* stirring *occasionally.* Allow to cool.

3—Remove pan lined with dough from refrigerator and spread the cooled mixture evenly over it.

4—Garnish with the sardines and sausages included in C. Cover with slices of Mozzarella cheese and sprinkle with the grated Parmesan cheese included in D.

5—Preheat oven to 375°F. and bake the pizza for *30 minutes.*

Note: The garnish may vary by using boiled lobster or shrimps, anchovies, etc.

CHAPTER VIII

Salads and Cold Dishes

Salads and Cold Dishes

PINK PARTY SALAD
Ensalada Rosada
(Serves 12)

A—3½ pounds potatoes, washed and halved
2 quarts (8 cups) water
4 tablespoons salt

B—1 can (1 pound) diced beets
1 can (1 pound) green peas (*Petit-Pois*)
6 hard-cooked eggs

C—3 apples
1 quart (4 cups) water
1 teaspoon salt

D—½ cup olive oil
¼ cup vinegar
2 tablespoons sugar
1¼ teaspoons salt

1—Place ingredients included in A in a deep kettle, *cover,* and cook over *moderate* heat for *45 minutes.* Drain and peel potatoes. When **thoroughly cool,** dice potatoes and place in a big bowl.

2—Add diced beets, **including liquid,** and mix.

3—Drain peas. Set aside about ½ cup peas for garnishing and add rest to the bowl.

4—Save 1 egg to use as garnish. Chop the rest and add to the bowl.

5—Peel apples, dice and rinse in water and salt included in *C*. Drain well and add to bowl.

6—Combine dressing ingredients included in *D*, pour over salad and mix.

7—Turn salad into salad bowl and arrange peas around in a border. Set in refrigerator. When ready to serve, garnish with reserved egg yolk pressed through a coarse sieve and with the egg white mashed with a fork.

WHITE SALAD
Ensalada Blanca
(Serves 12)

A—3 pounds potatoes, washed and halved
2 quarts (8 cups) water
4 tablespoons salt

B—6 hard-cooked eggs, chopped
1½ cups chopped onions
½ cup chopped celery
½ cup chopped sweet pickles

C—1 can (1 pound) green peas (*Petit-Pois*)
3 apples
1 quart (4 cups) water
1 teaspoon salt

D—½ cup olive oil
¼ cup vinegar
2 teaspoons salt
1 tablespoon sugar

E—3 tablespoons mayonnaise

1—Place ingredients included in *A* in a deep kettle, *cover,* and cook over *moderate* heat for *45 minutes*. Drain and peel potatoes. When **thoroughly cool,** dice potatoes and place in a big bowl.

2—Add ingredients included in *B* and mix.

3—Add contents of can of peas, **including liquid,** and mix. Peel apples, dice and rinse *rapidly* in water and salt included in *C*. Drain, add to bowl and mix.

4—Combine ingredients included in *D*, add and mix. Add mayonnaise, mix, spoon into a salad bowl and set in refrigerator.

IMPERIAL BUFFET SALAD

Ensalada Mixta

(Serves 12)

A—3 pounds potatoes, washed and halved
2 quarts (8 cups) water
4 tablespoons salt

B—4 hard-cooked eggs, chopped
½ pound carrots, scraped ⎫
¼ pound onions, peeled ⎬ ground
½ cup sweet pickles, chopped
1 can (1 pound) green peas (*Petit-Pois*), drained

C—2 tablespoons olive oil ⎫
1½ teaspoons vinegar ⎪
½ teaspoon salt ⎬ mix
⅛ teaspoon ground pepper ⎭

D—1 cup mayonnaise

1—Place ingredients included in *A* in a deep kettle, *cover,* and cook over *moderate* heat for *45 minutes.* Drain and peel potatoes. When **thoroughly cool,** dice potatoes and place in a big bowl.

2—Add ingredients included in *B*, and mix.

3—Combine dressing ingredients included in *C*. Pour over the salad and mix.

4—Add mayonnaise and mix. Spoon into a salad bowl and set in refrigerator.

PARTY CHICKEN SALAD
Ensalada de Pollo
(Serves 6)

A—2 pounds chicken breasts

B—2 peppercorns (whole black peppers) ⎫
   1 clove garlic, peeled   ⎬ crush and mix
   2 teaspoons salt   in a mortar
   1 teaspoon fresh lime juice ⎭

C—½ pound onions, peeled and sliced

D—1 pound potatoes, washed and halved
   2 quarts (8 cups) water | 1 tablespoon salt

E—3 apples
   1 quart (4 cups) water | 1 teaspoon salt

F—1 cup celery, finely chopped | 1 teaspoon fresh lime juice
   2 hard-cooked eggs, chopped | ¾ cup mayonnaise

G—1 can (1 pound) green peas (*Petit-Pois*)

1—Wash chicken breasts, dry and season with ingredients included in *B*.

2—Arrange onion slices in bottom of a glass baking dish. Add chicken breasts, *cover* and bake at 325°F., for *2 hours*.

3—Place ingredients included in *D* in a deep kettle, *cover,* and cook over *moderate* heat for *45 minutes*. Drain and peel potatoes. When **thoroughly cool,** dice potatoes and place in a big bowl.

4—Remove chicken, discard onions and add broth to bowl. Separate meat from bones of chicken. When **thoroughly cool,** mince chicken meat and add to bowl.

5—Peel apples, dice and rinse *rapidly* in water and salt included in *E*. Drain, add to bowl, and mix.

6—Add ingredients included in *F* and mix.

7—Add peas, *including liquid,* if salad looks dry. Mix, spoon into salad bowl and set in refrigerator.

FAMILY CHICKEN SALAD

Ensalada Sencilla de Pollo
(Serves 6)

A—1 pound chicken pieces

B—1 peppercorn (whole black pepper) ⎫
   1 clove garlic, peeled
   ½ teaspoon whole dried *orégano* ⎬ crush and mix
   1 teaspoon salt   in a mortar
   ¾ teaspoon olive oil
   ¼ teaspoon vinegar ⎭

C—1 pound medium-sized onions, peeled and halved
   2 bay leaves

D—4 hard-cooked eggs, chopped
   1 can (4 ounces) green peas (*Petit-Pois*), drained
   2 tablespoons sweet relish

E—2 apples
   1 quart (4 cups) water | 1 teaspoon salt

F—2 tablespoons mayonnaise
   ¼ cup olive oil | 1 teaspoon sugar
   2 tablespoons vinegar | 1 teaspoon salt

1—Wash chicken pieces, dry and rub with seasoning included in *B*.

2—Arrange onions in bottom of a pot. Add chicken pieces and bay leaves. *Cover* and cook over *moderate* heat for *5 minutes.* Reduce heat to *low* and cook for *1½ hours.*

3—Remove chicken and separate meat from bones. When **thoroughly cool,** dice meat and place in a bowl.

4—Add ingredients included in *D* and mix.

5—Peel apples, dice and rinse *rapidly* in water and salt included in *E*. Drain, add to bowl, and mix.

6—In a small bowl, blend ingredients included in *F*, add to bowl, and mix. Spoon into salad bowl and set in refrigerator.

MARGARITA'S SALAD

Ensalada Margarita

(Serves 12)

A—2 pounds potatoes, washed and halved
2 quarts (8 cups) water
3 tablespoons salt

B—6 hard-cooked eggs, (**reserve** 1 for garnishing)
1 small onion, peeled
3 large cloves garlic, peeled
1 can (4 ounces) pimientos, drained

C—2 apples
1 quart (4 cups) water
1 teaspoon salt

D—1 can (1 pound 1 ounce) green peas (*Petit-Pois*)

E—½ cup mayonnaise
1 teaspoon salt
1 teaspoon sugar
1 tablespoon olive oil
¼ cup vinegar

1—Place ingredients included in *A* in a deep kettle, *cover,* and cook over *moderate* heat for *45 minutes.* Drain and peel potatoes. When **thoroughly cool,** dice potatoes and place in a big bowl.

2—Chop 5 eggs and add to bowl. Chop onion and cloves garlic and add. **Reserve** part of pimientos for garnishing. Chop rest of pimientos and add.

3—Peel apples, dice and rinse **rapidly** in water and salt included in *C.* Drain, add to bowl, and mix.

4—Drain peas, **reserve** part for garnishing and add rest to bowl.

5—In a small bowl, mix ingredients included in *E,* and add to bowl. Mix and spoon mixture into salad bowl. Garnish with reserved egg, pimientos, and peas. Set in refrigerator.

PAPAYA SALAD

Ensalada de Lechosa Madura
(Serves 6)

A—1 ripe *papaya*, peeled and finely chopped
1½ cups chopped fresh pineapple

B—Lettuce leaves, washed and drained

C—½ cup mayonnaise | 1½ tablespoons fresh lime juice
2 tablespoons ketchup
¾ teaspoon Worcestershire sauce

1—Mix ingredients included in A and set in refrigerator.

2—When ready to serve, arrange on lettuce leaves and cover with dressing made by mixing ingredients included in C.

STUFFED AVOCADO SALAD

Ensalada de Aguacate y Frutas Frescas
(Serves 6)

A—3 ripe avocados
1 cup finely chopped fresh pineapple
2 oranges, peeled and separated into sections
12 *acerolas* or Maraschino cherries (see Glossary)

B—½ cup olive oil | ½ teaspoon salt
¼ cup vinegar | ⅛ teaspoon ground pepper
¼ teaspoon fresh lime juice | 1 tablespoon sugar (*optional*)

C—Lettuce leaves, washed and drained

1—Cut avocados into halves, *lengthwise.* Remove seeds and scoop out pulp, being careful not to break shells.

2—Cut avocado meat into ½-inch cubes and combine with pineapple. Mix *thoroughly* with dressing made by mixing ingredients included in B.

3—Fill shells with the mixture and serve on lettuce leaves on individual plates with orange sections around.

4—Garnish with *acerolas* or Maraschino cherries and serve cold.

TROPICAL SALAD

Ensalada Tropical
(Serves 6)

A—½ head cabbage, cored and shredded

B—**Slice thinly:**

1 cucumber, peeled	6 radishes
1 green pepper, seeded	1 large ripe avocado, peeled
6 onions, peeled	

C—½ cup olive oil   ¼ teaspoon fresh lime juice
  ¼ cup vinegar   ½ teaspoon salt
  ⅛ teaspoon ground pepper
  1 tablespoon sugar (*optional*)

1—Mix ingredients included in A and B.

2—Mix ingredients included in C and moisten vegetable mixture thoroughly with the dressing. Chill in the refrigerator.

CARROTS AND RAISIN SALAD

Ensalada de Zanahorias y Pasas
(Serves 4)

A—¾ pound carrots

B—½ cup seeded raisins

C—½ cup mayonnaise
  ⅛ teaspoon ground pepper
  1 teaspoon ground onion

D—Lettuce leaves, washed and drained

1—Scrape, wash and grate carrots. Place in a bowl.

2—Add raisins and mix.

3—Mix ingredients included in C and add to bowl. Mix **thoroughly** and set in refrigerator.

4—When ready to serve, spoon over lettuce leaves.

BAKED HAM WITH RED WINE

Jamón al Horno con Vino Tinto

(Serves 30)

A—1 can (12 pounds) boiled ham
Whole cloves

B—2 pounds (6 cups) brown sugar, firmly packed
2 cups red wine
1 can (12 ounces) pineapple juice
1 can (12 ounces) sliced pineapple
1 jar (4 ounces) Maraschino cherries

C—½ cup brown sugar, firmly packed

1—Preheat oven to 350°F.

2—After scraping off gelatin, place ham in a baking dish. Score the ham in diamonds and stud with cloves.

3—Mix sugar, wine, and pineapple juice. Drain liquid from cans of pineapple and cherries and add. **Reserve** pineapple slices and cherries for garnishing. Pour liquid over ham.

4—Bake ham for 45 minutes, basting occasionally. Remove from oven, garnish with pineapple slices and cherries. Sprinkle with brown sugar and broil about 3 minutes, or until golden.

5—Remove ham to a platter. Allow to cool and set in refrigerator. Strain the drippings and boil over high heat until syrup thickens to light stage (Candy Thermometer—220°F.). Allow to cool and set in refrigerator to serve with ham.

HAM IN APRICOT SAUCE

Jamón en Salsa de Albaricoque
(Serves 30)

A—1 can (12 pounds) boiled ham
Whole cloves

B—1 jar (12 ounces) apricot preserve
2 cans (7 ounces each) apricot nectar
1½ cups dry sherry
2 cups sugar

1—Preheat oven to 325°F.

2—Place ham in a baking pan, after scraping off the gelatin. Score the ham in diamonds and stud with cloves.

3—Mix ingredients included in B and pour over ham.

4—Bake for 2 *hours*, basting *occasionally*.

5—Remove from oven. Allow ham to cool and set in refrigerator. Pour sauce in a deep vessel, allow to cool and set in refrigerator, to serve with ham.

GLAZED HAM LOAF

Jamón Glaceado (Abrillantado o Confitado)
(Serves 8)

A—1½ pounds boiled ham
1 pound lean pork or beef
1 small onion, peeled
2 teaspoons salt
¼ teaspoon ground pepper
1 cup bread or cracker crumbs
1 cup milk
2 eggs, lightly beaten

B—1 can cranberry sauce
½ cup light corn syrup
½ cup water
1 can (12 ounces) pineapple slices

1—Grind together ham, meat, and onion.

2—Mix salt, pepper, and crumbs and add to meat mixture.

3—Add milk and eggs and mix well.

4—Pack the mixture into a greased baking dish and bake for *1½ hours* at preheated oven to *350°F.*

5—Remove from oven to a platter and allow to cool **thoroughly.** Garnish with pineapple slices.

6—Mix cranberry sauce, corn syrup, and water included in *B* and cook over *low* heat, stirring **constantly,** until sauce thickens.

7—Cool, but do not allow the sauce to jell. Cover the loaf with the sauce and set in refrigerator.

HAM IN WHITE WINE

Jamón al Horno con Vino Blanco
(Serves 30)

A—1 can (12 pounds) boiled ham
Whole cloves

B—1 pound (3 cups) brown sugar, firmly packed
2 tablespoons prepared mustard
¼ cup fresh orange juice
2 cups white wine

C—1 can (1 pound 4 ounces) pineapple slices
1 jar (4 ounces) Maraschino cherries
½ cup brown sugar

1—Preheat oven to *350°F.*

2—Place ham in an aluminum baking pan, after scraping off the gelatin. Score the ham in diamonds and stud with cloves.

3—Apart, mix ingredients included in *B.* Add liquid from contents of pineapple can and from jar of cherries. **Reserve** pineapple slices and cherries. Pour liquid over ham.

4—Bake for *45 minutes,* basting **occasionally.**

5—Remove from oven. Garnish ham with pineapple slices and cherries. Sprinkle with brown sugar. Preheat broiler and broil for a **few seconds**, until golden.

6—Remove ham to a platter, allow to cool and set in refrigerator. Strain drippings and boil over *high* heat, until syrup thickens to light stage (Candy Thermometer — 220°F.). Allow to cool and set in refrigerator to serve with ham.

PARTY HAM

Jamón Planchado y Almíbar

(Serves 30)

A—1 can (12 pounds) boiled ham
2 cups brown sugar, firmly packed

B—**Syrup:**
½ pound lean cured ham
5 cups brown sugar, firmly packed
3 cinnamon sticks
1 tablespoon whole cloves
¾ teaspoon salt
2½ cups water

1—Place ham in an aluminum baking pan, after scraping off the gelatin. Cover surface with sugar included in A and press **rapidly** to a golden brown with a hot old-fashioned iron. (If iron is not available, preheat broiler and broil for a **few seconds,** until golden.)

2—In a large saucepan, mix ingredients included in B and bring **rapidly** to a boil. Reduce heat to *moderate,* and boil until syrup thickens to light stage (Candy Thermometer — 220°F.). (Remove foam from edges as syrup boils.) Allow to cool, strain, and serve with cold ham.

COLD PORK OR BEEF SAUSAGE
Fiambre Italiano
(Serves 8)

A—¼ pound French bread or 4 slices of sandwich bread, crusts trimmed
1 cup milk

B—1 pound ground lean beef or pork
¼ cup onion, ground or finely minced
½ ounce (1 tablespoon) butter
1 tablespoon Worcestershire Sauce
2 cups freshly grated Parmesan cheese
5 eggs

1—Preheat oven to *350°F.* Grease a 9 x 5 x 3-inch glass baking dish.

2—Crumble bread over milk and soak. Mash bread **thoroughly** and drain in a colander, without squeezing.

3—Place meat in a bowl, add soaked bread and rest of ingredients included in *B.* Mix well.

4—Pack the mixture into baking dish and bake for *45 minutes.*

5—Remove from oven and drain fat from baking dish. Unmold and allow to cool. Wrap with wax paper, and set in refrigerator. Cut in slices for buffet supper, or serve in small cuts as an appetizer with crackers.

CHICKEN SAUSAGE
Embutido de Pollo
(Serves 8)

A—1½ pounds chicken breasts
½ pound boiled ham

B—¼ cup water
¼ teaspoon salt
¼ pound chicken livers (see Note)

C—3 eggs, lightly beaten
¼ teaspoon ground nutmeg
¼ teaspoon ground pepper
¾ teaspoon salt

D—¾ cup bread or cracker crumbs
3 eggs, lightly beaten

1—Wash and skin chicken breasts and separate meat from bones. **Reserve** bones.

2—Grind chicken meat and boiled ham through finest blade of a meat grinder.

3—Mix ingredients included in *B* and boil for 5 *minutes*. Drain and chop livers.

4—In a bowl, mix ingredients included in *C*. Add chopped livers. Mix with the ground meat and add 3 tablespoons of the crumbs included in *D*.

5—Mix well and place on a sheet of wax paper. Shape like a roll, about 2½ inches thick and about 12 inches long. Sprinkle with crumbs.

6—On another sheet of wax paper, spread the beaten egg. Add roll and cover well on all sides.

7—On a third sheet of wax paper, place roll and coat **generously** with crumbs.

8—Set on table a white cloth long enough to cover roll, and sprinkle with crumbs. Place roll on this cloth and wrap. Tie ends **securely.**

9—Cook for *1 hour* in a boiling stock made with the chicken bones, 5 tablespoons salt, and 4 quarts water. (The vessel should be rectangular to allow the roll to lie straight.) **Halfway,** turn the roll over. Remove from stock, allow to cool, and remove cloth. Wrap in wax paper and refrigerate overnight. Cut in narrow slices and serve cold in buffet supper, or as an appetizer.

Note: I can (1¼ ounces) truffles may be substituted for the liver. Include I tablespoon of liquid from can of truffles.

DELICIOUS CHICKEN ROLL

Embutido de Pollo Delicioso

(2 rolls)

A—2 ounces (4 tablespoons) butter
1 pound chicken meat, without bone (about 4 chicken breasts)
1 can (2¾ ounces) *Pâté de foie gras*
3 medium eggs, **very lightly** beaten
⅓ cup bread or cracker crumbs
1¼ teaspoons salt
⅛ teaspoon ground nutmeg
Pinch of white ground pepper

1—Cream butter in a bowl. Grind chicken meat, add, and mix. Add rest of ingredients and mix **thoroughly.** Divide mixture in two portions.

2—Place each portion over wax paper and roll into two 14-inch rolls.

3—Wrap each roll in parchment paper and cover **firmly** with heavy duty aluminum foil. Twist ends. Tie around rolls and ends **securely** with a string.

4—In a deep rectangular vessel, heat to boiling enough water to cover **generously** the two rolls.

5—Add rolls and boil for *1½ hours.* **Halfway,** turn the rolls over.

6—Remove from water, discard aluminum foil and parchment paper. Allow to cool. Wrap each roll in wax paper and set in refrigerator.

7—When ready to serve, cut in slices and serve in buffet supper, or as an appetizer.

PORK AND HAM SAUSAGE
Embutido de Cerdo y Jamón
(Serves 6)

A—¾ pound lean pork meat
¾ pound lean cured ham

B—5 ounces bread or cracker crumbs
¼ teaspoon ground nutmeg
1 egg, lightly beaten

1—Grind meat and cured ham included in A through the finest blade of a meat grinder.

2—Add cracker crumbs and nutmeg.

3—Mix well and turn out on wax paper. Shape into a roll.

4—On another sheet of wax paper spread the egg.

5—Roll the meat in the beaten egg, covering all sides.

6—On a third piece of wax paper, sprinkle additional cracker crumbs. Roll the meat on this sheet to coat it with crumbs.

7—Wrap meat in a piece of white cloth, which has been sprinkled with cracker crumbs, and tie ends **securely.**

8—In a deep rectangular vessel, heat to boiling enough water to cover roll. Add ½ teaspoon salt.

9—Add roll and boil for *2 hours.* **Halfway** turn the roll over. Add more boiling water, if necessary, to keep roll submerged during the entire cooking period.

10—Remove from water, allow to cool, and remove cloth. Wrap in wax paper and set in refrigerator overnight. Cut in narrow slices and serve cold.

TROPICAL MEAT PARTY LOAF
Butifarrón Tropical

A—¼ cup milk
½ teaspoon whole dried *orégano*
2¼ teaspoons salt
¼ teaspoon ground nutmeg
3 eggs
2 tablespoons ketchup
2 tablespoons butter or oleomargarine

B—1 onion, peeled and quartered
1 green pepper, seeded and quartered
4 sweet chili peppers, seeded
3 cloves garlic, peeled
1 package (4 ounces) liver sausage

C—3 slices sandwich bread, crumbled

D—1¾ pounds lean ground beef
3 bacon strips

E—Pickles, cut into strips
1 hard-cooked egg, quartered   } *for garnishing*
1 tomato, halved
Parsley sprigs

1—Preheat oven to 350°F. Grease a 9 x 5 x 3-inch glass baking dish.

2—In an electric blender, blend ingredients included in A. Add *gradually* ingredients included in B, *cover*, and blend. **Stop** blender, add crumbled bread, and mix with a spatula. *Cover* and blend again.

3—Place ground meat in a bowl, add blended ingredients and mix *thoroughly*. Spoon into baking dish and pack firmly. Cover with bacon strips and bake for *1½ hours*.

4—Remove from oven, discard bacon strips, and drain fat from baking dish. Turn into a platter. Allow to cool and wrap in wax paper. Set in refrigerator.

5—When ready to serve, divide in **two, lengthwise,** and cut in slices. Place pickle strips in center of a large serving platter. Surround with slices of meat and garnish with rest of ingredients included in E. Serve with apricot preserve.

Note: To serve as an appetizer, cut into squares and serve with crackers.

DANISH CABBAGE

Col Danesa

(Serves 8)

Cabbage:
1 cabbage, weighing about 4 pounds
5 quarts (20 cups) water
4 tablespoons salt

1—To soften the leaves **lightly,** place cabbage in a pot, **stem down,** in water and salt. Turn heat to *high, cover* and cook for *15 minutes.*

2—Drain and **reserve** the water to boil the stuffed cabbage later. Thrust a knife through center of cabbage, and remove leaves, **one at a time.**

3—Turn cabbage leaves over and slice most of the ribs, **carefully,** so as to keep the leaves intact.

4—Cover a soup plate with a large, damp cloth forming a base for the leaves.

5—Place two big cabbage leaves on center of cloth. Arrange cabbage leaves over them in a circular formation with stems toward center of plate. Use as many leaves as necessary, one overlapping the other, until the circle is formed. **Reserve** some leaves to cover filling.

Filling:
A—¼ pound butter
1 pound ground lean beef or pork

B—1 cup milk
4 sandwich slices, crusts trimmed

C—2½ teaspoons salt
¼ teaspoon ground pepper
1 teaspoon ground nutmeg
4 eggs, *lightly* beaten

D—2 tomatoes, thinly sliced
3 hard-cooked eggs, quartered } for garnishing
Parsley sprigs

1—Cream butter in a bowl. Add meat and mix.

2—Crumble bread over milk and blend well. To bread-milk mixture, add ingredients included in *C*, and mix. Add to bowl and mix *thoroughly*.

3—Spoon filling in center of cabbage leaves. Fold leaves up around filling and cover with the reserved leaves. Bring cloth up and tighten firmly at the top. Tie securely with string.

4—In a big kettle, bring to a boil reserved water. Add stuffed cabbage, *cover*, and boil at *moderate* heat for *30 minutes*. Turn cabbage over and boil for *30 minutes* more.

5—Drain very well, by placing cabbage in a colander until *thoroughly cool*.

6—Remove cloth, wrap in waxed paper and set in refrigerator overnight.

7—Cut in wedges and serve cold in a flat platter, garnished with sliced tomatoes, hard-cooked eggs, quartered and parsley sprigs.

MACARONI SURPRISE

Sorpresa de Macarrones
(Serves 8)

A—1 quart (4 cups) water
½ teaspoon salt
1 teaspoon vegetable oil

B—¼ pound macaroni

C—1 cup milk
¼ pound butter
¼ pound boiled ham, ground
⅔ cup freshly grated Parmesan cheese
4 eggs

D—2 tomatoes, sliced
3 hard-cooked eggs, quartered ⎫ for garnishing
Parsley sprigs ⎭

E—2 cans (10¾ ounces each) tomato soup
1 cup freshly grated Parmesan cheese

1—In a deep pan, bring **rapidly** to a boil ingredients included in *A*. Add macaroni, and boil over *moderate* heat for *20 minutes.* Drain well.

2—Grease a round 8 x 3-inch aluminum pan. Line bottom with brown paper. Grease paper.

3—In a saucepan, heat milk to boiling. Remove from heat, add butter and as soon as it melts, add rest of ingredients included in *C*. Mix **thoroughly.**

4—In pan, arrange alternate layers of sauce and macaroni, beginning and ending with sauce.

5—*Cover* pan and set in a large shallow baking pan containing about *1 inch* hot water. Cook over *moderate-high* heat about *1 hour 45 minutes,* or until set. (Replenish with boiling water, if necessary.)

6—Remove pan from water bath and place on wire rack. Allow to cool for *30 minutes.* Release edges of pan with a knife. Turn onto a flat platter. Remove paper and set in refrigerator.

7—When ready to serve, garnish with ingredients included in *D*. Serve accompanied by chilled contents of cans of tomato soup and with freshly grated Parmesan cheese on the side.

CHAPTER IX # Rice Dishes and Legumes

Rice Dishes and Legumes

CARIBBEAN RICE WITH CHICKEN

Arroz con Pollo
(Serves 8)

A—2½ pounds chicken pieces

B—2 peppercorns (whole black pepper) ⎱
2 cloves garlic, peeled
1 teaspoon whole dried *orégano*
4½ teaspoons salt   crush and mix in a mortar
2 teaspoons olive oil
1 teaspoon vinegar or fresh lime juice ⎰

C—1 tablespoon lard or vegetable oil
1 ounce salt pork ⎱
2 ounces lean cured ham ⎰   washed and diced

D—1 onion, peeled
1 green pepper, seeded
3 sweet chili peppers, seeded   chopped
1 tomato
6 fresh *culantro* leaves

E—½ teaspoon salt
10 olives, stuffed with pimientos
1 tablespoon capers
¼ cup tomato sauce
2 tablespoons fat or *Achiote Coloring* (see Index)
3 cups rice

F—1 can (1 pound 1 ounce) green peas (*Petit-Pois*)

G—1 can (4 ounces) pimientos

1—Wash chicken and divide each chicken piece in two. Dry and rub with seasoning included in *B*. Set in refrigerator for several hours or overnight.

2—In a *caldero* or heavy kettle, heat fat and brown **rapidly** salt pork and ham. Reduce heat to *moderate,* add chicken pieces, and cook for *5 minutes*.

3—Reduce heat to *low*, add ingredients included in *D*, and sauté for *10 minutes*, stirring **occasionally.**

4—Meanwhile, drain liquid from can of peas into a measuring cup and add enough water to measure **2½ cups, if regular rice** is used, or **3½ cups, if long grain rice** is used. **Reserve** peas. Heat liquid and **reserve.**

5—Add to kettle ingredients included in *E* and mix over *moderate* heat for *2 minutes*.

6—Add reserved hot liquid to kettle, mix well, and cook, *uncovered,* over *moderate* heat, until rice is dry.

7—With a fork, turn rice from bottom to top.

8—*Cover* kettle and cook over *low* heat for *40 minutes*. **Halfway** during this cooking period, turn rice over again.

9—Add peas, turn rice once more, *cover,* and cook for *15 minutes* over *low* heat.

10—Spoon rice into a serving platter.

11—Heat pimientos in their juice, drain, and garnish the rice. Serve at once.

WHITE RICE A LA CARIBE
Arroz Blanco
(Serves 6)

A—3 cups water (see Note 1) | 2 teaspoons salt
4 tablespoons lard, vegetable oil, butter or oleomargarine

B—2 cups rice

1—In a *caldero* or heavy kettle, heat to boiling the ingredients included in A.

2—Place rice in a colander and wash **thoroughly** under running water. Drain **well** and add to the boiling water. Mix and cook, *uncovered*, over *moderate* heat, until rice is dry.

3—Reduce heat to *low*. With a fork, turn rice from bottom to top, *cover*, and cook for *20 minutes* longer. **Halfway** during this cooking period, turn rice over again.

Note 1: Add 1 **cup** water if using **long grain rice.**

Note 2: To prevent a sticky consistency, it is important to avoid stirring the rice, but just to turn it over from bottom to top.

RICE WITH BUTTER AND GARLIC
Arroz con Mantequilla y Ajo
(Serves 6)

A—2 ounces (4 tablespoons) butter
1 tablespoon garlic salt | 2 cups long grain rice

B—1 quart (4 cups) boiling water

1—In a *caldero* or heavy kettle, melt butter **slowly.** Add garlic salt and rice and mix **well,** over *moderate-high* heat.

2—Add boiling water, mix, and bring to a boil over *moderate-high* heat. Reduce heat to *low, cover,* and cook for *25 minutes.*

3—*Uncover*, turn rice over with a fork, **from bottom to top,** and cook for *5 minutes.*

BASIC STEWED RICE

Arroz Guisado Básico

(Serves 6)

A—1 ounce salt pork
2 ounces lean cured ham } washed and diced

B—3 tablespoons lard or vegetable oil
1 green pepper, seeded
3 sweet chili peppers, seeded
1 clove garlic, peeled
6 fresh *culantro* leaves
1 onion, peeled
} ground or finely chopped

C—2 tablespoons tomato sauce
6 olives, stuffed with pimientos
2 teaspoons capers
2 teaspoons salt (amount varies according to basic ingredients used in preparing the stewed rice)

D—Basic ingredient (such as: cooked or canned shrimps, cuttlefish, Vienna sausages, beans, corn, etc.)

E—2¼ cups rice, **thoroughly** washed and drained
2¼ cups boiling water (use 3¼ cups water for long grain rice)

1—In a *caldero* or heavy kettle, brown **rapidly** salt pork and ham. Add ingredients included in *B* and sauté over *low* heat for *10 minutes*, stirring **occasionally.**

2—Add ingredients included in *C* and mix.

3—Add basic ingredient and mix. Add rice to kettle. Sauté for *2 or 3 minutes.*

4—Add boiling water, mix, and cook over *moderate* heat until rice is dry.

5—Turn rice over with a fork from bottom to top, *cover,* and cook for *30 minutes* at *low* heat. **Halfway** during this cooking period, turn rice over again.

PAELLA

(Serves 12)

A—2 pounds chicken pieces | 1 teaspoon fresh lime juice
2 teaspoons salt

B—3 cans (4¼ ounces each) *mejillones* (mussels)
2 cans (4¼ ounces each) *berberechos* (cockles)
2 cans (10 ounces each) *almejas* (clams)
3 quarts (12 cups) water (**including** drained liquid from cans included in *B*)
3 tablespoons salt
2 pounds frozen raw shrimp tails, medium size, **with shells**

C—1 cup olive oil
2 large cloves garlic, peeled and crushed
3 cans (5 ounces each) *chorizos* (Spanish sausages), cut in pieces

D—2 onions, peeled
2 green peppers, seeded
2 tomatoes   } finely chopped
6 large cloves garlic, peeled

E—1/16 ounce (½ teaspoon) *azafrán* (saffron threads)
2 tablespoons *pimentón* (paprika)
½ pound fresh string beans, trimmed and cut into ½-inch pieces

F—4 cups long grain rice

G—1 pound frozen lobster tail meat, **without shells**
1 box (10 ounce) frozen green peas
1 box (10 ounce) frozen *alcachofas* (artichoke hearts)

H—2 fresh limes

I—1 can (7 ounces) pimientos
1 can (10½ ounces) asparagus tips

1—Cut chicken pieces in half, wash, dry, and season with salt and lime juice included in *A*.

2—Drain cans included in *B* and measure the drained liquid. Add enough water to measure 3 quarts (12 cups) and **reserve. Reserve** contents of cans.

3—In a large pot, bring to a brisk boil reserved liquid, together with salt included in *B*. Wash shrimps **carefully,** add to pot, cover and cook at *low* heat for *5 minutes.* Strain and **reserve** liquid. **Reserve** shrimps.

4—Place a 20-inch *paellera* (see Glossary) over **two** coils of the electric stove. Heat olive oil included in *C* and add garlic cloves. Stir until **slightly** browned and discard.

5—Add chicken pieces and Spanish sausages to *paellera.* Cook for *10 minutes* at *moderate* heat, stirring **occasionally.**

6—Add chopped ingredients included in *D* to *paellera,* mix, and sauté at *low* heat for *10 minutes,* stirring **occasionally.**

7—In a very small frying pan, heat saffron over *moderate* heat until crispy. Remove, allow to cool slightly and crush, with the palms of the hands, over the *paellera.* Add paprika and string beans and mix.

8—Heat to boiling the reserved liquid, add to the *paellera,* mix, and cook at *moderate* heat for *45 minutes.* **Meanwhile, shell and devein the reserved shrimps.** Reserve to be added later.

9—Add rice included in *F*, mix, and cook over *moderate* heat for *30 minutes.*

10—Cut the lobster meat into 1½-inch chunks and add, together with other ingredients included in *G*. Mix and cook until rice is dry. (In the process of drying, it is convenient to spoon sections of dry rice over remaining pools of liquid.)

11—Turn rice over with a spoon, from bottom to top. Add shrimps and reserved contents of cans included in *B*. Mix and cook over *low* heat for 20 minutes.

12—Turn off heat on **both coils,** but allow *paellera* to rest on stove for *10 minutes.*

13—Sprinkle juice of ½ lime over *paellera.*

14—Heat pimientos and asparagus tips in their juice, drain, and garnish *paellera.* Garnish with remaining limes, cut into wedges.

PAELLITA

(Serves 6)

A—1 pound small chicken pieces

B—1 peppercorn (whole black pepper)
1 clove garlic, peeled
½ teaspoon whole dried *orégano*   crush and mix
1 teaspoon salt   in a mortar
¾ teaspoon olive oil
¼ teaspoon vinegar or fresh lime juice

C—½ cup olive oil
2 cloves garlic, peeled
1 onion, peeled   chopped
1 tomato

D—¼ teaspoon *azafrán* (saffron threads)

E—1 tablespoon *pimentón* (paprika)
1 tablespoon salt
5 cups boiling water

F—2 cups boiling water
2 cups long grain rice

G—1 pound frozen raw shrimp tails, medium size, **with shells**
½ of a 10-ounce box of frozen green peas

H—1 can (4 ounces) pimientos
1 can (10½ ounces) asparagus tips
2 fresh limes

1—Cut each chicken piece in two, wash, dry, and season with ingredients included in *B.*

2—In a 15-inch *paellera* (see Glossary) or frying pan, heat olive oil and sauté over *low* heat the ingredients included in *C*, for *10 minutes*, stirring *occasionally*.

3—Add chicken pieces and mix for *2 or 3 minutes*.

4—In a very small saucepan, heat saffron over *moderate* heat until crispy. Remove, allow to cool slightly, and crush with the palms of the hands over the *paellera*. Add ingredients included in *E* and mix *thoroughly*. Cook over *moderate-high* heat, *uncovered*, for *30 minutes*.

5—Add ingredients included in *F*, mix, and boil for *5 minutes*.

6—Wash shrimps *carefully*, drain, and distribute in *paellera*. Add frozen peas. Turn heat to *moderate*, and cook until rice is dry. (In the process of drying, it is convenient to spoon sections of dry rice over remaining pools of liquid.)

7—Turn rice over with a fork, from bottom to top. Cook at *low* heat for *20 minutes* more. During this time, remove shrimps from *paellera*, shell and devein. Return shrimps to *paellera* and arrange attractively.

8—Turn off heat, but allow *paellera* to rest on stove for *10 minutes*.

9—Sprinkle juice of ½ fresh lime over *paellera*.

10—Heat pimientos and asparagus tips in their juice, drain, and garnish *paellera*. Garnish with remaining limes, cut into wedges.

RICE APASTELADO

Arroz Apastelado

(Serves 8)

A—1 pound lean pork meat, washed and cubed
1 quart (4 cups) water
1 onion, peeled and halved
1½ teaspoons salt
1 small cured ham bone, washed

B—1 tablespoon lard or vegetable oil
 ¼ pound lean cured ham, washed and diced

C—1 small green pepper, seeded
 3 sweet chili peppers, seeded
 1 clove garlic, peeled
 1 tomato   } ground or chopped
 1 onion, peeled
 6 fresh *culantro* leaves

D—8 olives, stuffed with pimientos
 1 teaspoon capers
 1 teaspoon whole dried *orégano*
 ¼ cup tomato sauce
 3 tablespoons fat or *Achiote Coloring* (see Index)

E—2½ cups rice

F—1 can (1 pound 4 ounces) *garbanzos* (Chick-Peas)
 2 tablespoons seeded raisins
 ¼ cup juice of *naranja agria* (Sour Orange) (see Glossary)
 3½ teaspoons salt

G—1 plantain leaf, rinsed and drained

1—Combine ingredients included in A in a pot and boil, **un-covered,** for *30 minutes.* Discard ham bone. **Reserve** broth.

2—In a large *caldero* or heavy kettle, heat fat and brown diced ham **rapidly.** Turn heat to *low,* add ingredients included in C, and sauté for *10 minutes,* stirring **occasionally.**

3—Add ingredients included in D and mix.

4—Wash rice **thoroughly,** drain, add, and mix over *moderate* heat for *2 minutes.*

5—Add can of *garbanzos,* including liquid. Add rest of ingredients included in F and mix.

6—Add hot broth, mix, and cook over *moderate* heat until rice is dry.

7—Turn rice over with a fork, from bottom to top. *Cover* with piece of plantain leaf. Place a lid on top and cook over *low* heat for *30 minutes.* **Halfway** during this cooking period, turn rice over again.

RICE WITH SPARERIBS
Arroz con Costillitas de Cerdo

A—1 ounce salt pork ⎫
2 ounces lean cured ham ⎬ washed and diced
1½ pounds spareribs, washed and halved

B—1 onion, peeled ⎫
1 tomato ⎪
3 sweet chili peppers, seeded ⎬ chopped
1 green pepper, seeded ⎭

C—1 tablespoon fat or *Achiote Coloring* (see Index)
1 tablespoon capers
8 olives, stuffed with pimientos
1 teaspoon whole dried *orégano*
½ cup tomato sauce

D—1 can (1 pound 4 ounces) *garbanzos* (chick-peas)

E—2½ cups rice ⎪ 1 tablespoon salt
2½ cups water (use 3½ cups water for long grain rice)

1—In a *caldero* or heavy kettle, brown **rapidly** salt pork and ham. Add spareribs and brown **lightly** over *moderate* heat. Drain off excess fat.

2—Reduce heat to *low* and sauté ingredients included in *B* until tender.

3—Add ingredients included in *C* and mix. *Cover* and boil over *moderate* heat for *30 minutes.*

4—Drain can of chick-peas. **Reserve** liquid and add chick-peas to *caldero* and mix for *2 minutes.*

5—Wash **thoroughly** and drain rice. Add and mix well.

6—Combine reserved liquid with water and salt included in *E*. Bring **rapidly** to a boil over *high* heat. Add to *caldero* and mix. Reduce heat to *moderate* and boil until rice is dry.

7—Turn rice over, **from bottom to top.** Reduce heat to *low*, *cover*, and cook for *30 minutes.* **Halfway** during this cooking period, turn rice over again.

RICE WITH BUTTER AND VEGETABLES

Arroz con Mantequilla y Vegetales

A—1 can (1 pound) diced carrots
1 can (1 pound) green peas (*Petit-Pois*)
3 cups liquid | 2 ounces (4 tablespoons) butter
2 teaspoons salt

B—2 cups rice

1—Drain cans of carrots and peas. **Reserve** carrots and peas. Measure drained liquid. Add enough water to measure **3 cups** (**4 cups** for long grain rice). Pour into a *caldero,* or heavy kettle.

2—Add salt and butter included in A and bring **rapidly** to a boil.

3—Wash **thoroughly** and drain rice, add to *caldero,* mix, and cook *uncovered,* over *moderate* heat, until rice is dry.

4—Turn rice over **from bottom to top.** Add drained carrots and green peas, mix, *cover,* and cook over *low* heat for *30 minutes.* **Halfway** during this cooking period, turn rice over again.

RICE A LA REGENTA

Arroz a la Regenta
(Serves 6)

A—**Stock:**
6 cups water
2½ teaspoons salt
1 onion, peeled
2 cloves garlic, peeled
2 peppercorns (whole black peppers)
2 pounds chicken breasts

B—**Rice:**
1 pound small white onions, finely chopped
¼ pound butter
2½ cups rice, **thoroughly** washed and drained
½ cup freshly grated Parmesan cheese
3¾ cups chicken stock (see Instruction 2)

C—Sauce:

> ¼ pound butter
> 2 tablespoons flour
> ¼ teaspoon salt
> ⅛ teaspoon ground white pepper
> ½ cup white sweet wine
> 1 cup chicken stock (see Instruction 2)

D—1 can (4 ounces) pimientos
> 1 can (1 pound 1 ounce) green peas (*Petit-Pois*)

1—Combine A ingredients in a kettle, except chicken breasts. Heat to boiling. Add chicken breasts. When boiling, cover and cook over *moderate* heat for *45 minutes.*

2—Strain and **reserve** 3¾ cups stock (4¾ cups, if using long grain rice) to prepare rice and 1 cup to prepare sauce. Separate chicken meat from bones. Cut chicken meat into pieces and **reserve.**

3—Melt butter in a kettle and sauté onions included in B. Add rice and cheese, mix, and cook for *2 or 3 minutes.*

4—Add 3¾ cups of chicken stock and boil over *moderate* heat until rice is dry. With a fork, turn rice from bottom to top, *cover,* and cook over *low* heat for *20 minutes.*

5—Melt butter **slowly** in a saucepan. Add flour and stir until smooth. Add **gradually** rest of ingredients included in C. Cook, stirring, until sauce is medium thick. Add chicken meat, mix, and boil for *2 or 3 minutes.*

6—Pack the rice in a 9½ x 3½-inch ring mold. Turn out on a serving dish and fill the center with the sauce.

7—Heat pimientos in their juice and drain. Garnish rice with pimientos, thinly sliced. Heat green peas in their juice, drain and arrange around rice. Serve at once.

STUFFED CHEESE WITH RICE AND CHICKEN

Queso Relleno con Arroz con Pollo

(Serves 10)

This recipe is prepared with a Holland Edam cheese, after the interior has been scooped out through a small square opening on top. Avoid breaking rind by leaving about ¼ inch of cheese on the inside. The cheese removed may be used for snacks or cooking.

A—1 large Holland Edam cheese

B—1½ pounds chicken pieces

C—2 peppercorns (whole black pepper) ⎫
   1 teaspoon whole dried *orégano*
   1 clove garlic, peeled   ⎬ crush and mix
   3¼ teaspoons salt   in a mortar
   2 teaspoons olive oil
   1 teaspoon vinegar ⎭

D—1 tablespoon lard or vegetable oil
   1 ounce salt pork   ⎫
   1 ounce lean cured ham ⎬ washed and diced

E—1 onion, peeled   ⎫
   1 green pepper, seeded
   3 fresh *culantro* leaves   ⎬ chopped
   2 sweet chili peppers, seeded
   1 tomato   ⎭

F—6 olives, stuffed with pimientos, chopped
   1 teaspoon capers
   ¼ cup tomato sauce
   2 tablespoons fat or *Achiote Coloring* (see Index)

G—2¼ cups rice, **thoroughly** washed and drained
   3 cups boiling water

H—Plantain leaf

1—Scrape outer part of cheese, which is covered with red paraffin. Place cheese in a vessel with enough water to cover and soak **overnight.**

2—Drain cheese and **reserve,** ready to be stuffed.

3—Wash and dry chicken. Rub with seasoning included in C.

4—In a *caldero* or heavy kettle, heat fat included in D and brown *rapidly* salt pork and ham.

5—Reduce heat to *low* and sauté ingredients included in E, for *10 minutes,* stirring *occasionally.*

6—Add chicken pieces and ingredients included in F. Mix over *moderate* heat for *3 minutes.*

7—Add rice and stir for *2 minutes.*

8—Add boiling water, mix, and cook over *moderate* heat until rice is dry.

9—Turn rice over with a fork, from bottom to top. *Cover* and cook over *low* heat for *15 minutes.*

10—Remove pieces of chicken from rice. Separate meat from bones. Mince meat and add again to rice, mixing well.

11—Cover bottom of a large *caldero* or heavy kettle, with a piece of washed plantain leaf. Place cheese in the kettle and stuff with rice. Whatever rice is left, after cheese is filled, should be arranged around the cheese in the kettle.

12—*Cover* with a piece of washed plantain leaf. Place a lid on top. Bake in preheated oven to 350°F., about *45 minutes.* Serve in kettle.

CHICKEN ASOPAO
Asopao de Pollo
(Serves 6 to 8)

A—3 pounds dressed-weight whole chicken

B—2 peppercorns (whole black peppers) ⎫
  2 cloves garlic, peeled
  1 teaspoon whole dried *orégano*
  ⅛ teaspoon paprika   ⎬ crush and mix
  2½ teaspoons salt   in a mortar
  1¼ teaspoons olive oil
  1¼ teaspoons vinegar ⎭

C—2½ cups rice

D—9 cups water
  1 tablespoon salt

E—3 tablespoons vegetable oil
  1 ounce salt pork   ⎫ washed and diced
  2 ounces lean cured ham ⎭

F—1 green pepper, seeded   ⎫
  3 sweet chili peppers, seeded
  1 onion, peeled   ⎬ ground or chopped
  8 fresh *culantro* leaves ⎭

G—1 can (8 ounces) tomato sauce
  1 tomato, chopped
  8 olives, stuffed with pimientos
  1 *chorizo* (Spanish sausage), cut into ½-inch rounds
  1 tablespoon capers
  1 can (4 ounces) pimientos, chopped in their juice
    (**reserve** 1 pimiento for garnishing)
  2 tablespoons fat or *Achiote Coloring* (page xvi)

H—1 can (1 pound 1 ounce) green peas (*Petit-Pois*), drained
  1 can (10½ ounces) asparagus tips

1—Divide chicken into serving portions. Separate drumsticks from thighs and divide breast in two. Wash well chicken and giblets. Set in one plate drumsticks, thighs, breasts, and wings. Set in another plate carcass of chicken, neck, and giblets.

2—Rub contents of both plates with the seasoning included in *B*.

3—Wash rice **thoroughly** and soak in water to cover for *1 hour*.

4—In a 6-quart pot, combine ingredients included in *D* with the carcass of the chicken, the neck, and the giblets. *Cover* and boil over *moderate-high* heat for *15 minutes*. Reduce to *moderate*, and cook for *30 minutes*. Strain and **reserve** broth and giblets.

5—In a large *caldero* or heavy kettle, heat oil and brown **rapidly** salt pork and ham. Reduce heat to *low* and sauté ingredients included in *F* for *10 minutes*, stirring **occasionally**.

6—Add ingredients included in *G* and cook for *5 minutes*.

7—Add chicken pieces and mix over *moderate* heat until boiling. *Cover* and cook for *30 minutes* over *moderate* heat.

8—Add broth and giblets. Heat **rapidly** to boiling.

9—Drain rice, add and mix. Cook over *moderate* heat until boiling. Reduce heat to *low*, add peas, cover and cook until rice reaches soupy consistency to taste. (Occasionally, turn rice over to check soupy consistency and cover again.)

10—Serve **immediately** in soup plates. Heat reserved pimiento and asparagus tips in their juices, drain and garnish.

PIGEON PEA ASOPAO
Asopao de Gandules
(Serves 6)

A—1 can (1 pound) *gandules* (Pigeon Peas)
7 cups water | 1½ cups rice

B—1 ounce salt pork
2 ounces lean cured ham   } washed and diced

C—3 tablespoons fat or *Achiote Coloring* (see Index)
½ teaspoon whole dried *orégano,* crushed
2 cloves garlic, peeled ⎤
1 green pepper, seeded ⎥
3 sweet chili peppers, seeded ⎬ chopped
6 fresh *culantro* leaves ⎥
1 tomato ⎦

D—6 olives, stuffed with pimientos
½ teaspoon capers
¼ cup tomato sauce
1 tablespoon salt

1—Drain can of *gandules* (pigeon peas). Combine drained liquid with water included in *A.* Wash rice **thoroughly,** drain, and soak in the liquid for *30 minutes.*

2—In a *caldero* or heavy kettle, brown *rapidly* salt pork and ham. Reduce heat to *low,* add ingredients included in *B,* and sauté for *10 minutes,* stirring **occasionally.**

3—Add ingredients included in *D.* Add *gandules* and mix.

4—Drain rice and add to kettle. Heat the drained liquid to boiling and add to kettle. Cook over *moderate* heat, *uncovered,* for *20 minutes.* Serve immediately.

RICE WITH ROAST MEAT

Arroz Apastelado con Pernil

(Serves 6)

A—Left-overs from a roast leg of lamb, veal, or fresh pork, including both meat and bone

B—1 quart (4 cups) water
1 tablespoon salt

C—1 tablespoon lard or vegetable oil

1 ounce salt pork
2 ounces lean cured ham
} washed and diced

2 cloves garlic, peeled
1 green pepper, seeded
3 sweet chili peppers, seeded
1 onion, peeled
6 fresh *culantro* leaves
1 tomato
} chopped

1 teaspoon whole dried *orégano*, crushed

D—6 olives, stuffed with pimientos
1 teaspoon capers
3 tablespoons tomato sauce
2 tablespoons fat or *Achiote Coloring* (see Index)
1½ cups rice, **thoroughy** washed and drained

E—Plantain leaf

1—Separate meat from bone of roast. Cut meat into chunks and **reserve.**

2—Boil bone in water and salt included in B, for 15 *minutes,* to make a broth. Strain and **reserve** broth.

3—In a large *caldero* or heavy kettle, heat fat included in C and brown *rapidly* salt pork and ham. Reduce heat to *low* and sauté rest of ingredients included in C for 10 *minutes,* stirring **occasionally.**

4—Add chunks of meat and ingredients included in D. Mix and stir **occasionally** for 5 *minutes.*

5—Add boiling broth, mix, and boil over *moderate* heat until rice is dry.

6—Turn rice over with a fork, from bottom to top. Cover with piece of washed plantain leaf and place lid of kettle on top. Turn heat to *low* and cook for 30 *minutes.* **Halfway** during this cooking period, turn rice over again.

RICE WITH CRABS

Arroz con Jueyes
(Serves 8)

A—8 boiled land crabs

B—2 tablespoons fat or *Achiote Coloring* (see Index)
1 ounce salt pork }
2 ounces lean cured ham } washed and diced

C—2 cloves garlic, peeled ⎫
1 onion, peeled ⎪
3 sweet chili peppers, seeded ⎬ chopped
6 fresh *culantro* leaves ⎪
1 green pepper, seeded ⎭

D—6 olives, stuffed with pimientos
1 teaspoon capers
¼ cup tomato sauce
2 tablespoons salt
2 tablespoons fat or *Achiote Coloring* (see Index)

E—3 cups rice, **thoroughly** washed and drained

F—5 cups boiling water

1—Follow recipe on page 102 for Boiled Crabs.

2—Heat to boiling 5 cups water and soak crab shells.

3—In a *caldero* or heavy kettle, heat fat included in *B* and brown **rapidly** salt pork and ham. Reduce heat to *low*, add ingredients included in *C*, and sauté for *10 minutes*, stirring **occasionally.**

4—Add ingredients included in *D* and mix.

5—Add rice, mix, and cook for 5 *minutes* over *low* heat.

6—Add crab meat and mix.

7—Remove crab shells from the water in which they have been soaking. Heat the liquid, add to the kettle, and mix.

8—Boil over *moderate* heat until rice is dry.

9—Turn rice over with a fork, from bottom to top. *Cover* and cook over *low* heat for 25 *minutes*. **Halfway** during this cooking period, turn rice over again. Fill crab shells with rice and serve immediately.

GRANDMOTHER'S CREAMED RICE

Arroz con Leche

(Serves 6)

A—4 cups water
   2 teaspoons salt
   1 cup short-grain rice

B—1½ teaspoons vegetable lard or butter

C—½ cup sugar
   1 quart (4 cups) milk
   Peel of 1 fresh lime

1—In a deep kettle, heat to boiling the water and salt included in A.

2—Wash rice **thoroughly.** Drain and add.

3—Add vegetable lard or butter and mix. Heat **rapidly** to boiling. Reduce heat to *moderate* and cook until rice is dry. **Do not stir** during this cooking period.

4—Combine sugar and milk included in *C* and add. Add lime peel and mix all together.

5—Heat *rapidly* to boiling. Reduce heat to *low* and cook, *uncovered*, about 20 to 30 *minutes*, turning rice over, **occasionally**, from bottom to top.

Note: The consistency of this rice **should be creamy** and is served in cup bowls or soup plates.

LEGUMES

Legumbres ó Granos

Black beans	Habichuelas negras
Chick-peas	Garbanzos
Cow peas	Frijoles
Lentils	Lentejas
Lima beans	Habas
Navy or pea beans	Habichuelas blancas
Pigeon peas	Gandules
Red kidney beans	Habichuelas coloradas
Red small beans	Habichuelas rosadas

Legumes or *granos,* as these are called in Puerto Rico, are cooked either fresh or dried.

Dried legumes call for a longer cooking period than fresh legumes and are generally soaked in water, to cover, overnight to make them more tender. In this soaking period **no** salt should be added, except when cooking *garbanzos* (Chick-Peas) which **must** be soaked in water **with** salt to make them tender.

DRIED RED SMALL BEANS STEW

Habichuelas Rosadas Secas
(Serves 8)

A—1 pound dried red small beans (*habichuelas rosadas secas*)
  2 quarts (8 cups) water
  ¾ pound pumpkin, peeled and cut into pieces

B—**Sofrito:**
  1 tablespoon lard or vegetable oil
  1 ounce salt pork   ⎫
  2 ounces lean cured ham   ⎬ washed and diced

  1 onion, peeled   ⎫
  1 green pepper, seeded   ⎪
  2 sweet chili peppers, seeded   ⎬ ground or chopped
  2 cloves garlic, peeled   ⎪
  6 fresh *culantro* leaves   ⎭
  ¼ teaspoon whole dried *orégano,* crushed

C—¼ cup tomato sauce
2¾ teaspoons salt

1—Pick over beans, discarding any foreign particles or shriveled ones. Wash in several changes of water. Soak **overnight** in water to cover **generously.**

2—Drain beans and place in an 8-quart pot, together with rest of ingredients included in A. Heat to boiling, *cover*, and boil over *moderate* heat for *1 hour*, or until beans are almost tender.

3—Meanwhile, prepare *sofrito* as follows:
In a small *caldero* or heavy kettle, heat fat included in B. Brown *rapidly* salt pork and ham. Reduce heat to *low* and sauté rest of ingredients included in B for *10 minutes*, stirring *occasionally.*

4—When beans are almost tender, mash pumpkin inside kettle and add *sofrito* together with ingredients included in C. Mix and boil, *uncovered*, over *moderate* heat about *1 hour*, or until sauce thickens to taste.

DRIED KIDNEY BEANS STEW

Habichuelas Coloradas Grandes Secas
(**Marca Diablo**)

(Serves 8)

Proceed as with above recipe for Dried Red Small Beans, but add 1 **ripe** plantain, peeled and quartered.

DRIED NAVY OR PEA BEANS

Habichuelas Blancas Secas

(Serves 8)

Proceed as with recipe for Dried Red Small Beans, but add 1 teaspoon vinegar to the *sofrito*.

PUERTO RICAN CHICK-PEAS

Garbanzos Criollos
(Serves 8)

A—1 pound chick-peas (*garbanzos*)
   2½ quarts (10 cups) water
   2 tablespoons salt

B—2½ quarts (10 cups) water
   1¼ pound pumpkin, peeled and cut into pieces
   1 can (5 ounces) *chorizos* (Spanish sausages), halved and casings removed (fat in can **not** included)

C—**Sofrito:**
   1 teaspoon lard or vegetable oil
   ½ ounce salt pork   ⎱
   1 ounce lean cured ham ⎰ washed and diced

   1 onion, peeled   ⎫
   1 green pepper, seeded   ⎪
   3 sweet chili peppers, seeded ⎬ chopped
   2 cloves garlic, peeled   ⎪
   6 fresh *culantro* leaves   ⎭
   ¼ teaspoon whole dried *orégano*, crushed

D—¼ cup tomato sauce
   1 tablespoon salt
   ½ pound cabbage, quartered

1—Pick over chick-peas, discarding any foreign particles or shriveled peas. Wash in several changes of water. Soak **overnight** in water and salt included in *A*.

2—Drain chick-peas, rinse and place in 10-quart pot, together with ingredients included in *B*. Bring **rapidly** to a boil, *cover*, and boil over *moderate* heat *1½ hours*, or until chick-peas are almost tender.

3—*Uncover*, mash pumpkin and add ingredients included in *C* and *D*. Mix and boil over *moderate* heat, *uncovered*, about *1 hour*, or until sauce thickens to taste. (Raise or lower heat, if necessary.)

BLACK BEANS POTTAGE
Frijoles Negros
(Serves 8)

A—1 pound dried black beans (*frijoles negros*)
2 quarts (8 cups) water

B—⅔ cup olive oil
6 cloves garlic, peeled
2 onions, peeled } finely chopped or ground
6 sweet chili peppers, seeded

C—4 teaspoons salt | ¼ teaspoon ground pepper
¼ teaspoon whole dried *orégano*, crushed
2 tablespoons sugar | ¼ teaspoon ground cumin
2 bay leaves |

D—2 tablespoons dry wine | 1½ tablespoons vinegar

E—½ cup chopped onions

1—Pick over beans, discarding any shriveled ones or foreign particles. Wash well and soak **overnight** in water, to cover **generously.**

2—Drain beans, rinse in fresh water, and drain again. Place in a kettle, with water included in A. Bring *rapidly* to a boil. Reduce heat to *moderate, cover,* and cook about *45 minutes.*

3—In a skillet, heat ⅔ cups olive oil and sauté over *low* heat rest of ingredients included in B for *10 minutes,* stirring *occasionally.*

4—Add to skillet, 1 drained cup of the boiled black beans and mash *thoroughly* with rest of the ingredients in the skillet. Add this mixture to the kettle, together with ingredients included in C. *Cover,* and boil for *1 hour* at *moderate* heat.

5—Add ingredients included in D, *cover,* and cook over *low* heat for *1 hour.*

6—*Uncover* and cook until sauce thickens to taste.

7—Serve individually in cup bowls or soup plates and sprinkle with chopped onions.

BASIC RECIPE FOR FRESH LEGUME STEW

Receta Básica para Legumbres o Granos Frescos

(Serves 6)

A—1 pound **fresh** legumes | 6 cups water
¾ pound pumpkin, peeled and cut into pieces

B—**Sofrito:**
1 tablespoon lard or vegetable oil
1 ounce salt pork   ⎫
2 ounces lean cured ham   ⎬ washed and diced
                           ⎭
1 onion, peeled   ⎫
1 green pepper, seeded |
3 sweet chili peppers, seeded ⎬ chopped
2 cloves garlic, peeled |
6 fresh *culantro* leaves ⎭
¼ teaspoon whole dried *orágano*, crushed

C—¼ cup tomato sauce | 2 teaspoons salt

1—Pick over beans, discarding any foreign particles or shriveled ones. Wash in several changes of water.

2—Drain beans and place in an 8-quart pot, together with rest of ingredients included in A. Heat to boiling, *cover,* and cook over *moderate* heat for *45 minutes,* or until beans are almost tender.

3—Meanwhile, prepare *sofrito* as follows:
In a small *caldero* or heavy kettle, heat fat included in B. Brown *rapidly* salt pork and ham. Reduce heat to *low,* and sauté rest of ingredients included in B, for *10 minutes,* stirring *occasionally.*

4—When legumes are almost tender, mash pumpkin inside kettle and add *sofrito,* together with ingredients included in C. Mix and boil, *uncovered,* over *moderate* heat, about *30 minutes,* or until sauce thickens to taste.

Note: Cooking time might vary in instruction 2, according to tenderness of legumes.

CHAPTER X

Cakes and Icings

Cakes and Icings

FRESH ORANGE CAKE

Bizcocho de Chinas (Naranjas Dulces) Frescas

A—2½ cups sifted cake flour
  4 teaspoons baking powder
  ¼ teaspoon salt

B—½ pound butter
  1½ cups sugar
  2 tablespoons grated fresh orange rind
  ⅔ cup fresh orange juice
  5 eggs (recipe calls for 2 egg whites **only**)

1—Preheat oven to 325°F. Grease a round 9 x 3½-inch aluminum tube cake pan and sprinkle *lightly* with flour.

2—Sift together dry ingredients included in A.

3—Cream butter and sugar *thoroughly*. Add egg yolks, **one at a time,** and mix. Add grated orange rind and mix.

4—Add *alternately* sifted ingredients and orange juice and mix.

5—Beat 2 egg whites until stiff, and fold into the batter.

6—Turn batter into pan and bake about *45 minutes*, or until toothpick, inserted in center, comes out clean.

7—Set pan on wire rack for *5 minutes*. Remove from pan and allow to cool on wire rack, top side up.

ORANGE LAYER CAKE

Bizcocho de Chinas (Naranjas Dulces)

A—¼ pound butter
1½ cups sugar
3 eggs
1 cup fresh orange juice

B—3 cups sifted cake flour
1 tablespoon baking powder
1 teaspoon salt

C—Orange Icing (see Index)

1—Preheat oven to 375°F. Grease two 9-inch aluminum layer cake pans.

2—Cream butter *thoroughly*. Add sugar *gradually* and mix well. Add eggs, **one at a time,** and mix.

3—Sift together dry ingredients included in B **3 times** and add to batter, alternating with the orange juice.

4—Turn batter into pans and bake about 30 *minutes,* or until toothpick, inserted in the center, comes out clean.

5—Set pans on wire racks for 5 *minutes.* Remove from pans and allow to cool on wire racks, top side up.

6—Spread Orange Icing between layers and over top and sides of cake.

BANANA CUPCAKES

Bizcochitos de Guineo

(12 cupcakes)

A—½ cup evaporated milk, **undiluted** | 1 teaspoon vinegar

B—½ cup vegetable lard
1 cup brown sugar, firmly packed
1 egg
1 teaspoon vanilla extract

C—1½ cups flour | 1 teaspoon baking soda
1 teaspoon baking powder | ½ teaspoon salt

D—½ cup finely chopped walnuts

E—1 cup mashed ripe bananas

F—½ cup sifted confectioners' powdered sugar ⎫
½ teaspoon vanilla extract   ⎬ mix together
1 teaspoon evaporated milk, **undiluted**   ⎭

1—Preheat oven to *350°F.*

2—Combine ingredients included in A.

3—In a bowl, mix ingredients included in B.

4—Sift together ingredients included in C. Dredge walnuts with 1 tablespoon of sifted ingredients and **reserve.**

5—Add to bowl sifted ingredients, alternating with ingredients included in A and with mashed bananas, beginning and ending with sifted ingredients.

6—Add dredged walnuts and mix.

7—Line muffin pan with cupcake liners. Spoon batter into cupcake liners, filling each **two-thirds** full.

8—Bake about *30 minutes,* or until golden.

9—Remove from oven, place on a platter, and garnish with ingredients included in F, by dropping with a tablespoon, strips of icing over cakes.

DELIGHTFUL CAKE

Bizcocho Sabroso

A—6 ounces (¾ cup) butter
6 eggs
1⅓ cups sugar

B—1⅓ cups sifted cake flour
1½ teaspoons fresh lime juice
¼ teaspoon grated lime rind

1—Preheat oven to 350°F. Grease a round 9 x 3½-inch aluminum tube cake pan and sprinkle **lightly** with flour. In a sauce pan, melt butter **slowly.**

2—In the large bowl of an electric mixer beat eggs at *high speed* for *10 minutes.* Add sugar **gradually** at *low speed.* Beat at *high speed* for *10 minutes.*

3—Remove bowl from mixer. Blend in flour and add melted butter **slowly.** Mix **gently.** Add lime juice and rind, stirring just enough to mix. Turn batter into pan and bake in preheated oven about *45 minutes* or until toothpick inserted into center comes out clean. Set pan on wire rack for *5 minutes.* Remove from pan and allow to cool on wire rack, top side up.

WHITE CAKE

Bizcocho Blanco

A—¼ pound butter
1¼ cups sugar

B—1½ cups sifted cake flour
2½ teaspoons baking powder

C—½ cup milk
1 teaspoon almond or vanilla extract } mix together

D—⅔ cup egg whites

1—Preheat oven to *350°F.* Grease a round 8 x 3-inch aluminum tube cake pan and sprinkle **lightly** with flour.

2—Cream butter and sugar **thoroughly.**

3—Sift together dry ingredients included in *B* and add, **alternately,** with milk, flavored with almond or vanilla.

4—Beat egg whites until stiff, but not dry, and fold into mixture.

5—Turn batter into pan and bake in preheated oven about *45 minutes,* or until toothpick, inserted in the center, comes out clean.

6—Set pan on wire rack for *5 minutes.* Remove from pan and allow to cool on wire rack, top side up.

GOLDEN CAKE
Ponqué

A—1 pound butter (*at room temperature*)
2 cups sugar
12 eggs (recipe requires 12 egg yolks and **only** 8 egg whites)
1 tablespoon fresh lime juice, or 2 teaspoons vanilla or almond extract

B—3 cups sifted cake flour
1 teaspoon baking powder
½ teaspoon salt

1—Preheat oven to *350°F.* Grease a round 10 x 4-inch aluminum tube cake pan and sprinkle **lightly** with flour.

2—Cream butter **thoroughly.** Add sugar **gradually** and mix. Add 12 egg yolks, **one at a time,** and beat well together. Add lime juice, vanilla, or almond extract, and mix.

3—Sift together dry ingredients included in *B* **3 times** and add.

4—Beat 8 egg whites until stiff. Fold into the mixture.

5—Turn batter into pan and bake about *1 hour,* or until toothpick, inserted in the center, comes out clean.

6—Set pan on wire rack for *5 minutes.* Remove from pan and allow to cool on wire rack, **top side up.**

SPONGY CHOCOLATE CAKE

Bizcocho Esponjoso de Chocolate

A—2 cups sifted cake flour
1 teaspoon baking soda
¾ teaspoon salt

B—2 cups brown sugar, firmly packed
¼ pound butter
1 teaspoon vanilla extract

C—1 cup milk
1 tablespoon fresh lime juice

D—¾ cup whole eggs
2 ounces (2 squares) **unsweetened** chocolate, melted

E—Spongy Chocolate Icing (see Index)

1—Preheat oven to 350°F. Grease and flour *lightly* two 9-inch aluminum layer cake pans.

2—Sift together ingredients included in A into the large bowl of electric mixer. Add ingredients in B. Combine milk and lime juice, stir, and add to bowl.

3—Beat at *moderate* speed for *2 minutes.*

4—Add ingredients included in D and beat for *2 minutes.*

5—Turn batter into pans and bake about *30 minutes,* or until toothpick, inserted in the center, comes out clean.

6—Set pans on wire racks for *5 minutes.* Remove from pans and allow to cool on wire racks, top side up.

7—Spread Spongy Chocolate Icing between layers and over top and sides of cake.

CHOCOLATE CAKE WITH CREAM FILLING

Bizcocho de Chocolate

Cake:

A—3 ounces (3 squares) **unsweetened** chocolate

B—2 cups sifted cake flour
2½ teaspoons baking powder
¼ teaspoon baking soda
½ teaspoon salt

C—¼ pound butter
1¼ cups sugar
2 eggs
1 cup milk
1 teaspoon vanilla extract   } mix together

D—Chocolate Icing (see Index)

1—Melt chocolate in saucepan over simmering water. Preheat oven to 350°F.

2—Sift together dry ingredients included in B **3 times.**

3—Cream butter and *gradually* beat in sugar. Add eggs and beat well. Add melted chocolate. Stir in milk flavored with vanilla extract, *alternately,* with sifted dry ingredients.

4—Turn batter into 2 greased and floured aluminum layer-cake pans and bake in preheated oven about *30 minutes,* or until toothpick, inserted in the center, comes out clean.

5—Set pan on wire rack for *5 minutes.* Remove from pan and allow to cool on wire rack, top side up.

Filling:

A—½ cup sugar
¼ cup flour
¼ teaspoon salt

B—1½ cups milk
2 egg yolks, lightly beaten

C—1 teaspoon vanilla extract

1—Put A ingredients in upper part of double boiler. Add B ingredients and cook, **stirring constantly,** for *10 minutes.*

2—Cool *slightly.* Stir in vanilla.

3—Spread filling between layers of cake.

4—Spread Chocolate Icing over top and sides of cake.

DATE CAKE
Bizcocho de Dátiles

A—3 ounces (6 tablespoons) butter
1⅓ cups brown sugar, firmly packed

B—1¾ cups cake flour
1 tablespoon baking powder
½ teaspoon ground cinnamon
½ teaspoon ground nutmeg
½ teaspoon salt

C—1 pound dates, pitted and chopped

D—½ cup milk
2 eggs

1—Preheat oven to 350°F. Grease a round 9 x 3½-inch aluminum tube cake pan and sprinkle *lightly* with flour.

2—Cream butter and *gradually* beat in sugar.

3—Sift together dry ingredients included in B **3 times.** Dredge dates with part of the sifted dry ingredients and **reserve.** Add rest of sifted ingredients to butter-sugar mixture, *alternately,* with the milk. Add dredged dates and stir *just enough* to mix.

4—Beat eggs and fold into batter. Turn batter into pan and bake in preheated oven about *1 hour,* or until toothpick, inserted in the center, comes out clean.

5—Set pan on wire rack for *5 minutes.* Remove from pan and allow to cool on wire rack, top side up.

WHITE GLACÉED FRUIT CAKE

Bizcocho con Frutitas Abrillantadas

A—¼ pound butter
1 cup sugar
2 eggs

B—2 cups flour
1 tablespoon baking powder
1 teaspoon salt
¾ teaspoon ground nutmeg
¾ teaspoon ground cinnamon

C—1 pound glacé mixed fruits
¾ cup milk

1—Preheat oven to *350°F*. Grease a round 9 x 3½-inch aluminum tube cake pan and sprinkle *lightly* with flour.

2—Cream butter and sugar *thoroughly*.

3—Add eggs and mix well.

4—Sift together dry ingredients included in *B* **3 times.** Dredge fruits included in *C* in part of the sifted ingredients and **reserve.**

5—Add rest of sifted ingredients to the butter-sugar mixture, *alternately*, with the milk.

6—Add the dredged fruits and stir *just enough* to mix.

7—Turn batter into pan and bake in preheated oven about *1 hour*, or until toothpick, inserted in the center, comes out clean.

8—Set pan on wire rack for *5 minutes*. Remove from pan and allow to cool on wire rack, top side up.

DOÑA CARMEN'S FRUIT CAKE
Bizcocho de Pascua

A—¼ pound butter

B—1¾ cups flour
¼ teaspoon salt
1 tablespoon baking powder
¾ teaspoon ground cinnamon
¼ teaspoon ground cloves
¼ teaspoon ground nutmeg

C—8 dry prunes, pitted and quartered
½ cup seeded white raisins
1 package (8 ounces) chopped dates
1 box (4 ounces) diced citron
1 box (4 ounces) glacé cherries
1 box (1 pound) glacé mixed fruits
½ cup slivered almonds

D—1½ cups brown sugar, firmly packed
½ cup dark Puerto Rican rum | 2 large eggs

1—Preheat oven to 350°F. Grease with butter and flour **lightly** three 8½ x 4½ x 2½ inches disposable aluminum pans.

2—Melt butter over *low* heat.

3—In a big bowl, sift together ingredients included in B. Measure 1 cup of sifted ingredients and dredge ingredients included in C. **Reserve.**

4—Add to bowl ingredients included in D and mix. Add melted butter and mix. Add dredged ingredients and mix. Spoon batter into pans.

5—Bake in preheated oven for *45 minutes*. Reduce temperature of oven to 325°F. and bake about *15 minutes*, or until toothpick, inserted in the center, comes out clean.

6—Remove from oven and allow to cool over wire racks for *5 minutes*. Release edges of cakes with a knife and turn cakes, top side up.

SPICE-BREAD CAKE
Bizcocho Apanado de Especies

A—1¾ cups flour
1 tablespoon baking powder
⅛ teaspoon salt
¾ teaspoon ground cinnamon
¼ teaspoon ground cloves
¼ teaspoon ground nutmeg

B—1 cup seeded raisins

C—1½ cups brown sugar, firmly packed
½ cup water, chilled
2 eggs
¼ pound butter, melted

1—Preheat oven to 350°F.

2—Grease and flour *lightly* a 9 x 5 x 2¾-inch aluminum pan.

3—Sift together into a bowl ingredients included in A. Measure *½ cup* of sifted ingredients, dredge raisins, and **reserve.**

4—Add to the bowl, *gradually*, ingredients included in C and mix.

5—Add dredged raisins, stir just enough to mix, and spoon batter into pan.

6—Bake about *1 hour*, or until toothpick, inserted in the center, comes out clean.

7—Set on wire rack for *5 minutes*. Remove from pan and set on a platter, top side up. Serve warm, together with butter and preserve.

HOJALDRE

A—½ pound butter
  2 cups brown sugar, firmly packed
  6 eggs

B—3 cups flour
  1 tablespoon baking powder
  2 teaspoons ground cinnamon
  2 teaspoons ground nutmeg
  1 teaspoon ground cloves
  ¼ teaspoon salt

C—1 cup milk
  ⅓ cup sweet wine

D—Confectioners' powdered sugar, sifted (*to garnish*)

1—Preheat oven to *350°F.*

2—Grease and flour *lightly* a round 9 x 3½-inch aluminum tube cake pan.

3—In a bowl, cream butter and sugar, until light and fluffy. Add eggs, **one at a time,** beating well after each addition.

4—Sift together ingredients included in B **3 times,** and add to egg mixture, *alternately,* with ingredients included in C.

5—Turn batter into pan and bake in preheated oven about *1 hour,* or until toothpick, inserted in the center, comes out clean.

6—Remove from oven and allow to cool on wire rack for *5 minutes.* Remove from pan and cool on wire rack, top side up.

7—Set on a platter and sprinkle with confectioners' sugar.

GUAVA CAKES DELIGHTS

Delicias de Guayaba

(16 cakes)

A—¼ pound butter
2 tablespoons vegetable lard
1 cup sugar

B—2 cups flour
1 tablespoon baking powder
¼ teaspoon salt

C—2 large eggs

D—Guava paste (1 pound), cut into 16 slices

1—Preheat oven to *350°F.*

2—Grease an 8 x 8 x 2-inch glass or aluminum baking dish.

3—In a bowl, cream butter, vegetable lard, and sugar, until light and fluffy.

4—Sift together **twice** ingredients included in *B,* add, and mix.

5—Add eggs, **one at a time,** and mix.

6—Spoon half of batter into baking dish. Top with guava paste slices. Cover with remaining batter.

7—Bake in preheated oven about *35 to 40 minutes,* or until golden. **Cool thoroughly** on a wire rack before dividing into 16 cakes. Remove each cake with a metal spatula and place on a serving platter.

PINEAPPLE UP-SIDE-DOWN CAKE
Bizcocho de Piña

A—1½ ounces (3 tablespoons) butter
½ cup brown sugar, firmly packed
1 can (1 pound 4 ounces) sliced pineapples
9 Maraschino cherries

B—3 ounces (6 tablespoons) butter
½ cup sugar | 1 egg
1 teaspoon vanilla extract

C—1¼ cups sifted flour | ¼ teaspoon salt
2 teaspoons baking powder
½ cup drained syrup (*from can of pineapples*)

1—Preheat oven to 350°F.

2—Melt butter included in A over *low* heat in an 8 x 8 x 2-inch aluminum pan.

3—Remove from heat, and sprinkle brown sugar included in A over butter.

4—Drain can of pineapple. Measure *½ cup* syrup and **reserve.**

5—Arrange 9 slices of pineapple at bottom of pan, removing wedges from slices to fit. Place a cherry in center of each slice.

6—In a bowl, cream butter and add rest of ingredients included in B.

7—Sift together ingredients included in C and add to bowl, *alternately*, with *½ cup* of the reserved syrup.

8—Spoon batter into pan, spreading to cover pineapple slices and cherries.

9—Bake in preheated oven about *45 minutes*, or until done and golden.

10—Set pan on wire rack for *10 minutes*. Release edges of cake with a knife and turn cake over into platter. Serve warm.

CHEESECAKE
Bizcocho de Queso

A—1 package (8 ounces) Philadelphia cream cheese

B—1 jar (6 ounces) Avoset cream (*blue label*) or heavy cream
1 cup sifted confectioners' powdered sugar
¼ teaspoon vanilla extract
½ teaspoon fresh lime juice

C—Graham cracker crumbs (*to line pie plate*)

D—1 jar (12 ounces) guava preserve (or any other preserve to taste)

1—In a bowl, cream cheese. Beat cream until stiff and blend into bowl, together with rest of ingredients included in B.

2—Line a 9-inch glass pie plate with Graham cracker crumbs, firmly packed.

3—Cover with preserve and top with mixed ingredients in bowl.

4—Set overnight in refrigerator.

CREAM ROLL
Brazo de Gitana
(Serves 16)

Recipe makes a large cream roll, that should be divided into **two 9-inch** rolls.

Cake:

A—1⅓ cups sifted flour   ½ teaspoon salt
2 teaspoons baking powder

B—⅓ cup water, chilled
½ teaspoon vanilla extract
½ teaspoon fresh lime juice

C—4 eggs | 1⅓ cups sugar

D—Confectioners' powdered sugar, sifted (*for garnishing*)

1—Preheat oven to *350°F.*

2—Grease with oleomargarine an 18 x 12 x 1-inch aluminum pan. Line with brown paper and grease paper *generously* with oleomargarine.

3—Sift together dry ingredients included in *A* **3 times,** and **reserve.**

4—Combine water, vanilla, and lime juice and **reserve.**

5—**Immediately,** in the small bowl of an electric mixer, beat eggs at **full speed** for *1 minute.* Reduce speed to *moderate* and add sugar *gradually.*

6—Turn speed to *low* and add, *alternating,* sifted ingredients and reserved water.

7—Turn batter into pan and bake for *20 minutes.* (While cake is baking, prepare cream filling.)

8—A few minutes before removing cake from oven, place a large damp cloth on a table and sprinkle *generously* with sifted confectioners' sugar.

9—Remove cake from oven. Release edges of cake with a knife. Turn cake over cloth, remove paper, and trim edges of cake.

10—Pour cream filling over cake *immediately* and spread almost to the edges. Roll cake from bottom up.

11—Cut roll in the middle, to divide into two 9-inch Cream Rolls. Lift rolls with two wide spatulas, to set on flat platters. Set in refrigerator and remove *1 hour* before serving. When ready to serve, sprinkle rolls with sifted confectioners' powdered sugar.

Cream Filling:
⅓ cup cornstarch
2 cups milk
2 egg yolks
¾ cup sugar
¼ teaspoon salt
Peel of 1 small fresh lime

1—Place cornstarch in a saucepan and dissolve in part of the milk, until well blended. Add egg yolks and mix well. Add remaining milk and rest of ingredients. Mix with a wooden spoon over *moderate* heat, until it boils. **Immediately,** remove from heat and spread over cake. (If cake is still baking when cream is ready, reserve cream over stove in *warm* heat.)

SPONGE CAKE WITH FROZEN CREAM

Bizcocho Esponjoso con Crema Helada

This dessert is made in an ice-cube tray.

A—2 cups milk
   1 teaspoon cornstarch
   2 egg yolks
   ¼ teaspoon salt
   3 tablespoons sugar
   ½ teaspoon grated lime rind
   1 teaspoon vanilla extract

B—½-pound sponge cake, sliced

1—Use ½ cup of the milk to dissolve the cornstarch. Add egg yolks and mix well. Stir in salt and sugar.

2—In a saucepan, bring remaining milk to a boil with lime rind. When boiling, stir in cornstarch mixture and cook over *moderate* heat, stirring *constantly* with a wooden spoon, until mixture boils and thickens. Stir in vanilla.

3—Pour half the vanilla cream in an ice-cube tray. Cover with slices of cake and pour rest of cream over cake. Allow to cool.

4—Set into freezing compartment of refrigerator. Half an hour before serving, place tray in lower part of refrigerator.

SOPA BORRACHA

(Serves 8)

A—2½ cups sugar | 2 cups water

B—½ pound sponge cake

C—1½ cups muscatel wine

D—2 egg whites | ½ cup sugar

E—Cake decors (*for garnishing*)

1—In a saucepan, mix ingredients included in A, and boil over *high* heat, **without stirring,** until syrup thickens to the soft ball stage. (Candy Thermometer — *240°F.*)

2—Remove from heat and allow to cool. Add wine, and mix.

3—Divide cake into 8 portions and place in individual cups.

4—Cover cakes with syrup.

5—Beat egg whites until stiff, add sugar *gradually,* and beat until fluffy. Garnish each cup with meringue and set in refrigerator.

6—When ready to serve, sprinkle meringue with cake decors.

STRAWBERRY CREAM DELICACY

Delicia de Fresas con Crema

A—2 boxes (1 pound each) frozen strawberries
¼ cup sugar

B—1 box (11¼ to 12 ounces) pound cake

C—1 pint (16 ounces) non-dairy whipped topping

1—Thaw strawberries and drain well. **Reserve** strawberries. Mix drained liquid with sugar included in A, and boil over *moderate* heat for *15 minutes.* Allow to cool.

2—Meanwhile, trim edges from cake and divide cake into **10 slices.** Arrange slices to cover bottom of a 12 x 7½ x 2-inch glass baking dish.

3—Pour syrup over cake slices. Cover **lightly** with whipped topping.

4—**Reserve** 6 strawberries for garnishing. Distribute rest of strawberries over surface.

5—Top with remaining whipped topping. Garnish with reserved strawberries and chill in refrigerator.

FRUIT COCKTAIL CAKE

Bizcocho de Frutitas Surtidas Enlatadas

A—½ cup sugar (*to caramelize pan*)
1 pound sponge cake
1 can (1 pound 14 ounces) fruit cocktail

B—1 teaspoon cornstarch	½ cup sugar
3 cups milk	½ teaspoon salt
3 egg yolks	1 teaspoon vanilla extract

1—Preheat oven to 350°F.

2—Caramelize an 8 x 8 x 2-inch aluminum pan, by melting ½ cup sugar, **slowly,** in the pan to a light gold. Swirl the pan to coat bottom and sides with caramel. Set on wire rack.

3—In a saucepan, dissolve cornstarch in part of milk. Add egg yolks and blend. Add remaining milk and rest of ingredients included in *B.* Cook over *moderate* heat, stirring **constantly** with a wooden spoon, until mixture boils and thickens.

4—Drain can of fruit cocktail and **reserve** fruits and syrup.

5—Cover bottom and sides of caramelized pan with thin slices of cake.

6—Arrange over cake slices, alternate layers of vanilla cream and drained fruits, beginning and ending with cream.

7—Set caramelized pan in a large shallow baking pan containing about *1 inch* of hot water and bake about *1 hour,* or until set. Remove pan from water bath. Cool **slightly** on wire rack and turn onto a deep serving platter. Pour reserved syrup into caramelized pan and bring to a boil, scraping sides and bottom of pan. Pour syrup over cake and allow to chill overnight in refrigerator.

BORINQUEN'S SWEET POTATO CAKE

Bizcocho de Batata Borinquen

A—1 quart (4 cups) water
1 tablespoon salt
2 pounds sweet potatoes, scrubbed and halved

B—1 cup flour
½ teaspoon salt
2 cups milk

C—2 cans (6¼ ounces each) Danish butter (see Note)
2¼ cups sugar
8 eggs, lightly beaten

1—In a kettle, bring to a boil water and salt included in A. Add
sweet potatoes, *cover*, and boil for *30 minutes*, or until fork-
tender.

2—Preheat oven to *350°F.*

3—Grease a round 9 x 3½-inch aluminum pan (*without tube*).

4—Blend flour and salt in part of milk and when well blended,
add remaining milk and mix well.

5—As soon as sweet potatoes are done, drain, peel, and put
through a ricer into a bowl.

6—Add to bowl milk mixture *gradually,* to form a smooth batter.

7—Add *gradually* butter, sugar, and eggs.

8—Press mixture through a sieve and turn into pan.

9—Bake about *1 hour 45 minutes,* or until toothpick, inserted in
the center, comes out clean.

Note: Instructions 5 and 6 can be worked in a blender. Danish butter can
be substituted by ¾ pound butter at room temperature.

PUMPKIN CAKE
Bizcocho de Calabaza

A—1½ pounds pumpkin, peeled and cut into pieces
1 quart (4 cups) water
1 teaspoon salt

B—1 cup sugar (*to caramelize pan*)

C—1 ounce (2 tablespoons) butter
½ cup flour
2 cups milk
1 teaspoon salt
½ teaspoon vanilla extract
1 cup sugar

D—4 eggs

1—In a kettle, combine ingredients included in A. *Cover,* and boil about *30 minutes,* or until fork-tender.

2—Meanwhile, caramelize a round 8 x 3-inch aluminum pan, **without tube,** by melting, **slowly,** sugar included in B to a light gold. Swirl pan to coat bottom and sides of pan with caramel. Set on a wire rack.

3—Preheat oven to *350°F.*

4—Drain pumpkin, place in a bowl, and mash with butter. Blend flour in part of milk and add to bowl, together with rest of milk and remaining ingredients included in C.

5—Add eggs **gradually,** and mix. Press mixture through a sieve and turn into caramelized pan.

6—Set pan in a large shallow baking pan containing about *1 inch* of hot water and bake about *2 hours,* or until toothpick, inserted in the center, comes out clean. Remove pan from water bath and allow to cool on wire rack.

FLUFFY ICING
Azucarado Esponjoso

A—½ cup water | Rind of 1 lime
1½ cups sugar |

B—4 egg whites

1—In a saucepan, bring to a boil over *high* heat ingredients included in A. Boil until syrup thickens to the soft ball stage. (Candy Thermometer — 240°F.)

2—In large bowl of electric mixer, beat at *high* speed egg whites until stiff. Continue beating while pouring syrup **slowly.** Beat until fluffy. Spread over top and sides of cake.

ORANGE ICING
Azucarado de China (Naranja Dulce)

¼ cup fresh orange juice
¼ cup melted butter
1 tablespoon grated orange rind
3 cups sifted confectioners' powdered sugar

1—Put all ingredients into a bowl, mix and beat until smooth.

2—Spread over top and sides of cake.

BIRTHDAY CAKE ICING
Azucarado para Bizcocho de Cumpleaños

A—¾ cup water | ½ teaspoon almond extract
2½ cups sugar |

B—¾ cup egg whites

1—In a saucepan, combine ingredients included in A. Boil **rapidly** until syrup thickens to the soft ball stage. (Candy Thermometer — 240°F.)

2—In large bowl of electric mixer, beat at **high** speed egg whites until stiff. Continue beating while pouring syrup **slowly.** Beat until fluffy. Spread over top and sides of cake.

SPONGY CHOCOLATE ICING

Azucarado Esponjoso de Chocolate

A—6 ounces (6 squares) unsweetened chocolate

B—¼ pound butter or oleomargarine
2⅔ cups sifted confectioners' powdered sugar
⅛ teaspoon salt
1 egg
¼ cup milk
2 teaspoons vanilla extract

1—Melt chocolate in upper part of double boiler.

2—Cream butter in the small bowl of electric mixer. Add melted chocolate and rest of ingredients included in B. Beat to mix **thoroughly.** Set in the freezer and when it reaches a good spreading consistency, spread **lightly** between layers of cake and cover top and sides of cake with remaining icing.

CHOCOLATE ICING I

Azucarado de Chocolate I

2 ounces (2 squares) unsweetened chocolate
1 can (14 ounces) sweetened condensed milk, **undiluted**

1—Melt chocolate in upper part of double boiler.

2—Add **undiluted** condensed milk and cook for *10 minutes,* stirring **occasionally.**

3—Set in freezer and when it reaches a good spreading consistency, spread **lightly** between layers of cake and cover top and sides of cake with remaining icing.

CHOCOLATE ICING II
Azucarado de Chocolate II

A—4 tablespoons shaved, unsweetened chocolate

B—3 ounces (6 tablespoons) butter
¾ cup sifted confectioners' powdered sugar
1½ teaspoons vanilla extract | ¼ teaspoon salt

C—3 egg whites
1¼ cups sifted confectioners' powdered sugar

1—Melt chocolate in upper part of double boiler.

2—Cream butter. Add sugar included in *B* and blend well. Add vanilla and salt and mix *thoroughly*.

3—Beat egg whites until stiff, *but not dry*. Add sugar included in *C*, *gradually*, and beat until fluffy.

4—Add chocolate mixture and beat until well blended and of good spreading consistency.

CHOCOLATE ICING III
Azucarado de Chocolate III

A—2 cups sugar
2 ounces (2 squares) unsweetened chocolate
2 tablespoons white corn syrup | ¾ cup milk

B—1 ounce (2 tablespoons) butter
1 tablespoon vanilla extract

1—In a saucepan, place ingredients included in *A* over *low* heat and stir *constantly*, until sugar is dissolved.

2—Continue to cook, **without stirring,** until syrup thickens to soft ball stage (Candy Thermometer — *240°F.*).

3—Add butter, remove from heat, and place pan inside a larger pan filled with cold water.

4—When lukewarm, add vanilla extract and beat until thickened to a soft and creamy consistency.

CHAPTER XI Pies, Custards, and Creams

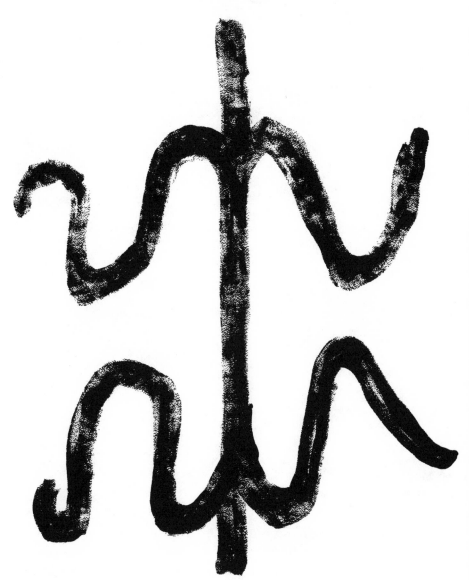

Pies, Custards, and Creams

APPLE PIE A LA CARIBE

Pastel (Pie) *de Manzana a la Caribe*

(Serves 12)

Apple filling:

A—3 pounds medium-sized apples (red, heavy, and slightly sour)
1 quart (4 cups) water
1 tablespoon salt

B—2 cups water
2½ cups sugar

C—2 ounces (4 tablespoons) butter

1—Wash and peel apples, cut each into 8 wedges and core wedges. Rinse *rapidly* in water and salt included in A. Drain well.

2—Place ingredients included in B in a deep pan. Add drained apple wedges and bring *rapidly* to a boil. Reduce heat to *moderate* and boil until syrup thickens to light stage (Candy Thermometer — 220°F.).

3—Add butter and cook just until butter melts. Remove from heat and **reserve** to fill unbaked pie crust. (If apple filling renders too much syrup, drain and pour over drained apple wedges only ¼ cup syrup.)

Pastry for a 2-crust pie (bottom and top):
A—3 cups flour
1½ teaspoons salt

B—1 cup vegetable shortening, chilled
½ cup milk, chilled

1—Preheat oven to 350°F.

2—Sift together dry ingredients included in *A* into a bowl.

3—With a dough blender, or two knives, cut in shortening until mixture resembles coarse meal.

4—Add milk *gradually* and mix *rapidly* with a fork, until all flour is moistened. Knead *lightly* with hands, handling dough gently and quickly.

5—Gather dough into a ball and cut in half.

6—Place on a lightly floured board. With a floured rolling pin, roll out half of dough into a circle about 1-inch larger than a 10-inch pie plate. Cover dough with waxed paper, roll and unroll over plate, **without stretching.** Remove waxed paper. Prick dough in several places.

7—Roll out remaining dough into a circle. Roll in waxed paper and **reserve** to cover pie after filling is spooned in the pastry-lined plate.

8—Spoon filling into pastry-lined plate. Cover with reserved dough and discard waxed paper. Prick again in several places, and press edges together with prongs of fork, moistened in milk or water.

9—Bake in preheated oven for *45 minutes,* or until golden brown. Serve warm.

COCONUT PIE

Pastel (Pie) *de Coco*
(Serves 12)

Pastry for a 1-crust pie:
A—1½ cups flour | ¾ teaspoon salt

B—½ cup vegetable shortening, chilled
¼ cup milk, chilled

1—Preheat oven to *350°F.*

2—Sift together dry ingredients included in A into a bowl.

3—With a dough blender, or two knives, cut in shortening until mixture resembles coarse meal.

4—Add milk **gradually** and mix **rapidly** with a fork, until all flour is moistened. Knead *lightly* with hands, handling dough gently and quickly.

5—Gather dough into a ball and place over a **lightly** floured board. With a floured rolling pin, roll out dough into a circle about 1-inch larger than a 10-inch pie plate. Cover dough with waxed paper, roll and unroll over plate, **without stretching.** Remove paper. Prick dough in several places and trim edges with fork, moistened in milk or water.

6—Bake in preheated oven around *30 minutes,* or until golden brown. Allow to cool and **reserve** to be filled.

Coconut filling:
6 tablespoons cornstarch
1¾ cups milk
2 egg yolks
½ cup **undiluted** coconut milk (see page 289)
¾ cup sugar
¼ teaspoon salt

1—In a saucepan, dissolve cornstarch **thoroughly** in part of milk. Add egg yolks and blend well. Add remaining milk and rest of ingredients. Mix and cook over *moderate-high* heat, stirring **constantly** with a wooden spoon until it begins to thicken. Turn heat to *moderate* and stir **vigorously** until it boils. Remove from heat and pour **immediately** into baked pastry shell.

Meringue:
A—1 cup sugar
   ¼ teaspoon Baking Powder } mixed together

B—⅔ cup egg whites (about 4 large eggs)

1—Preheat oven to *350°F.*

2—In the large bowl of an electric mixer, beat whites at high speed until stiff. Continue beating *at same speed* while adding slowly the mixture of sugar and baking powder. Beat until fluffy.

3—Top pie filling with the meringue, spreading until it touches the edges of pastry.

4—Bake in preheated oven about *15 minutes* or until slightly golden. (Meringue will crack when cut if it is too brown.)

5—Remove from oven and allow to cool on wire rack. Set in refrigerator until ready to serve.

LIME PIE

Pastel (Pie) *de Limón*
(Serves 12)

Pastry for 1-crust pie:
Follow recipe for Pastry in Coconut Pie (see page 272)

Lime filling:
A—¾ cup cornstarch
4 egg yolks (*reserve white for meringue topping*)
2½ cups water | 2 cups sugar
¼ cup fresh lime juice | 1½ teaspoons salt

B—2 ounces (4 tablespoons) butter

1—Dissolve cornstarch in part of the water. Blend in egg yolks. Add remaining water and rest of ingredients included in A. Strain into a saucepan. Add butter and cook **slowly**, stirring **constantly** with a wooden spoon, until mixture boils and thickens.

2—Pour into baked pastry shell.

Meringue:
Follow recipe for Meringue in Coconut Pie (*page 273*), but add 1 tablespoon fresh lime juice after adding sugar and baking powder.

MARISOL FRESH STRAWBERRY PIE

Pastel (Pie) *Marisol*

(Serves 12)

Pastry for a 1-crust pie:
Follow recipe for Pastry in Coconut Pie (see page 272)

Strawberry filling:

A—1 cup sugar
1 cup water
2 tablespoons cornstarch
4 tablespoons strawberry-flavored gelatin
1 tablespoon fresh lime juice

B—3 boxes (1 quart each) fresh strawberries

C—½ pint (8 ounces) whipping cream or non-dairy whipped
     topping
2 tablespoons sugar

1—Place ingredients included in *A* in a saucepan and stir with a wooden spoon over *high* heat, until mixture boils. Remove from heat and allow to cool.

2—Wash strawberries, with stems, once or twice, handling *carefully*. Remove stems and wash strawberries *lightly*. Line bottom of pastry shell with strawberries, placing wide side down, until bottom is fully covered. **Reserve** 13 strawberries for garnishing.

3—Pour syrup over strawberries and refrigerate for at least *3 hours*.

4—When ready to serve, whip cream and sugar. (If using non-dairy whipped topping, add sugar and mix.) Cover strawberries and garnish with reserved strawberries, placing the largest one in the center and the rest in a circle. Serve *immediately*.

Note: This recipe was developed in honor of Marisol Malaret, of Puerto Rico, Miss Universe 1970.

BUTTER PIE

Pastel (Pie) *de Mantequilla*

(Serves 12)

Pastry for 1-crust pie:
Follow recipe for Pastry in Coconut Pie (see page 272)

Butter filling:
A—4 tablespoons cornstarch
 2 cups milk
 4 egg yolks (*reserve whites for meringue topping*)
 ½ cup sugar
 ¼ teaspoon salt

B—½ pound butter, chilled

1—In a saucepan, dissolve cornstarch with part of the milk. Blend in egg yolks. Add remaining milk and rest of ingredients included in A. Mix over *moderate* heat, stirring *constantly* with a wooden spoon, until it boils and thickens and mixture separates from bottom and sides of pan.

2—Divide butter into **four portions,** and add **one** at a time. Mix vigorously after each addition and **do not proceed** with the other until the first one is **thoroughly blended.**

3—Pour **immediately** into baked pastry shell.

Meringue:
Follow recipe for Meringue in Coconut Pie (see page 273)

CHOCOLATE PIE

Pastel (Pie) *de Chocolate*

(Serves 12)

Pastry for 1-crust pie:
Follow recipe for Pastry in Coconut Pie (see page 272)

Chocolate filling:

A—2 ounces (2 squares) unsweetened chocolate

B—2 cups milk

C—1 cup sugar ⎫
  ⅓ cup flour ⎬ sift together
  ⅛ teaspoon salt ⎭

D—3 egg yolks
  ½ teaspoon vanilla extract

1—In a saucepan, melt chocolate over *low* heat.

2—In the lower part of a double boiler, bring water to a boil. In the upper part, heat milk.

3—Add sifted ingredients and mix with a wooden spoon, over *moderate* heat, until mixture boils and thickens.

4—Remove from double boiler. Add melted chocolate, mix, and cook, *covered*, over *moderate* heat, for *15 minutes*.

5—Beat egg yolks, add, and stir *constantly*.

6—Place again over double boiler and cook for *5 minutes*.

7—Remove, add vanilla extract, and mix.

8—Pour **immediately** into baked pastry shell.

Meringue:
Follow recipe for Meringue in Coconut Pie (see page 273)

PUERTO RICAN BAKED CUSTARD

Flán de Leche
(Serves 12)

A—6 cups milk   ¼ teaspoon salt
  1 cup sugar   Peel of fresh lime, rinsed

B—7 eggs

C—1 cup sugar (*to caramelize pan*)

1—Combine ingredients included in A and bring *rapidly* to a boil. Reduce heat to *moderate* and cook for *15 minutes,* stirring **occasionally.** Strain and allow to cool.

2—Preheat oven to *350°F.*

3—Caramelize a round 9 x 3½-inch aluminum pan **without tube,** by melting 1 cup sugar, **slowly,** in the pan to a light gold. Swirl the pan to coat bottom and sides with caramel. Set on wire rack.

4—In a saucepan, blend egg yolks and whites with a rubber spatula. Mix milk **gradually,** and strain.

5—Pour strained mixture into caramelized pan. Set pan in a large shallow baking pan containing about *1 inch* of hot water. Bake about *1 hour,* or until set and golden. Remove pan from water bath.

6—Allow to cool on wire rack. *Cover,* and set in refrigerator. When ready to serve, turn custard onto a platter.

FRESH PINEAPPLE CUSTARD

Flán de Piña Fresca
(Serves 8)

A—2 cups fresh pineapple juice | 2 cups sugar

B—¼ teaspoon salt | 8 eggs

C—1 cup sugar (*to caramelize pan*)

1—In a large saucepan, mix ingredients included in A and boil, **without stirring,** until syrup thickens to light stage (Candy Thermometer — 222°F.). Remove from heat and allow to cool.

2—Preheat oven to *350°F.*

3—Caramelize a round 8 x 3-inch aluminum pan **without tube,** by melting 1 cup sugar, **slowly,** in the pan to a light gold. Swirl the pan to coat bottom and sides with caramel. Set on wire rack.

4—In another saucepan, mix salt with eggs, blending egg yolks and whites with a rubber spatula. Add syrup **slowly,** mix and strain.

5—Pour strained mixture into the caramelized pan. Set pan in a large shallow baking pan containing about *1 inch* of hot water. Bake about *1 hour,* or until set and golden. Remove pan from water bath.

6—Allow to cool on wire rack. *Cover,* and set in refrigerator. When ready to serve, turn custard onto serving platter.

CANNED PINEAPPLE CUSTARD

Flán de Jugo de Piña Enlatado
(Serves 8)

A—1 cup sugar (*to caramelize pan*)

B—2 teaspoons cornstarch
¼ teaspoon salt
2 cans (7½ ounces each) pineapple juice
8 eggs
2 cups sugar

1—Preheat oven to *350°F.*

2—Caramelize a round 8 x 3-inch aluminum pan **without tube,** by melting 1 cup sugar, **slowly,** in the pan to a light gold. Swirl the pan to coat bottom and sides with caramel. Set on wire rack.

3—In a saucepan, dissolve cornstarch and salt in part of pineapple juice.

4—Add eggs, **two at a time,** and blend well, **without beating.**

5—In another saucepan, combine sugar and remaining pineapple juice. Mix with a rubber spatula until sugar dissolves. Pour **slowly** over first sauce pan. Mix and strain.

6—Pour strained mixture into caramelized pan. Set pan in a large shallow baking pan containing about *1 inch* of hot water. Bake about *1 hour,* or until set and golden. Remove pan from water bath.

7—Allow to cool on wire rack. *Cover,* and set in refrigerator. When ready to serve, turn custard onto a platter.

CONDENSED MILK CUSTARD

Flán de Leche Condensada
(Serves 8)

A—1 cup sugar (*to caramelize pan*)

B—8 eggs (yolks and whites blended)
2 cans (14 ounces each) condensed milk, **undiluted**
3½ cups water
¼ teaspoon salt
1 teaspoon vanilla extract

1—Preheat oven to *350°F.*

2—Caramelize a round 8 x 3-inch aluminum pan **without tube,** by melting 1 cup sugar, **slowly,** in the pan to a light gold. Swirl the pan to coat bottom and sides with caramel. Set on wire rack.

3—In a saucepan, mix *gradually* ingredients included in *B.* Strain.

4—Pour strained mixture into caramelized pan. Set pan in a large shallow baking pan containing about *1 inch* of hot water. Bake about *1 hour,* or until set and golden. Remove pan from water bath.

5—Allow to cool on wire rack. *Cover,* and set in refrigerator. When ready to serve, turn custard onto a platter.

CREAM CHEESE CUSTARD
Flán de Queso-Crema
(Serves 8)

A—1 cup sugar (*to caramelize pan*)

B—1 can (13 ounces) evaporated milk, **undiluted**
2 packages (8 ounces each) Philadelphia cream cheese
1 cup sugar
4 eggs
1 teaspoon vanilla extract

1—Preheat oven to *350°F.*

2—Caramelize a round 8 x 3-inch aluminum pan **without tube,** by melting 1 cup sugar, **slowly,** in the pan to a light gold. Swirl the pan to coat bottom and sides with caramel. Set on wire rack.

3—Blend ingredients included in *B* in an electric blender.

4—Pour mixture into the caramelized pan. Set pan in a large shallow baking pan containing about *1 inch* of hot water and bake about *1 hour,* or until set and golden. Remove pan from water bath.

5—Allow to cool on wire rack. *Cover,* and set in refrigerator. When ready to serve, turn custard onto a platter.

COCONUT CUSTARD
Flán de Coco
(Serves 8)

A—1 cup sugar (*to caramelize pan*)

B—2 cans (8¾ ounces each) cream of coconut
1 can (14 ounces) condensed milk, **undiluted**
2 tablespoons milk
¼ teaspoon salt

C—8 eggs

1—Preheat oven to *350°F.*

2—Caramelize a round 8 x 3-inch aluminum pan **without tube,** by melting 1 cup sugar, **slowly,** in the pan to a light gold. Swirl the pan to coat bottom and sides with caramel. Set on wire rack.

3—Blend ingredients included in *B* in an electric blender.

4—In a saucepan, break eggs, **without beating,** just enough to mix egg yolks and whites. Add blended ingredients *slowly* and mix. Strain and pour into the caramelized pan.

5—Set pan in a large shallow baking pan containing about *1 inch* of hot water and bake about *1 hour,* or until set and golden. Remove pan from water bath.

6—Allow to cool on wire rack. *Cover,* and set in refrigerator. When ready to serve, turn custard onto a platter.

EVAPORATED MILK CUSTARD

Flán de Leche Evaporada
(Serves 8)

A—1 cup sugar (*to caramelize pan*)

B—5 eggs
1 can (13 ounces) evaporated milk, **undiluted**
1 teaspoon vanilla extract
1¼ cups sugar

1—Preheat oven to *350°F.*

2—Caramelize a round 8 x 3-inch aluminum pan **without tube,** by melting 1 cup sugar, **slowly,** in the pan to a light gold. Swirl the pan to coat bottom and sides with caramel. Set on wire rack.

3—In a saucepan, break eggs, **without beating,** just enough to mix egg yolks and whites. Add rest of ingredients and mix. Strain.

4—Pour strained mixture into the caramelized pan. Set pan in a large shallow baking pan containing about *1 inch* of hot water and bake about *1 hour,* or until set and golden. Remove pan from water bath.

5—Allow to cool on wire rack. *Cover,* and set in refrigerator. When ready to serve, turn custard onto a platter.

CARACA'S CUSTARD

Flán Caraqueño

(Serves 12)

A—1 cup sugar (*to caramelize pan*)

B—¼ pound blanched almonds
13 soda crackers
8 eggs (yolks and whites blended)

C—2 ounces (4 tablespoons) butter
½ teaspoon salt
1½ cups sugar
1 quart (4 cups) milk
1 tablespoon vanilla extract

1—Preheat oven to 350°F.

2—Caramelize a round 9 x 3½-inch aluminum pan **without tube,** by melting 1 cup sugar, **slowly,** in the pan to a light gold. Swirl the pan to coat bottom and sides with caramel. Set on wire rack.

3—Grind almonds and crackers, and combine in a bowl. Add eggs and mix all together.

4—Melt butter over *low* heat. Add remaining ingredients included in C and pour over egg mixture.

5—Pour egg mixture into the caramelized pan. Set pan in a large shallow baking pan containing about *1 inch* of hot water, and bake in preheated oven about *1 hour*, or until set and golden. Remove pan from water bath.

6—Allow to cool on wire rack. *Cover*, and set in refrigerator. When ready to serve, turn custard onto a platter.

FLOATING ISLAND

Isla Flotante

(Serves 12)

Custard:

A—2 tablespoons cornstarch
6 cups milk
4 egg yolks (*reserve whites for meringue topping*)

B—½ teaspoon salt
⅔ cup sugar
1 cinnamon stick or 1 teaspoon vanilla extract

1—Dissolve cornstarch in part of the milk. Add egg yolks and blend.

2—In a large saucepan, mix rest of milk with ingredients included in *B*, and bring *rapidly* to a boil, **without stirring.**

3—*Gradually*, add milk-yolk mixture and cook over *moderate* heat, stirring *rapidly* with a wooden spoon, until custard boils.

4—Strain into bowl or into individual custard cups. Garnish with the following meringue:

Meringue:

A—4 egg whites (*reserved from Custard*)

B—1 cup sugar
1 tablespoon lime juice

1—Beat egg whites until stiff. *Gradually*, beat in sugar and lime juice. Beat until fluffy.

2—Garnish custard with meringue, cool, and chill in refrigerator.

CANDIED MILK
Leche Costrada

(Serves 8)

A—1 quart (4 cups) milk
⅓ cup sugar
½ teaspoon salt

B—4 eggs (use **only** 3 egg whites)
1 teaspoon vanilla extract

1—Preheat oven to 350°F.

2—In a large saucepan, mix and bring *rapidly* to a boil ingredients included in A.

3—Stir eggs just to mix lightly egg yolks and whites, **without beating.** Pour hot milk over eggs, *stirring rapidly.* Add vanilla and mix.

4—Strain mixture into a glass baking dish, or into 8 individual custard cups, and bake about *30 minutes,* or until set and golden brown.

5—Allow to cool and chill in refrigerator.

EVAPORATED MILK DESSERT
Dulce de Leche Evaporada

A—1 can (13 ounces) evaporated milk, **undiluted**
1 teaspoon fresh lime juice
Peel of fresh lime, rinsed

B—1½ cups sugar

1—Pour evaporated milk into a saucepan.

2—Add lime juice and lime peel, mix, and set aside for *10 minutes.*

3—Add sugar and blend well with a rubber spatula. Set sauce-pan over *moderate* heat and bring to a boil, **without stirring.**

4—Reduce heat to *low* and cook from *1 hour to 1½ hours*, de-pending upon how much syrup is preferred. During this cooking period, stir **only twice** with a wooden spoon in a back-and-forth motion, to separate dessert from bottom and sides of saucepan. (In this way, the dessert will come out in lumps.)

5—As soon as dessert is done, remove lime peel and allow dessert to cool on wire rack. Pour into dessert bowl, *cover,* and set in refrigerator.

NATILLA
(Serves 4)

A—1 tablespoon cornstarch
⅛ teaspoon salt
2 egg yolks
2 cups milk

B—½ cup sugar
1 thin cinnamon stick
1 lime peel, rinsed and drained

1—In a saucepan, blend cornstarch and salt with part of milk. Add egg yolks and mix well. Add remaining milk and in-gredients included in *B.*

2—Place saucepan over *moderate-high* heat and bring to a brisk boil, stirring **constantly** with a wooden spoon.

3—Remove **immediately** and strain into a dessert bowl or 4 indi-vidual cups. Allow to cool and set in refrigerator.

CHAPTER XII *Coconut Desserts*

Coconut Desserts

COCONUT MILK
Leche de Coco

Delicious desserts are made with coconut milk. It can be used **undiluted** or **diluted,** by adding hot water to the grated coconut meat.

The quantity of coconut milk rendered by a coconut depends on its size and on the ripeness of the nut. As a rule, ½ cup **undiluted** milk can be obtained from 1 large coconut.

APPROXIMATE YIELD FROM A LARGE *RIPE* COCONUT

1 ripe coconut yields 1 pound coconut meat
1 pound coconut meat yields 5 cups grated coconut
5 cups grated coconut yields ½ cup **undiluted** coconut milk

HOW TO EXTRACT COCONUT MILK

Undiluted coconut milk:

1—Crack number of ripe coconuts called for in the recipe. Separate the meat from the shells. Remove the brown skin, unless the recipe indicates otherwise.

2—Wash, drain, and grate the coconut meat.

3—Squeeze grated coconut meat through a muslin cloth. Strain and measure the **undiluted** coconut milk rendered. **Reserve** the grated coconut meat to obtain **diluted** coconut milk.

289

Diluted coconut milk:

To obtain **diluted** coconut milk, measure amount of **undiluted** coconut milk rendered by coconuts. Add to the reserved grated coconut meat enough hot water to complete the difference of amount of **diluted** coconut milk required in the recipe. Squeeze through a muslin cloth and mix with the **undiluted** coconut milk.

Coconut Milk in Electric Blender:

Dice coconut meat and blend *gradually* with hot water. Squeeze through a muslin cloth, until required amount of coconut milk in recipe is obtained.

Note: The grated coconut meat, after milk has been extracted, can be used to prepare recipe for Love Powder (see Index).

CAZUELA

(Serves 12)

A—2 quarts (8 cups) water
  1 tablespoon salt
  2¼ pounds pumpkin   ⎫ scrubbed, peeled, washed,
  2¼ pounds sweet potatoes ⎬ and cut into pieces

B—½ cup water
  1 small piece ginger, washed and crushed
  1 large cinnamon stick
  ¼ teaspoon aniseeds
  5 whole cloves

C—2 ounces (4 tablespoons) butter
  3 eggs
  2 cups sugar

D—4 tablespoons flour
  1 teaspoon salt
  1 large ripe coconut, to make **1 cup diluted** coconut milk (see Index)

E—Plantain leaves

1—In a large pot, bring to a boil water and salt included in *A*. Add sweet potatoes and pumpkin, *cover*, and boil at *moderate* heat for *45 minutes*, or until fork-tender.

2—Meanwhile, combine ingredients included in *B* in a small saucepan. Cover and cook over *moderate* heat for *5 minutes*. Strain and **reserve** liquid.

3—Drain sweet potatoes and pumpkin and put **immediately** through a potato ricer into a bowl.

4—Add **gradually** ingredients included in *C* and mix.

5—Add strained liquid and mix.

6—Blend flour and salt with coconut milk, add to bowl, and mix **thoroughly.**

7—Butter generously a 9½-inch earthenware casserole and cover bottom and sides with plantain leaves, washed and buttered.

8—Preheat oven to *350°F.*, and bake about *2 hours,* or until set. Cool **thoroughly** on wire rack before turning into serving platter. Remove plantain leaves.

COCONUT DELIGHT

Bien-Me-Sabe

(Serves 8)

A—2 large ripe coconuts, to make **2 cups diluted** coconut milk (see Index)
3⅓ cups sugar

B—6 egg yolks

C—16 lady fingers

D—3 egg whites | 3 tablespoons sugar

1—Combine coconut milk and sugar in a saucepan, and cook over *high* heat, **without stirring,** until boiling. Reduce heat to *moderate* and boil until syrup thickens to a light stage (Candy Thermometer —*220°F.*). Remove from heat and allow to cool.

2—Place egg yolks in a saucepan and blend the syrup **gradually.** Cook over *moderate* heat, stirring *constantly* with a wooden spoon, until it boils. Remove **immediately** from heat and strain.

3—Place 2 lady fingers in deep dessert plates, and spoon coconut cream over them.

4—Beat egg whites until stiff, add sugar **gradually,** and beat. Garnish dessert with the meringue.

COCONUT CREAM DESSERT

Bien-me Sabe Sencillo

(Serves 12)

A—2½ cups sugar
  1 cup water

B—2 cans (8¾ ounces each) cream of coconut

C—8 egg yolks

D—24 lady fingers

E—3 egg whites

F—¾ cup sugar
  ¼ cup water

1—In a saucepan, combine sugar and water included in A. Cook over *high* heat, **without stirring,** until syrup thickens to light stage (Candy Thermometer — 222°F.). Remove from heat and allow to cool.

2—Add to saucepan, *gradually,* ingredients included in B and mix.

3—In another saucepan, break egg yolks with a rubber spatula. Blend in contents of first saucepan.

4—Place saucepan over *high* heat, stirring *constantly,* for *5 minutes.* Reduce heat to *moderate* and stir until boiling. **Immediately,** remove saucepan from heat and strain coconut cream.

5—Arrange lady fingers in bottom of a 13 x 9 x 2-inch glass baking dish.

6—Cover lady fingers with coconut cream.

7—In a saucepan, bring to a boil ingredients included in F, until syrup thickens to the soft ball stage (Candy Thermometer— 240°F.).

8—Meanwhile, in the small bowl of the electric mixer, beat egg whites until stiff. Add syrup **slowly** and beat until foamy. Garnish dessert with the meringue and chill until serving.

CRUNCHY COCONUT SQUARES

Cuadritos de Coco Amelcochados

(Makes 48 squares)

A—¼ pound butter (*at room temperature*)
½ cup brown sugar, firmly packed
1 cup flour

B—1 cup brown sugar, firmly packed
2 teaspoons flour
½ teaspoon salt
1 teaspoon vanilla extract
2 eggs
1½ cup fresh grated coconut meat or 1 can (3½ ounces) Baker's *Angel Flake Coconut, Sweetened*
2 tablespoons molasses

1—Preheat oven to 350°F. Butter a shallow aluminum pan, either 8 x 12-inch, or 9 x 10-inch.

2—Combine ingredients included in A and spread into pan. Bake for *10 minutes.*

3—Combine ingredients included in B and spread over baked mixture. Bake again about *15 to 20 minutes,* or until golden brown.

4—Remove from oven. Allow to cool on wire rack for *10 minutes.* Cut into 48 squares, and place on serving platter.

COCONUT CUSTARD-PUDDING

Budín-Flán de Coco

(Serves 8)

A—1 cup sugar (*to caramelize pan*)

B—1 can (1 pound 2 ounces) Grated Coconut in Heavy Syrup
1 can (14 ounces) condensed milk, **undiluted**
½ cup water   ¼ teaspoon salt
½ teaspoon vanilla

C—4 eggs

1—Preheat oven to 350° F. Caramelize a round 8 x 3-inch aluminum pan, **without tube,** following Instruction 2 on page 280.

2—Blend ingredients included in *B* in an electric blender. In a saucepan, blend eggs, **without beating,** just enough to mix egg yolks and whites. Add blended ingredients, mix, strain and pour into caramelized pan.

3—Set pan in a large, shallow baking pan containing about an inch of hot water and bake about *1 hour*, or until set and golden. Remove pan from water. Allow to cool on wire rack. *Cover* and set in refrigerator. When ready to serve, turn custard onto a platter.

TEMBLEQUE

(Serves 8)

A—2 large ripe coconuts, to make 4 **cups diluted** coconut milk (see pages 289 and 290)

B—½ cup cornstarch   ½ teaspoon salt
⅔ cup sugar   1 tablespoon orange blossom water

1—In a saucepan, dissolve cornstarch in part of the coconut milk. Add remaining coconut milk and rest of ingredients included in *B* and mix.

2—Cook over *moderate-high* heat, stirring **constantly** with a wooden spoon until it begins to thicken.

3—As soon as it begins to thicken, reduce heat to *moderate* and stir **vigorously** until it boils. Pour **immediately** into a round 6 x 3-inch fluted or 8 x 6 x 1½-inch plain aluminum pan, rinsed in cold water. Allow to cool **slightly** and place in refrigerator.

4—When **thoroughly** cool, separate edges with a knife. Turn into a flat platter and let stand until it drops from pan. Set in refrigerator until ready to serve.

GOLDEN COCONUT DESSERT

Dulce de Coco Dorado

A—5 cups fresh grated coconut (see page 289)
 1⅓ cups water
 2⅔ cups sugar

B—2 eggs, lightly beaten

1—In a saucepan, combine ingredients included in A. Cook over *high* heat for 5 *minutes*. Turn heat to *low* and cook until syrup thickens to a light stage (Candy Thermometer — 222°F.), stirring **once** or **twice** only.

2—Add eggs, stirring *vigorously*, until blended. Cook for 5 *minutes*.

3—Remove from heat and allow to cool. Serve in a deep platter.

COCONUT DESSERT WITH MERINGUE

Dulce de Coco con Merengue

A—5 cups fresh grated coconut (see page 289)
 3 eggs
 1½ cups sugar
 1 cup evaporated milk, **undiluted**
 ¼ teaspoon grated lime peel

B—1 cup sugar
 ½ teaspoon baking powder
 ¼ teaspoon grated lime peel
 1 teaspoon vanilla extract

1—Preheat oven to *375°F.* Butter a round 2-quart glass baking dish.

2—In a bowl, combine 3 egg yolks with rest of ingredients included in A. Spoon mixture into baking dish and bake for *45 minutes.*

3—Beat egg whites until stiff. Add ingredients included in **B** *gradually* and beat. Spoon over baked mixture and set in oven, heated to *425°F.,* about *10 minutes,* or until meringue goldens on top.

SWEET POTATO PUDDING

Budín de Batata

(Serves 8)

A—1¾ pounds sweet potatoes
1 quart (4 cups) boiling water
1 tablespoon salt

B—1 cup sugar (*to caramelize pan*)

C—2 large ripe coconuts, to make **2 cups diluted** coconut milk (see Index)

D—8 eggs, lightly beaten
2¼ cups sugar
½ teaspoon salt
¾ pound butter, melted
1 cup flour

1—Scrub, cut into pieces, and wash sweet potatoes. Boil in water and salt included in A, *covered,* about *40 minutes,* or until fork-tender.

2—Meanwhile, caramelize a round 9 x 3½-inch aluminum pan *without tube,* by melting sugar included in B in the pan over *low* heat until light gold. Swirl pan to coat bottom and sides. Set on a wire rack.

3—Preheat oven to *350°F.*

4—Drain sweet potatoes, put through a potato ricer **immediately,** and add coconut milk.

5—**Gradually,** add ingredients included in *D*, and mix **thoroughly.** Press mixture through a sieve and pour into the caramelized pan.

6—Set pan in a large shallow baking pan containing about *1 inch* of hot water and bake in preheated oven about 2 *hours,* or until toothpick, inserted in the center, comes out clean. Remove pan from water bath.

7—Allow to cool on wire rack and turn onto a serving platter.

COCONUT CRUNCH

Turroncitos de Coco

A—2 large ripe coconuts, to make **2 cups diluted** coconut milk (see Index)

B—3 cups sugar

1—In a deep kettle, combine coconut milk and sugar and bring **rapidly** to a boil. Turn heat to *moderate* and cook syrup, **without stirring,** until syrup thickens to hard ball stage (Candy Thermometer —258°*F.*).

2—Grease a marble slab and pour mixture onto it, to cool **slightly.** When syrup is set but not hardened, begin to pull, as for taffy. Pull mixture out as far as arms can reach, double back, and pull again. Repeat until mixture turns whitish in color.

3—**Immediately,** form into long rolls about 1-inch thick. Place on marble slab.

4—Rub the palm of the hands **rapidly** over the candy, to flatten and make it glossy. Cut into pieces 1-inch long. Wrap pieces in waxed paper or tissue paper of different colors.

CANDIED COCONUT RICE

Arroz con Coco

(Serves 12)

A—1½ cups rice

B—¾ cup **undiluted** coconut milk ⎱
    4¼ cups **diluted** coconut milk ⎰ see Index
    1½ teaspoons salt
    3 cinnamon sticks
    2 ounces fresh ginger, scrubbed under running water (Cut into 6 pieces about 1 inch long, 1 inch wide and ¼ inch thick. Crush well.)
    6 whole cloves ⎱ *optional*
    Pinch of nutmeg ⎰

C—1½ cups either white granulated or brown sugar
    ½ cup seeded raisins

1—Wash rice and soak in water to *cover*, **generously**, for *2 hours*.

2—**Twenty minutes** before soaked rice is ready, proceed as follows: **Reserve** the ¾ cup **undiluted** coconut milk included in *B* and combine rest of ingredients in *B* in an 11-inch *caldero* or heavy kettle. Bring to a boil over *high* heat. Reduce heat to *moderate, cover* and boil for *15 minutes*.

3—Drain rice **thoroughly** and add to *caldero*. Mix and bring to a boil over *moderate* heat. Reduce heat to *low* and cook until rice is **completely dry,** *without stirring*.

4—Add ingredients included in *C*, mix and bring to a boil over *moderate heat*. Reduce heat to *low* and cook for *15 minutes, without stirring*.

5—Add reserved ¾ cup of **undiluted** coconut milk and mix. Turn heat to *moderate* and boil about *30 minutes*, or until rice dries again. In this cooking period, turn rice over **occasionally** and scrape bottom of *caldero*.

6—Remove spices. Spoon rice into a flat serving platter. Allow to cool at *room temperature*.

SWEET POTATO BALLS

Nísperos de Batata

(Makes 16)

A—2 pounds white sweet potatoes
1½ quarts (6 cups) water
1 teaspoon salt

B—2 large ripe coconuts, to make ¾ **cup undiluted** coconut milk
(see Index)
3 cups sugar
1 egg yolk

C—Ground cinnamon ⎫
Whole cloves ⎬ (*for garnishing*)
⎭

1—Scrub, cut into pieces, and wash sweet potatoes. Boil in water and salt included in A, over *moderate* heat, *covered*, about *40 minutes*, or until fork-tender. Drain, peel, and **immediately** put through a ricer.

2—Add ingredients included in B, mixing well with a wooden spoon.

3—Turn mixture into a *caldero* or heavy kettle. Bring *rapidly* to a boil, **stirring constantly** with a wooden spoon in a *back-and-forth* movement. Lower heat to *moderate* and cook in the same way, until mixture separates completely from bottom and sides of kettle. (Control heat to avoid spattering.)

4—Remove from heat and cool *slightly*. Shape mixture into small balls. Dust *lightly* with ground cinnamon and garnish each ball with a whole clove.

COCONUT MOLASSES TAFFY

Mampostial

A—1½ cups grated coconut meat, firmly packed
1½ cups molasses

1—Mix coconut and molasses in a *caldero* or heavy kettle. Cook over *moderate* heat, stirring *constantly* with a wooden spoon, about 20 *minutes,* or until mixture separates from bottom and sides of kettle.

2—Turn onto a greased table or marble slab. Allow to cool and cut into bars, about 1 inch square and 3 inches long. (The taffy will have a sticky consistency.)

LOVE POWDER
Polvo de Amor

This recipe is made with the grated meat of a coconut, after the milk has been extracted and used in other recipes.

A—5 cups grated coconut meat (after milk has been extracted)
2¼ cups sugar

1—Mix grated coconut meat and sugar. Place in a kettle and cook *rapidly* for 5 *minutes,* **stirring constantly.**

2—Turn heat to *moderate* and cook about 10 *minutes,* or until grated coconut meat turns golden brown and crispy.

YELLOW CORNMEAL TEMBLEQUE
Tembleque de Maíz

A—1¼ cups yellow cornmeal   ½ teaspoon salt
1 teaspoon aniseeds   1 cup sugar
2 large ripe coconuts, to make **2½ cups diluted** coconut milk
(see Index)

1—In a saucepan, combine ingredients included in A and cook over *moderate* heat, **stirring constantly** with a wooden spoon, until mixture boils and separates from bottom and sides of saucepan.

2—Pour **immediately** into a round 6 x 3-inch fluted or plain aluminum pan and when *thoroughly* cool, turn onto serving platter.

COCONUT BREAD PUDDING

Budín de Pasas con Coco

A—1 pound French bread, crust trimmed

B—2 large ripe coconuts, to make 1¾ **cups diluted** coconut milk (see Index)

C—1 cup sugar (*to caramelize pan*)

D—4 eggs
3 ounces (6 tablespoons) butter
1½ cups sugar
¾ teaspoon salt
½ teaspoon ground cinnamon
½ teaspoon ground cloves
1 cup milk
½ cup seeded raisins

E—¼ cup blanched almonds

1—Preheat oven to 375°F.

2—Have ready to use 1¾ cups **diluted** coconut milk.

3—Caramelize a round 9 x 3½-inch aluminum pan without tube, by placing sugar on pan and melting over *low* heat until light gold. Swirl pan to coat bottom and sides. Set on a wire rack.

4—Crumble bread over a bowl, cover with water, and soak for *15 minutes.* Squeeze well and drain. Place bread in a bowl and mash **thoroughly.**

5—Add coconut milk and mix. Add eggs, **one at a time,** and mix. Add rest of ingredients included in *D* and mix.

6—Crush half of almonds. Add to bowl, together with whole almonds. Mix **thoroughly** and pour mixture into caramelized pan.

7—Set pan in a large shallow baking pan containing about *1 inch* of hot water. Bake about *2 hours,* or until set. Remove pan from water bath.

8—Allow to cool on a wire rack. Turn onto serving platter.

COCONUT KISSES

Besitos de Coco

(24 Kisses)

A—3 cups grated ripe coconut (see page 289), firmly packed, or 2 cans (3½ ounces each) Baker's *Angel Flake Coconut, Sweetened*

B—2 ounces (4 tablespoons) butter (at room temperature)
4 egg yolks
8 tablespoons flour
¼ teaspoon salt
½ teaspoon vanilla extract
1 cup brown sugar, firmly packed

1—Preheat oven at *350°F.* Grease a 13 x 9 x 2-inch glass baking dish.

2—In a bowl, place butter and blend egg yolks well with a wooden spoon. Add **gradually** rest of ingredients included in *B* and mix.

3—Add grated coconut and mix **thoroughly.** Take mixture by teaspoonsful, place in palm of the hand and turn into balls. Arrange in baking dish, 4 rows of 6 balls each. (During this process, wash palms of hands frequently, to make shaping of balls easier.)

4—Bake in preheated oven about *30 to 40 minutes* or until golden brown.

5—Remove from oven and allow to cool **upside down** on a platter. Turn over and serve.

CHAPTER XIII

Preserves and Other Desserts

℘reserves and
Other ℘esserts

GUAVA JELLY
Jalea de Guayaba

Select both sweet and sour **guavas.** The **sour,** for acid and pectin essential to a good jelly; the **sweet,** for flavor. **Do not** cook more than **3 pounds** of *guavas* at a time.

A—3 pounds ripe, firm guavas
    6 cups water

B—3 cups sugar

1—Wash guavas *thoroughly.* Peel and **reserve** peelings. Cut guavas in halves and remove seeds **carefully,** without breaking shells. **Reserve** guava shells to make Guava Shells in Syrup (see Index). Combine peelings and seeds with water included in *A* and cook over *moderate* heat for *1 hour,* stirring *occasionally.*

2—Strain liquid through a sieve, lined with cheesecloth.

3—Measure 3 cups of the strained liquid. Pour into a very large, deep kettle, so that liquid may boil freely, and add sugar included in *B.* Mix well.

4—Boil over *high* heat, *without stirring,* until syrup thickens to a heavy stage (Candy Thermometer — *224°F.*).

5—Have ready two jars with a silver fork inside each, to prevent jars from breaking by the hot liquid. **Immediately,** pour liquid into jars and remove fork as soon as jars are filled. (When **totally** cool, liquid will turn into jelly.)

GUAVA SHELLS IN SYRUP

Dulce de Casquitos de Guayaba en Almíbar
(Serves 12)

Select large, sweet, ripe, and firm guavas.

A—3 pounds guavas
7 cups water

B—4 cups sugar

1—Wash guavas *thoroughly*. Peel and **reserve** peelings. Cut guavas in halves and remove seeds **carefully,** without breaking the shells. **Reserve** shells.

2—Combine peelings and water included in A, and cook over *high* heat, *uncovered,* for *25 minutes.*

3—Strain liquid into a pot and mix with sugar included in B. Add reserved shells. Bring *rapidly* to a boil. Reduce heat to *moderate* and cook, **without stirring,** about *1½ hours,* or until syrup thickens to light stage (Candy Thermometer — *222°F.*).

4—Allow to cool and pour shells and syrup into dessert bowl.

GUAVA PASTE

Pasta de Guayaba

Select both sweet and sour, ripe (soft to the touch), guavas

A—Guavas — sufficient to make **2 cups** guava purée
¼ cup water
1 teaspoon fresh lime juice

B—2 cups sugar

1—Wash guavas carefully, remove stems and chop, **without** peeling.

2—In a pan, mix water and lime juice included in A. Add chopped guavas, *cover,* and cook over *moderate* heat for *5 minutes.*

3—Remove from heat, and in same pan, **immediately** mash guavas **thoroughly** with potato masher.

4—Press **gradually** through a sieve, and measure **2 cups** of guava purée. Mix well with sugar in a *caldero*, or heavy kettle.

5—Boil over *moderate-high* heat, stirring **constantly** with a large wooden spoon, in a back-and-forth motion.

6—Cook until mixture separates from bottom and bubbles around sides of *caldero*. Rinse a shallow pan with cold water and pour mixture. **Do not scrape** bottom of *caldero*, to avoid crystallization.

7—Allow to cool. Unmold and wrap in wax paper.

Note: In making guava paste, it is recommended to cook **not** more than **4 cups** guava purée at a time.

PAPAYA PRESERVE

Dulce de Lechosa en Almíbar

(Serves 6)

Papaya furnishes its own juice when cooked. Therefore, the fruit should be chosen carefully. Too young *papaya* will be almost tasteless and will yield too much juice. Too ripe, *papaya* will be almost dehydrated, and will yield little or no juice. Since some *papayas* are more watery than others, cooking time should be adjusted accordingly.

A—2 pounds green, peeled and seeded *papaya*, cut into 1 inch squares
2 quarts (8 cups) water
2 tablespoons baking powder

B—4½ cups sugar

C—2 cinnamon sticks or 1 teaspoon vanilla extract

1—Combine ingredients included in *A* and soak for 1 hour. (Baking powder will turn *papaya* pieces hard on the outside, but soft on the inside.)

2—Strain, wash **carefully**, and place papaya pieces in a *caldero*, or deep heavy kettle.

3—Add sugar included in *B*, mix, and cook over *low* heat, *covered*, for *30 minutes*. (During this cooking period, *papaya* should render the necessary juice to make a syrup. If *papaya* does not render juice, add water.)

4—*Uncover*, add either cinnamon sticks or vanilla extract, and cook over *low* heat, **stirring occasionally**, about *1 hour* or until *papayas* turn golden and syrup thickens to light stage (Candy Thermometer—*222°F.*). Remove cinnamon sticks.

5—Allow to cool and pour into dessert bowl.

GROUND PAPAYA DESSERT

Dulce de Lechosa Rallado
(Serves 6)

A—2 pounds green, peeled and seeded *papayas*
4½ cups sugar

B—2 cinnamon sticks or 1 teaspoon vanilla extract

1—Grate *papaya* and mix with sugar, *cover*, and cook over *low* heat for *30 minutes*.

2—*Uncover*, and cook until *papaya* turns light golden and syrup thickens to light stage (Candy Thermometer — *222°F.*). (When dessert is ready, it should have a scanty syrup, almost dry.)

3—Allow to cool and pour into dessert bowl.

MANGO PRESERVE

Dulce de Mangó en Almíbar

Select mangoes that are not fibrous. The most acceptable variety of mangoes for this dessert are those that are round in shape and green in color, in spite of being almost ripe.

A—1½ pounds mangoes, washed, peeled, and sliced
    3 cups water

B—4½ cups sugar

1—Place mangoes into a pot, with water included in A, and bring *rapidly* to a boil.

2—Turn heat to *low* and cook for *10 minutes.*

3—Add sugar, mix, and bring *rapidly* to a boil.

4—Reduce heat to *moderate,* and cook until syrup thickens to light stage (Candy Thermometer — 222°F.). (While cooking, remove foam that forms around sides of pot.)

5—Allow to cool and pour into dessert bowl.

MANGO DESSERT

Dulce de Mangó

A—6 mangoes (**non fibrous**)

B—4 cups water
    4 cups sugar

C—1 teaspoon vanilla extract

1—Wash and peel mangoes. Place in a pot and cover with water. Bring *rapidly* to a boil. Remove mangoes and measure **4 cups of liquid.**

2—Combine liquid with sugar in a pot. Add mangoes and boil over *moderate* heat until syrup thickens to light stage (Candy Thermometer — 222°F.). Add vanilla when almost done, and mix.

3—Allow to cool and turn into dessert bowl.

MAMEY PRESERVE

Dulce de Mamey

A—1 ripe *mamey* (see Glossary), about 3½ pounds (Select *mamey* that is not **too** ripe)
1 quart (4 cups) water
1 tablespoon salt

B—3 cups water

C—4 cups sugar

1—Peel, wash, and dice *mamey*. Soak in water and salt included in *A* for *30 minutes*.

2—Drain and place in a pot with water included in *B*. Bring *rapidly* to a boil. Reduce heat to *low* and cook for *10 minutes*.

3—Add sugar, mix, and bring *rapidly* to a boil. Reduce heat to *moderate* and cook until syrup thickens to light stage (Candy Thermometer — 222°F.). (While cooking, remove foam that forms around sides of pot.)

4—Allow to cool and pour into dessert bowl.

GRAPEFRUIT DESSERT

Dulce de Toronja

A—6 large ripe grapefruits

B—4 cups sugar
3 cups water

C—1 teaspoon vanilla extract

1—Peel *carefully* grapefruits, so as not to break the pulp. Slit pulp into 1½-inch wedges. Remove pulp wedges from grapefruit and place in a pot, cover with water, and soak *overnight*. (**Reserve** inside of grapefruits for other use.)

2—Drain and place in a pot, cover with water, and bring *rapidly* to a boil. Drain and cool *slightly*. Roll each wedge and squeeze to drain. Place wedges back into pan, cover again with water, and repeat procedure once again.

3—The third time, drain but **do not squeeze.** Place in a pot, together with ingredients included in *B*. Bring to a boil over *moderate* heat. Cook for *15 minutes* over *moderate* heat.

4—Reduce heat to *low*, add vanilla extract, mix, and cook until syrup thickens to light stage (Candy Thermometer — *222°F.*). (Dessert takes a long cooking period to allow wedges to soak through delicately.)

5—Allow to cool and pour into dessert bowl.

CASHEW PRESERVE

Dulce de Pajuil

A—30 ripe *pajuiles* (cashews), without nuts (see Glossary)

B—3 cups water
    4 cups sugar

1—Cut cashews *lengthwise* and soak overnight in salted water to cover.

2—Drain, peel, cover with water, and bring *rapidly* to a boil. **Drain.**

3—Place in a pot with ingredients included in *B*, and bring *rapidly* to a boil. Reduce heat to *low* and cook about *3 hours*, or until syrup thickens to light stage (Candy Thermometer — *222°F.*).

4—Allow to cool and pour into dessert bowl.

COCO PLUM PRESERVE

Dulce de Hicacos

A—4 cups water
    2 pounds ripe *hicacos* (coco plums) (see Glossary)

B—3 cups water
    4 cups sugar

1—In a pot, bring water included in *A* to a boil. Remove from heat, add coco plums, and soak for *5 minutes*. Drain, rinse in fresh water, and peel *immediately*.

2–In a pot, mix peeled coco plums with water and sugar included in B. Bring *rapidly* to a boil, turn heat to *moderate*, and cook until syrup thickens to light stage (Candy Thermometer — *222°F.*).

3–Allow to cool and pour into dessert bowl.

ANGEL'S HAIR
Cabello de Angel
(Serves 6)

A–3 large *chayotes* (see Glossary) | 2¼ cups sugar

B–½ teaspoon vanilla extract

1–Wash *chayotes*, pare, and shred or cut into very thin slices.

2–Place *chayotes* in a pot together with sugar, *cover*, and cook over *low* heat for 30 *minutes*, stirring *occasionally*. (By this time *chayotes* should render enough juice to make syrup.)

3–*Uncover*, add vanilla extract, mix, and boil over *moderate* heat until syrup thickens to light stage (Candy Thermometer — *222°F.*).

4–Allow to cool and pour into dessert bowl.

BUÑUELOS DE VIENTO
(Makes 18)

A–1 cup water | ½ teaspoon salt
¼ pound butter |

B–1 cup flour | 4 eggs

C–Lard or vegetable oil (*for deep-frying*)

D–3 cups sugar | 4 cups water
½ teaspoon vanilla extract, or 1 lime peel, rinsed and drained

1–Place ingredients included in A in a saucepan, and bring *rapidly* to a boil.

2—Remove from heat and add flour all at once, **stirring vigorously** with a wooden spoon, until well blended.

3—Add eggs, **one at a time,** and mix until well blended after each addition.

4—Deep-fry, by tablespoons, in fat heated to 375°F., until golden brown.

5—Remove and drain on absorbent paper and place in dessert bowl.

6—In a saucepan, mix ingredients included in *D*, and boil over *high* heat, until syrup thickens to light stage (Candy Thermometer—222°F.). Allow to cool.

7—When ready to serve, pour syrup over the fried *buñuelos*.

Note: For more flavor, add individually either anisette, or cherry liqueur.

TORREJAS GALLEGAS

A—½ pound French bread, crust trimmed

B—1 cup milk
½ cup sweet wine

C—½ teaspoon ground cinnamon

D—3 eggs, lightly beaten

E—Lard or vegetable oil (*for pan-frying*)

F—2 cups sugar
1 cup water
¼ teaspoon salt
1 thin cinnamon stick or 1 lime peel, rinsed and drained

1—Cut bread into ½ inch slices.

2—Mix milk and wine and dip each slice **gradually.** Remove with a slotted spoon and place on an aluminum sheet.

3—Sprinkle slices with ground cinnamon.

4—Dip into beaten eggs and drain with a slotted spoon.

5—Fry in hot fat until golden brown. Remove, drain on absorbent paper and place in dessert bowl.

6—In a saucepan, mix ingredients included in *F* and boil over *high* heat, **without stirring,** until syrup thickens to light stage (Candy Thermometer — 222°F.).

7—Pour syrup over *torrejas.* Allow to cool before serving.

BREAD PUDDING

Budín de Pan Sencillo

(Serves 12)

A—1½ pounds French bread, crust trimmed
2 quarts (8 cups) milk

B—¼ pound butter

C—2½ cups sugar
½ teaspoon salt
1 tablespoon vanilla extract

D—4 eggs

1—Preheat oven to 375°F. Grease a 13 x 9 x 2-inch glass baking dish. Melt butter over *low* heat.

2—Crumble bread into a big bowl. Add milk and mix *thoroughly.* until well blended.

3—Add ingredients included in *C* and mix.

4—Beat eggs *lightly,* add and mix.

5—Add melted butter, mix *thoroughly* and pour into baking dish.

6—Bake for *1½ hours* on the middle rack of the oven. (Put a large aluminum pan on the rack beneath to collect drippings.)

7—Allow to cool on wire rack and serve in the baking dish.

GUAVA PUDDING
Budín de Guayaba

A—1 quart (4 cups) milk
1 can (6¼ ounces) Danish butter, or 6 ounces butter

B—1 pound sandwich bread, crust trimmed
2¼ cups sugar

C—4 egg yolks (*reserve whites for meringue*)
8 whole eggs
¼ teaspoon salt
1 teaspoon vanilla extract

D—1 pound guava paste

E—**Meringue:**
4 egg whites
½ cup sugar
¼ teaspoon baking powder

1—Preheat oven to *300°F*. Grease a 13 x 9 x 2-inch glass baking dish.

2—Bring milk to a boil. Remove from heat, add butter and mix.

3—Crumble bread over milk and mix. Add sugar and mix.

4—In a bowl, mix ingredients included in C, and add to milk mixture. Mix well, pour into baking dish and bake for *1½ hours*.

5—Remove from oven. Divide guava paste into 32 slices and arrange to cover dish.

6—Beat egg whites until stiff. Add sugar *gradually*. Add baking powder and beat until well blended.

7—Top with meringue and bake for *30 minutes*. Allow to cool on wire rack and serve in the baking dish.

HEAVEN'S DELIGHT
Tocino del Cielo

A—½ cup sugar (*to caramelize pan*)

B—2 whole eggs
16 egg yolks (*about*)

C—2½ cups sugar
1 cup water
1 thin cinnamon stick
1 lime peel, rinsed and drained

1—Preheat oven to *350°F.*

2—Caramelize a round 1-quart aluminum pan, by placing sugar in pan, and melting over *low* heat until light gold. Swirl pan to coat bottom and sides. Set on a wire rack.

3—Break 2 whole eggs into a measuring cup and blend with a rubber spatula. Add and mix egg yolks sufficient to total 1½ cups. Place in a saucepan.

4—In another saucepan, mix ingredients included in *C* and boil over *high* heat, **without stirring,** until syrup thickens to thread stage (Candy Thermometer — *230°F.*).

5—Remove from heat and discard cinnamon stick and lime peel.

6—Add **slowly** to egg mixture and blend with a rubber spatula. Strain and pour over caramelized pan.

7—Cover pan with aluminum foil and set in a large shallow baking pan containing about *1 inch* of hot water.

8—Bake for *2 hours.* Remove pan from water bath. Remove aluminum foil, allow to cool on wire rack and unmold onto serving platter.

ROYAL YOLKS

Yemas Reales

(Serves 8)

A—2 whole eggs | 10 egg yolks

B—¼ teaspoon salt | 2 teaspoons cornstarch
½ teaspoon baking powder |

C—4 cups sugar | 1 lime peel, rinsed and drained
3 cups water |

1—Preheat oven to *300°F.*

2—Grease with oleomargarine a 12 x 7½ x 2-inch glass baking dish. Line bottom of dish with brown paper. Grease paper *generously* with oleomargarine.

3—In the small bowl of the electric mixer, beat ingredients included in A over *high speed* for *1 minute.*

4—Reduce speed to *low* and add ingredients included in B, turn speed to *high* and beat for *5 minutes.*

5—Pour mixture into baking dish and bake about *25 minutes.*

6—Remove dish from oven, release edges of cake with a knife, and turn dish. Remove paper and discard. With a sandwich knife, trim crusts. Divide into 32 squares or "royal yolks."

7—In a large saucepan, combine ingredients included in C and boil *rapidly* until syrup thickens to a very light stage (Candy Thermometer — *218°F.*).

8—Drop the squares, **eight at a time,** into the boiling syrup, and boil for *1 minute.*

9—Remove with a slotted spoon and arrange the "royal yolks" in a deep serving dish.

10—Allow syrup to thicken to light stage (Candy Thermometer — 222°F.), and pour over squares. Allow to cool and set in refrigerator.

MERINGUES
Merengues
(Makes 40)

(Meringues are baked on **special wooden non-resinous board**)

A—2¼ cups sugar   1 lime peel, rinsed and drained
1 cup water

B—⅔ cup egg whites

1—In a small saucepan, mix sugar, water and lime peel. Boil until syrup thickens to soft crack stage (Candy Thermometer — *270°F.*). Remove lime peel.

2—In large bowl of electric mixer, beat at *high* speed egg whites until stiff. Continue beating while pouring the syrup **slowly.** Beat at *high* speed for *20 minutes* longer.

3—Drop mixture, by teaspoonfuls, 1 inch apart, on a dampened 11 x 18-inch **wooden non-resinous board.** (Mixture will yield two batches.)

4—Heat oven to *325°F.* and bake the meringues for *20 minutes,* or until golden.

5—Remove meringues from board **immediately** and place upside down. Press two meringues *flat sides* together, to make a whole meringue.

SNOWBALLS
Bolas de Nieve

A—½ cup water   1 lime peel, rinsed and drained
2¼ cups sugar

B—2 egg whites

1—In a small saucepan, combine water, sugar, and lime peel. Boil, **without stirring,** until syrup thickens to hard ball stage (Candy Thermometer — *265°F.*).

2—In large bowl of electric mixer, beat at *high* speed egg whites until stiff. Continue beating while pouring syrup *slowly*. Beat until mixture becomes thick enough to be handled and shaped into small balls.

3—Wrap in tissue paper of different colors.

PEACHES A LA GRAND MARNIER

Melocotones a la Grand Marnier

(Serves 12)

A—1 box (11¼ ounces) pound cake

B—2 cans (1 pound 13 ounces each) sliced Yellow Cling peaches
8 tablespoons Grand Marnier | 15 Maraschino cherries

C—½ cup cornstarch
½ teaspoon salt
1 quart (4 cups) milk

4 egg yolks
1½ cups sugar
1 lime peel, rinsed and drained

1—Remove brown top from cake and slice cake into 12 slices.

2—Line bottom of a 13 x 9 x 2-inch glass baking dish with cake slices.

3—Drain liquid from 1 can of peaches. **Reserve** peaches. Add to drained liquid, 8 tablespoons of Grand Marnier and mix. Pour over cake slices.

4—Drain other can of peaches and **reserve** liquid for other use. Add drained peaches to reserved peaches.

5—**Select** and **reserve** 15 peach slices for garnishing. Place 2 peach slices over each slice of cake.

6—Prepare cream as follows: In a saucepan, blend cornstarch and salt with part of milk. Add egg yolks and mix well. Add remaining milk and rest of ingredients included in *C*. Stir with a wooden spoon, over *moderate* heat, until mixture boils. Remove **immediately** from heat, discard lime peel, and pour over contents in dish.

7—Garnish dish with reserved peach slices. Drain and wipe dry cherries and garnish.

8—Allow to cool, cover, and set in refrigerator.

MANJAR BLANCO

(Serves 6)

A—1 cup ricemeal
  4 cups milk
  1 cup sugar
  ½ teaspoon salt
  1½ tablespoons orange blossom water
  1 tablespoon butter

1—Mix ingredients in a pot.

2—Cook over *moderate* heat, **stirring constantly** with a wooden spoon, until mixture separates from bottom and sides of pot.

3—Pour **immediately** into a shallow serving dish. Allow to cool.

MAJARETE

A—5 cups milk
  1 cup ricemeal
  1 teaspoon salt
  1½ cups sugar
  3 thin cinnamon sticks
  3 tablespoons orange blossom water
  2 tablespoons vegetable shortening or butter

B—Ground cinnamon (*for dusting*)

1—In a saucepan, mix ingredients included in A and stir **constantly,** with a wooden spoon over *medium-high* heat until boiling.

2—**Immediately** reduce heat to *moderate* and continue stirring for 2 *minutes.*

3—Remove from heat. Discard cinnamon sticks and spoon mixture into individual small deep plates.

4—Dust **lightly** with ground cinnamon, and allow to cool.

TASTY COOKIES
Mantecaditos

A—¼ pound butter
½ cup vegetable shortening
½ cup sugar
1 teaspoon almond extract
2¼ cups flour

B—5 Maraschino cherries

1—Preheat oven to 350°F.

2—In a bowl, cream butter and vegetable shortening. Blend in sugar and rest of ingredients included in A.

3—Take mixture by teaspoonfuls and rub with the palm of the hands to form balls.

4—Arrange in an *ungreased* aluminum sheet. Press each ball *gently* with the palm of the hand to form the cookie.

5—Cut each cherry into 8 pieces and garnish each cookie with a piece in the center.

6—Bake about *20 minutes*, or until golden.

7—Remove to a serving platter and allow to cool. Store in air-tight container until ready to serve.

OATMEAL MACAROONS
Macaroons de Avena
(65 to 70)

A—½ cup shortening, chilled
½ teaspoon salt
1 teaspoon ground cinnamon
1 teaspoon vanilla extract
1 tablespoon molasses
1 cup brown sugar, firmly packed
1 egg

B—1 cup flour | ¾ teaspoon baking soda

C—1 cup oatmeal (Quaker Quick Instant)

1—Preheat oven to *350°F.*

2—Grease an aluminum pan *very lightly.*

3—In a bowl, cream shortening and mix together with rest of ingredients included in A.

4—Sift ingredients included in B, add, and mix.

5—Add oatmeal and mix.

6—Take mixture by teaspoonfuls, rub with the palm of the hands to form balls the size of a large grape, and arrange on an aluminum sheet, in columns 1 inch apart.

7—Bake about *12 to 15 minutes,* or until golden brown.

8—Set on a wire rack for *10 minutes.* Remove from pan, allow to cool **up-side-down,** and store in airtight container until ready to serve.

ECLAIRS
Palitos de Jacob

Pastry:
A—1 cup flour
¼ teaspoon salt

B—1 cup water
¼ pound butter

C—4 eggs

1—Preheat oven to *375°F.*

2—Grease an aluminum pan *lightly.*

3—Sift together dry ingredients included in A.

4—In a saucepan, bring *rapidly* to a boil water and butter. Turn heat to *moderate* and add, **all at once,** sifted ingredients. Mix **vigorously** with a wooden spoon. Almost *immediately,* mixture will separate from bottom and sides of saucepan and will look somewhat like a ball. **At once,** remove from heat and continue mixing **vigorously** until mixture is smooth and well blended. Set on wire rack and allow to cool for *5 minutes.*

5—Add eggs, **one at a time,** beating **vigorously** after each addition. Allow mixture to rest for *15 minutes.*

6—Take mixture by tablespoons and arrange on aluminum sheet in eclairs, 4 inches long by 1 inch wide by 1 inch high.

7—Bake about *40 minutes,* or until set and golden brown. (To make smaller eclairs, take mixture by teaspoons and bake about *35 minutes,* or until set and golden brown.)

8—Set on wire rack and allow to cool for *5 minutes.* Remove from pan, set on a platter, and when thoroughly cool, make a deep gash in each eclair, ready to be filled.

Cream filling:
⅓ cup cornstarch
2 cups milk
2 egg yolks
¾ cup sugar
¼ teaspoon salt
1 lime peel, rinsed and drained

1—Place cornstarch in a saucepan and dissolve in part of the milk, until well blended. Add egg yolks and mix well. Add remaining milk and rest of ingredients. Mix with a wooden spoon over *moderate* heat, until it boils. *Immediately,* remove from heat and fill eclairs.

Icing:
2 cups sifted confectioners' powdered sugar
2½ tablespoons evaporated milk, **undiluted**
¼ teaspoon vanilla extract

1—Mix ingredients *thoroughly* and garnish eclairs.

CHAPTER XIV Ice Creams, Sherbets, Sandwiches, and Beverages

Ice Creams, Sherbets, Sandwiches, and Beverages

GRANDFATHER'S ICE CREAM
Mantecado del Abuelo

A—2 quarts (8 cups) milk
¼ cup cornstarch
6 eggs

B—2½ cups sugar
¾ teaspoon salt
½ lime peel, rinsed and drained
1 cinnamon stick

1—In a saucepan, dissolve cornstarch in part of milk included in A. Blend in egg yolks. Place 3 egg whites in a bowl and reserve rest for other use.

2—In a large saucepan, mix rest of milk together with ingredients included in B and bring rapidly to a boil. Add yolk mixture and stir vigorously over *moderate* heat until boiling. Strain and allow to cool.

3—Beat egg whites until stiff and fold into mixture.

4—Freeze until firm in an ice cream freezer.

VANILLA ICE CREAM
Mantecado de Vainilla

A—10 tablespoons cornstarch
3 cans (13 ounces each) evaporated milk, **diluted**
8 egg yolks (see Note)
1 teaspoon salt
3 cups sugar

B—2 teaspoons vanilla extract

1—In a large saucepan, dissolve cornstarch in part of milk. Blend in egg yolks. Add rest of milk together with salt and sugar.

2—Start mixing over *moderate-high* heat, stirring *constantly* with a wooden spoon. Reduce heat to *moderate* and continue stirring until boiling.

3—Remove from heat, add vanilla extract, mix, and strain.

4—Allow to cool. Freeze until firm in an ice cream freezer.

Note: Egg whites can be used for meringue or white cake (see Index)

COCONUT SHERBET
Helado de Coco

A—2 large ripe coconuts | 2 quarts (8 cups) water

B—¼ teaspoon salt | Grated rind of ¼ lime
3 cups sugar

1—Crack coconuts. Separate coconut meat from the shells. Pare the brown skin, wash, dry, and grate the meat. Set in pan.

2—Heat the water included in A and pour over the grated coconut. Mix well.

3—Pour mixture *gradually* in a muslin cloth and squeeze out the coconut milk. Strain.

4—Add ingredients included in B, mix, and freeze until firm in an ice cream freezer.

GUAVA SHERBET

Helado de Guayaba

Select both sweet and sour, ripe (soft to the touch), guavas

A—Guavas — sufficient to make 4 **cups** guava purée
¼ cup water

B—3 cups water
3½ cups sugar

1—Wash guavas carefully, remove stems and chop, **without** peeling.

2—In a pan, place water included in *A*. Add chopped guavas, *cover*, and cook over *moderate* heat for *5 minutes*.

3—Remove from heat, and in same pan, **immediately** mash guavas *thoroughly* with potato masher.

4—Press *gradually* through a sieve, and measure 4 **cups** purée.

5—Combine purée with water and sugar included in *B*. Freeze until firm in an ice cream freezer.

SOURSOP SHERBET

Helado de Guanábana

A—3 pounds ripe *guanábanas* (see Glossary)

B—3 cups water
2½ cups sugar

1—Cut *guanábanas* in two, *lengthwise*. Core and remove pulp and seeds.

2—In a large saucepan, mash pulp and seeds with *1 cup* of the water included in *B*.

3—Strain through a sieve. Put pulp and seeds back into saucepan, and proceed as above, adding water *gradually,* until all the pulp has been removed from the seeds.

4—Add sugar, mix, and freeze until firm in an ice cream freezer.

CANNED FRUIT SHERBET
Helado de Frutas Enlatadas

A—2 cans (1 pound 14 ounces each) *Fruits in Syrup* (either Pears, Peaches, Pineapples, Fruit Cocktail, etc.)
4 cans (12 ounces each) *Fruit Juice* in accord with the Fruits in Syrup selected.
2 cups sugar

1—In a pot, drain cans of *Fruits in Syrup*. Dice fruits and add to the pot.

2—Add rest of ingredients, mix, and freeze until firm in an ice cream freezer.

FANCY SANDWICHES
Emparedados Descubiertos

A—2 jars (8 ounces each) pimiento cheese spread
2 teaspoons mayonnaise
Vegetable color (*for garnishing*)

B—2 cans (2¼ ounces each) deviled ham
1 ounce (2 tablespoons) butter (at room temperature)

C—1 can (7 ounces) pimientos, drained
1 small jar olives, stuffed with pimientos

D—4 hard-cooked eggs

E—4 pounds sandwich bread, crusts trimmed
½ pound butter (at room temperature)

1—In a small bowl, mix pimiento cheese spread with mayonnaise. Divide in *4 portions* and set on individual plates. Pour over each plate a few drops of different vegetable colors. Mix and **reserve.**

2—Mix deviled ham with creamed butter included in *B* and **reserve.**

3—Cut pimientos in thin slices and **reserve.**

4—Cut stuffed olives in rounds and **reserve.**

5—Set on the table sandwich slices. Cover *lightly* with butter. Top slices with different spreads and garnish some with strips of pimiento and others with rounds of olives.

6—With a spoon, press egg yolks through a sieve over sandwich slices. Break egg whites with a fork and garnish.

7—Cut slices in different shapes. Set on a platter. Refrigerate until ready to serve.

PARTY CHICKEN SANDWICHES

Emparedados de Pollo

A—1 pound chicken breasts | 2 teaspoons salt
1 quart (4 cups) water | 1 onion, peeled and halved
½ pound string beans, trimmed
½ pound carrots, scraped and chopped

B—2 cans (10½ ounces each) asparagus tips

C—2 apples | 1 teaspoon salt
1 cup water |

D—3 hard-cooked eggs } chopped
4 sweet pickles }
1 can (1 pound) green peas (*Petit-Pois*), drained

E—½ cup mayonnaise | 1 pound butter (at room temperature)

F—10 pounds sandwich bread, crusts trimmed
Light mayonnaise (*for spreading bread slices*) (**optional**)

1—Wash and dry chicken breasts. Place in a pot, together with rest of ingredients included in A. *Cover* and cook over *high* heat for *15 minutes.* Reduce heat to *moderate* and cook for *30 minutes.*

2—Strain and measure ¼ *cup* broth. Pour into a bowl.

3—Separate meat from bones of chicken. Grind meat, together with onion, string beans and carrots. Add to the bowl.

4—Drain asparagus, grind and add to bowl.

5—Peel apples and rinse **rapidly** in water and salt included in C. Drain, mince and add to bowl. Add ingredients included in D and mix. Add ingredients included in E and blend **thoroughly.**

6—Spread mayonnaise **lightly** over one side of each bread slice. Spread filling between slices of bread and cut in half. Set on a platter and cover with a damp cloth. Refrigerate until ready to serve.

FRESH CALF'S LIVER SANDWICHES

Emparedados de Hígado Fresco

A—1 pound calf's liver, trimmed   1 fresh lime, rinsed
1 cup water

B—1 clove garlic, peeled
1 sweet chili pepper, seeded
1 onion, peeled, chopped   crush and mix
1 parsley sprig, chopped   in a mortar
1 teaspoon salt
⅓ cup vinegar

C—1 tablespoon olive oil | 1 teaspoon tomato sauce
2 ounces (4 tablespoons) butter (at room temperature)
5 tablespoons freshly grated Parmesan cheese

D—4 pounds sandwich bread, crusts trimmed
Light mayonnaise *(for spreading bread slices)* **(optional)**

1—Cut liver into pieces and rinse in water and lime included in A. Drain, wipe dry, and season with ingredients included in B. Allow to stand for *15 minutes.*

2—In a small *caldero* or heavy kettle, heat olive oil. Add seasoned liver and tomato sauce included in C. Mix and bring *rapidly* to a boil. Reduce heat to *low* and cook for *30 minutes.*

3—Remove from heat and allow to cool. Remove and grind liver. Add again to *caldero*, together with butter and grated cheese. Mix *thoroughly.*

4—Spread mayonnaise **lightly** over one side of each bread slice. Spread filling between slices of bread and cut in half. Set on a platter and cover with a damp cloth. Refrigerate until ready to serve.

BONED TURKEY OR CHICKEN SANDWICHES

Emparedados de Pavo o Pollo Enlatado

A—2 cans (5 ounces each) boned turkey or chicken

B—¼ cup minced onions
¼ cup finely chopped sweet pickles
6 hard-cooked eggs, chopped

C—½ teaspoon salt
¼ teaspoon ground white pepper
2 tablespoons vinegar

D—⅔ cup mayonnaise

E—4 pounds sandwich bread, crusts trimmed
Light mayonnaise *(for spreading bread slices)* (**optional**)

1—Place contents of cans of boned turkey or chicken in a bowl.
Mince. Add and mix ingredients included in *B*.

2—In a cup, mix together ingredients included in *C*. Add to bowl
and mix. Add mayonnaise in *D* and mix **thoroughly.**

3—Spread mayonnaise **lightly** over one side of each bread slice.
Spread mixture between slices of bread and cut in half. Set
on a platter and cover with a damp cloth. Refrigerate until
ready to serve.

MIXED VEGETABLES SANDWICHES

Emparedados de Vegetales Enlatados

A—1 can (1 pound 4 ounces) mixed vegetables
¼ teaspoon salt
2 teaspoons vinegar
1 tablespoon mayonnaise
¼ pound butter (at room temperature)

B—2 pounds sandwich bread, crusts trimmed
Light mayonnaise *(for spreading bread slices)* (**optional**)

1—Drain mixed vegetables and grind. (When using an electric
blender, blend mixed vegetables, including liquid, and drain.)
Place in a bowl and mix with the rest of the ingredients.

2—Spread mayonnaise **lightly** over one side of each bread slice (**optional**).

3—Spread filling between slices of bread and cut in half. Set on a platter and cover with a damp cloth. Refrigerate until ready to serve.

LIVERWURST SANDWICHES

Emparedados de Hígado de Ganso

A—¼ pound Swiss cheese⎤
   (*Gruyère*)   ⎬ grind
   ½ pound liverwurst⎦
   ½ pound boiled ham

B—¼ pound butter (at room temperature)
   2 tablespoons vinegar
   2 tablespoons mayonnaise

C—4 pounds sandwich bread, crusts trimmed
   6 ounces butter (at room temperature)

1—Place ground ingredients in a bowl. Add ingredients included in *B* and mix.

2—Spread butter included in *C* over bread slices and spread filling between slices. Cut in half. Set on a platter and cover with a damp cloth. Refrigerate until ready to serve.

ASPARAGUS SANDWICHES

Emparedados de Espárragos

A—2 cans (10½ ounces each) asparagus tips
   4 hard-cooked eggs (at room temperature)

B—3 pounds sandwich bread, crusts trimmed
   Light mayonnaise (*for spreading bread slices*) (**optional**)

1—Pour contents of cans of asparagus tips in the electric blender, liquid included. Blend and drain well over a sieve, **without squeezing.**

2—Place drained asparagus in a bowl, together with rest of ingredients, and mix **thoroughly.**

3—Spread mayonnaise **lightly** over one side of each bread slice. Spread mixture between bread slices and cut in half. Set on a platter and cover with a damp cloth. Refrigerate until ready to serve.

PIMIENTO AND VELVEETA CHEESE SANDWICHES

Emparedados de Queso Velveeta y Pimientos Morrones

A—½ pound butter (at room temperature)
1 package (8 ounces) *Velveeta* cheese, chilled ⎫
1 can (7 ounces) pimientos, drained   ⎬ grind
8 hard-cooked eggs   ⎭

B— 2 tablespoons vinegar │ 2 tablespoons mayonnaise
1 teaspoon salt │

C—5 pounds sandwich bread, crusts trimmed
Light mayonnaise *(for spreading bread slices)* (**optional**)

1—Mix in a bowl ingredients included in *A*. Add and mix ingredients included in *B*.

2—Spread mayonnaise **lightly** over one side of each bread slice. Spread filling between slices of bread and cut in half. Set on a platter and cover with a damp cloth. Refrigerate until ready to serve.

PÂTÉ DE FOIE SANDWICHES

Emparedados de Pâté de Foie

A—2 cans (4½ ounces each) *Pâté de Foie* (see note)
4 hard-cooked eggs, finely chopped │ ½ cup mayonnaise
2 tablespoons sweet relish │

B—3 pounds sandwich bread, crusts trimmed
Light mayonnaise *(for spreading bread slices)* (**optional**)

1—In a bowl, mix together ingredients included in *A*.

2—Spread mayonnaise **lightly** over one side of each bread slice. Spread filling between slices of bread and cut in half. Set on a platter and cover with a damp cloth. Refrigerate until ready to serve.

Note: Recipe can be made with 2 cans (4½ ounces each) *Deviled Ham.*

PUERTO RICAN PARTY PIZZITAS

Pizzitas Jíbaras

A—1 pound French bread

B—½ cup olive oil
¼ teaspoon salt
8 cloves garlic, peeled and very finely crushed in a mortar and pestle

C—1 cup prepared pizza sauce

D—2 packages (4 ounces each) shredded Mozzarella cheese
½ cup freshly grated Parmesan cheese

1—Preheat oven to 375°F.

2—Line with aluminum foil an aluminum sheet.

3—Trim ends of bread and cut loaf in half. Divide both in two, *lengthwise.*

4—Mix ingredients included in *B* and spread over bread slices.

5—Distribute pizza sauce over bread slices.

6—Cover pizza sauce with shredded Mozzarella cheese, and sprinkle with grated Parmesan cheese.

7—Set bread slices on aluminum sheet and bake for *12 minutes.*

8—Remove from oven. Cut breads into 1-inch slices, set on a platter, and serve **immediately** as an appetizer.

PARTY PUNCH
Ponche para Fiestas

(30 cups, 6 ounces each)

A—1 bottle (24 ounces) grape juice
¼ cup fresh lime juice
2 cups sugar
6 cups fresh orange juice or 2 cans (6 ounces each) frozen
orange juice concentrate, diluted in *4½ cups* water

B—4 bottles or cans (10 ounces each) beer
1 bottle or can (12 ounces) soda water

C—Ice

1—In a large pot, mix ingredients included in A.

2—When ready to serve, add and mix ingredients included in B.

3—Pour into a bowl with ice, and serve.

FRESH FRUIT PUNCH
Refresco de Frutas Frescas

A—1 cup fresh orange juice
1 cup fresh pineapple juice
1 cup fresh grapefruit juice

B—1 can (12 ounces) ginger ale
Sugar (*to taste*)

C—Ice

1—In a saucepan, mix ingredients included in A. Pour into a
glass jar and set in refrigerator. When ready to serve, add
ingredients included in B, mix, and serve with ice.

BUL

A—1 can (10 ounces) beer
2 bottles (12 ounces each) soda water
4 tablespoons sugar
2 tablespoons fresh lime juice

B—Ice

1—Mix ingredients included in A in a bowl. Add ice and serve.

CANNED FRUIT JUICE PUNCH
Refresco de Jugo de Fruta Enlatado

A—1 can (10 ounces) beer
1 can (12 ounces) ginger ale
1 can (12 ounces) any fruit juice
5 tablespoons sugar
2 tablespoons fresh lime juice

B—Ice

1—When ready to serve, mix ingredients in a pot.

2—Pour into punch bowl and serve, chilled with ice.

BIÈRE PANACHÉE

A—1 can (10 ounces) beer
1 can (12 ounces) lime soda or limeade
1 teaspoon fresh lime juice
2 tablespoons sugar

B—Ice

1—Mix ingredients in a pot. Serve **immediately,** chilled with ice.

FRESH LIMEADE

Refresco de Limón

(1 cup)

A—2 tablespoons fresh lime juice
½ cup water
2 tablespoons sugar

B—Ice

1—Mix ingredients in a pot. Serve chilled with ice.

Note: Limeade can be sweetened with molasses, instead of sugar.

EGG TISANA

Tisana de Huevo

A—2 egg whites | 1 lime peel, rinsed and drained

B—1 cup sugar | 5 cups water, chilled

1—Wash lime peel and wipe dry. Beat egg whites, together with lime peel, until stiff, **but not dry.**

2—Add sugar *gradually* and beat until stiff.

3—Add chilled water *slowly* and beat. Serve cool *immediately*.

AGUA LOJA

A—1 ounce fresh ginger, washed and crushed
¼ ounce cinnamon sticks
5 cups water

B—1½ cups molasses

1—In a pot, mix ingredients included in *A*, and boil for *15 minutes.*

2—Strain and allow to cool. Add molasses, mix, and set in refrigerator in a glass jar. Serve chilled.

MABI BEVERAGE
Mabí

(Makes 4 quarts)

A—1 ounce *mabí* bark (see Glossary)
　1 ounce fresh ginger (after peeled, about 4 slices 1 inch long,
　　1 inch wide and ¼ inch thick)
　1 cinnamon stick
　1½ cups water

B—3 quarts (12 cups) water ⎤　or
　2½ cups granulated sugar ⎬ 5 cups either granulated
　2½ cups brown sugar ⎦　or brown sugar, firmly packed

C—2 cups ready-to-drink *mabí* beverage (*to serve as a base*)

1—Wash and drain *mabí* bark. Place in a large kettle (to avoid
　spilling in the process of free boiling).

2—Wash ginger and peel with a vegetable peeler. Divide into
　pieces and crush well. Add to kettle.

3—Add cinnamon stick and water included in A. Bring to a boil
　over *high* heat. Reduce heat to *moderate, cover* and boil for
　5 minutes. Strain through a sieve and allow to cool *thoroughly.*

4—In a large 12-quart kettle, mix well ingredients included in B.
　Add cool liquid to kettle and mix. Add ingredient included
　in C and mix. Strain beverage through sieve covered with a
　cheesecloth.

5—With a laddle, or *preferably with a saucepan,* dip out high the
　liquid in the kettle, as many times as required, until beverage
　becomes **real foamy.** Pour beverage into glass bottles ¾
　full. Place a *loose* paper in the shape of a cone on top of
　bottle. **Never cover mabi tightly.** Let rest for 3 days at *room
　temperature,* to allow beverage to ferment.

6—Set bottles in refrigerator, **uncovered.** Serve chilled.

FRESH COCONUT BEVERAGE

Refresco de Coco Tierno

6 cups green coconut water | ½ cup sugar
Fresh coconut pulp (*from coconuts*)

1—Mix ingredients in a pot, and set in refrigerator in a glass jar. Serve chilled.

RIPE COCONUT BEVERAGE

Refresco de Coco Seco

(Serves 4)

A—1 cup grated ripe coconut | 3 cups lukewarm water

B—¼ cup sugar

1—In a saucepan, mix ingredients included in A. Squeeze through a muslin cloth into pot.

2—Add sugar, mix, and set in refrigerator in a glass jar. Serve chilled.

TAMARIND BEVERAGE

Refresco de Tamarindo

A—1 pound tamarind seeds, with pulp (see Glossary)
1 quart (4 cups) water
2 cups sugar

B—Ice

1—In a large saucepan, place tamarind seeds. Add water and mash seeds *thoroughly* with the hands, until seeds are *almost* free from pulp.

2—Set over *high heat* and bring to a boil.

3—Strain well, add sugar and mix.

4—Set in refrigerator in a covered glass jar. Serve in highball glasses on the-rocks, or *frappé* in electric blender, and spoon into cocktail glasses.

Note: Beverage may be diluted and sweetened to taste.

ALMOND BEVERAGE

Horchata de Almendras

(Serves 4)

A—½ pound almonds | 2 cups hot water

B—1 quart (4 cups) lukewarm water

C—½ cup sugar

D—Ice

1—In a saucepan, mix almonds and hot water and bring *rapidly* to a boil. Boil for *3 minutes*. Remove from heat, drain, and peel almonds.

2—Crush almonds in a mortar. Add lukewarm water, mix, and squeeze through a muslin cloth into a pot.

3—Add sugar, mix, and set in refrigerator in a glass jar. Serve chilled with ice.

SESAME SEEDS BEVERAGE

Horchata de Ajonjolí

(Serves 4)

A—1 cup *ajonjolí* (sesame seeds) (see Glossary)
   1 quart (4 cups) water

B—2 cups lukewarm water

C—½ cup sugar

D—Ice

1—Soak *ajonjolí* in water included in A for various hours. Drain well and crush *ajonjolí* in a mortar.

2—Add lukewarm water, mix, and squeeze through a muslin cloth into a pot.

3—Add sugar, mix, and set in refrigerator in a glass jar. Serve chilled with ice.

OATMEAL BEVERAGE

Refresco de Avena

(Serves 4)

A—½ cup oatmeal
1 quart (4 cups) water
1 lime peel, rinsed and drained

B—½ cup sugar

1—Soak oatmeal in water and lime peel included in A for *30 minutes.*

2—Strain, add sugar, mix, and set in refrigerator in a glass jar. Serve chilled.

BARLEY BEVERAGE

Refresco de Cebada

(Serves 4)

6 cups water
¼ cup ground barley
¼ cup sugar
1 lime peel, rinsed and drained

1—Mix ingredients in a pot, and boil for a few minutes, stirring *constantly,* until barley is cooked.

2—Strain and serve chilled.

SOURSOP BEVERAGE

Refresco de Guanábana

A—2 pounds ripe *guanábanas* (soursop) (see Glossary)

B—2 cups water

C—¾ cup sugar

D—Ice

1—Cut *guanábanas* in two, *lengthwise*. Core and remove pulp and seeds.

2—In a large saucepan, mash pulp and seeds with *1 cup* of the water included in *B*.

3—Press through a sieve. Place pulp and seeds back into saucepan and proceed as above, adding water *gradually*, until all the pulp has been removed from the seeds.

4—Add sugar, mix, and set in refrigerator in a glass jar. Serve chilled with ice.

Note: Beverage can be sweetened or diluted to taste.

SOURSOP CHAMPOLA

Champola de Guanábana

Proceed as in above recipe for Soursop Beverage, but substitute water with milk.

GINGER TEA

Té de Gengibre

(1 cup)

A—1 piece fresh ginger | 1 cup water

B—1 teaspoon sugar

1—Scrub, wash, and crush ginger. Bring to a boil in water included in *A*. Strain.

2—Add sugar, mix, and serve hot.

SOUR ORANGE TEA
Té de Naranja Agria

(1 cup)

A—2 fresh *naranja agria* leaves (sour orange leaves) (see Glossary)
1 cup water

B—1 teaspoon sugar

1—Wash leaves, crush and bring to a boil in water included in A.

2—Add sugar, mix, and serve hot.

PUERTO RICAN DRIP COFFEE
Café Puertorriqueño

1 cup ground coffee, Puerto Rican style, *firmly packed*
1½ cups **boiling** water

1—In a drip coffee pot, place the ground coffee in the strainer and *pack firmly*.

2—Pour over the coffee ¼ *cup* of the boiling water and allow to drip **slowly.** When dripping stops, continue adding boiling water, **¼ cup at a time.**

Note: Puerto Rican drip coffee is very strong. It is usually served in cups, almost full with hot milk, sugar to taste, and a few teaspoons of the coffee extract. It is also served as an extract, sweetened to taste, in demi-tasse cups. For more diluted coffee, add more boiling water to the ground coffee.

347

Rum Drinks

RUM DRINKS FROM THE CARIBBEAN

The word RUM brings to our minds romance under a tropical moon — its light filtering through the feathery leaves of palm trees strewn along a white-sand beach — with the rumbling and musical cadence of the waves. Refreshing!

A few years after Christopher Columbus landed in the sunny shores of Hispaniola (and stopped for water in Puerto Rico during his second voyage), the colonizers brought from the other side of the world the first sugar-cane seedlings. The virgin lands of the West Indies soon started yielding the golden-brown sugar obtained from the cane and the residue, black-strap molasses, was fermented and distilled into a powerful beverage — rum-bullion.

Since the late sixteenth century "rum" has played a very important role in the history of the New World. Wars, slavery, rum-bootlegging, Yankee traders, and pirates from the seventeenth and eighteenth centuries have done their share in creating a large rum industry in the islands. The rum barons — Bacardí, Barceló, Clemente, González, Myers, Oliver, Serrallés — have upgraded the rum from the saloons to the salons.

When my husband and I entertain at home — and this is almost always — Luis takes care of the drinks. I, in the kitchen, supervise Francisca, our dear and loyal cook.

Rum drinks — *Daiquirí on-the-Rocks* or *Pineapple-Rum Punch*, served with *Corn Meal Sticks* and *Gallician Turnovers*, put our guests in the mood for the Caribbean food to follow. After dessert and coffee, we serve a homemade rum-orange cordial which Luis picked up on one of his trips — I do not know when or where. We used to call it *Show-Time*. Lights are turned off; Luis lights a match and *flambés* the rum-orange cordial, which, to the astonishment of all the guests, gives off a rainbow of beautiful colors.

One day, we had the pleasure of preparing this cordial at our home for the late Miss Clementine Paddleford. To our delight she gave a name to our *Show-Time* piece — *Sugar Loaf Cordial* — when she published the recipe in the New York *Herald Tribune*. Try it, it's fantastic!

Our favorite before-dinner drink is *White Dove*. Sweet and powerful! If you like only one long drink to relax before dinner, this is it! You can vary the quantities of the ingredients — there are just two — to suit your taste, whether it be masculine or feminine.

During Prohibition (Puerto Rico was involved in this, too) our farmers prepared a "moonshine" rum called *cañita* or *mamplé*. The *tufo* was so strong, that the federal agents could detect the illicit stills miles away. To drink the *cañita* it was necessary to mix it with a fruit juice. And that's how *Coquito* was born! Today, we prepare *Coquito* with the excellent Puerto Rican rums and serve it during the Christmas holidays. We invite you to try this, our Tropical Eggnog.

Today, Puerto Rico is the world's leading producer of rum. In this land of enchantment, nature and climate blend to make it ideal for growing cane. The green-clad mountains give rise to fresh water streams and rivers whence comes the pure water essential to fine rum making. The trade winds perpetually fan the island. The climate is soft, spring-like all year round. In these surroundings, the rums of the island, resting in oak casks, age to maturity without artificial temperature control. Thereby, they acquire a natural softness which contributes greatly to your drinking pleasure.

The words **Puerto Rican Rum** on the label, assures you that the rum was distilled, aged and bottled in Puerto Rico and has the maturity and quality required by law. These rums are characterized by their exceptional lightness of body, dryness, and potability.

There are three types of Puerto Rican rums. *White* or *silver* labels, which are very dry, pale of color and light-bodied, are recommended for cocktails and flavored mixed drinks. *Gold* or *amber* labels, which acquire their color from the charred oak casks in which they are aged, are recommended for straight drinks, on-the-rocks, or in highballs. *Black* or *purple* labels, which are very strong, *151 proof,* are used only for certain powerful *mixed* drinks and to *flambé* food.

In this chapter we offer our favorite rum drinks. They might differ somewhat from other texts, but that is the prerogative of the bartender . . . or is it the effect of our Spanish inheritance — individuality?

Here's to you!

¡ *Salud, amor, dinero y tiempo para gastarlo!*

TROPICAL EGGNOG

Coquito
(Serves 16)

2 ripe coconuts	4 egg yolks
2 cups white Puerto Rican rum	
1 can (14 ounces) condensed milk, **undiluted**	
Ground nutmeg	

1—Crack coconuts. Separate the meat from the shell and remove brown skin. Wash, drain, and grate the meat.

2—In an electric blender, pour 1 cup of the rum and add about ⅓ of the grated coconut meat. Crush *thoroughly* at *high* speed. Strain and squeeze through muslin cloth.

3—Pour the strained liquid back into the blender, add ⅓ grated coconut meat and repeat.

4—Pour liquid again in blender, add balance of grated coconut meat and repeat. Strain and measure **2 cups.**

5—Pour liquid back into blender, add egg yolks, and mix.

6—Add condensed milk and mix well.

7—In a large bowl, mix the liquid *thoroughly* with 1 cup rum.

8—Bottle and store in refrigerator. Remove from refrigerator ½ *hour before serving.* Shake bottle well, pour into punch cups and sprinkle the top with ground nutmeg.

Note: To separate coconut meat from shell, break coconut in large pieces and heat in preheated oven to *350°F.,* about *5 to 10 minutes.*

CHRISTMAS DELIGHT

Ponche de Navidad

A—3 egg yolks | 1 cup sugar
1 can (13 ounces) evaporated milk, **undiluted**

B—1 teaspoon vanilla extract
1¼ cups white Puerto Rican rum

1—In a small saucepan, blend egg yolks and sugar. Add milk *gradually* and mix.

2—Heat a coil in the stove until it is red. Place over it the saucepan and stir mixture **rapidly** for 2 *minutes*. Remove from heat, add vanilla extract and rum, and mix.

3—Pour into glass bottle and store in refrigerator. When ready to serve, shake bottle and pour into cocktail glasses.

THREE KING'S PUNCH

Ponche de los Reyes Magos

A—1 cup sugar | 1 cinnamon stick
1 cup water |

B—1 can (13 ounces) evaporated milk, **undiluted**
1 cup white Puerto Rican rum | 1 cup anisette

C—4 egg yolks

D—Ground cinnamon (*for garnishing*)

1—Combine ingredients included in A in a saucepan and bring to a boil. Remove from heat, discard cinnamon stick and allow to cool.

2—Mix ingredients included in B and add *gradually*.

3—Beat egg yolks and fold into mixture. Pour into glass bottle and store in refrigerator.

4—When ready to serve, pour into punch cups and sprinkle the top with ground cinnamon.

LIME-RUM PUNCH

Ponche de Limón con Ron

(Serves 12 to 15)

A—1 cup sugar
   1 cup water

B—1 cup fresh lime juice
   1 bottle (4/5 quart) white Puerto Rican rum

1—Dissolve sugar in water over *low* heat. Remove from heat.

2—Add lime juice and rum. Mix well and pour into glass bowl.

3—Store in freezer. When ready to serve, mix well and scoop into cocktail glasses.

PINEAPPLE-RUM PUNCH

Ponche de Piña con Ron

(Serves 20)

A—1 can (1 quart 14 ounces) pineapple juice
   2 cups sugar

B—½ cup fresh lime juice
   5 cups white Puerto Rican rum

1—In a saucepan, dissolve sugar in 2 cups of pineapple juice over *low* heat. Remove from heat and mix with balance of juice.

2—Add lime juice and rum. Mix well. Pour into glass or porcelain bowl, ¾ full.

3—Store in freezer. When ready to serve, mix well and scoop into cocktail glasses.

RUM PUNCH

Ponche con Ron
(Serves 1)

A—2 ounces (4 tablespoons) dark Puerto Rican rum
⅟₂ ounce (1 tablespoon) fresh lime juice
1 teaspoon sugar | 1 dash Curaçao
1 teaspoon grenadine |

B—Crushed ice

C—Pineapple slice ⎫
   Orange slice   ⎬ *for garnishing*
   Maraschino cherry ⎭

1—Shake all ingredients included in A in a cocktail shaker.

2—Fill tall glass with crushed ice and pour mixture.

3—Garnish with pineapple and orange slices. Add Maraschino cherry and serve with straw.

PLANTER'S PUNCH

(Serves 1)

A—Cracked ice

B—1 ounce (2 tablespoons) fresh lime juice
6 dashes Angostura bitters
2 teaspoons sugar
2 ounces (4 tablespoons) dark Puerto Rican rum
1 ounce (2 tablespoons) Myer's Jamaican rum

C—1 bottle carbonated water, chilled

D—Lime slice   ⎫
   Orange slice ⎬ *for garnishing*

1—Fill tall glass with cracked ice.

2—Mix ingredients included in B and pour over ice.

3—Add chilled carbonated water and stir *lightly*.

4—Garnish with lime and orange slices and serve with straw.

PUNCH MARTINIQUAIS
(Serves 1)

A—**Sugar syrup:**
    2 cups sugar | 2 cups water

B—Dark Puerto Rican rum | Lime peels, rinsed

1—Prepare beforehand sugar syrup by boiling ingredients included in *A* about *10 minutes* (Candy Thermometer — 220°F.). Allow to cool and store, sealed, to be used as required.

2—In an Old-Fashioned glass, pour syrup and rum to taste (usually *1 ounce* syrup to *2 ounces* rum).

3—Twist lime peel over mixture and add peel.

4—Add two or three ice cubes, stir, and serve.

Note: This drink is usually prepared individually, to taste.

SUGAR LOAF CORDIAL*
(Serves 8)

1 large ripe orange | 1 cup sugar
1 cup white Puerto Rican 86 proof rum
1 tablespoon Puerto Rican 151 proof rum

1—Wash and scrub orange. Peel around in one long, thin slice *without breaking*. Discard the peeled orange.

2—In the center of a heat-proof deep dish, arrange the peel to simulate the orange and fill the interior with the sugar.

3—Pour rum around sugar loaf to form an island.

4—Saturate the sugar mound and orange peel with 1 tablespoon of 151 proof rum. Ignite. (In case 151 proof rum is not available, the 86 proof rum can be used, but will take longer to ignite.)

* Named by the late Miss Clementine Paddleford of the New York *Herald Tribune*.

5—With long-handled fork and spoon, lift flaming peel and dip into rum. Move it around in the sugar and lift peel again. Repeat until the sugar is dissolved. (For better effect, turn off lights while igniting and mixing.)

6—Allow to cool *slightly* before serving in cordial glasses.

ORANGE AND ROCK CANDY CORDIAL

Cordial de China (Naranja Dulce) y Azúcar Candy

A—1 large ripe orange | 1 pound rock candy
1 bottle (4/5 quart) dark Puerto Rican rum

1—Wash and scrub orange. Wipe dry, and with an icepick, pierce all over, deep into the orange.
2—Place **whole** orange in a glass jar with a wide lid.
3—Add the rock candy to the jar.
4—Pour contents of the bottle of rum over the rock candy and cover *tightly*.
5—Allow to stand for *at least one month* at room temperature.
6—Strain, discard orange, and bottle orange liqueur with remaining rock candy in decanter, to serve as a cordial.

COCONUT CORDIAL

Cordial de Coco

1 large, ripe coconut | Sugar
White Puerto Rican rum |

1—With a sharp knife, pierce hole on top of coconut and discard water.
2—Fill coconut with water. Drain and measure water.
3—In a saucepan, put rum and add sugar in the amount of **one part sugar** to **two parts rum.** Dissolve sugar with a rubber spatula. Pour syrup into coconut.
4—Seal with cork and wax. Store at room temperature for *at least one month.*
5—Strain and bottle, to serve as a cordial.

DAIQUIRI
(Serves 1)

2 ounces (4 tablespoons) white Puerto Rican rum
1½ teaspoons fresh lime juice
1 teaspoon sugar | Cracked ice

1—Shake all ingredients well with cracked ice.

2—Strain into chilled cocktail glass.

FROZEN DAIQUIRI
Daiquirí Frappé
(Serves 1)

2 ounces (4 tablespoons) white Puerto Rican rum
2 tablespoons fresh lime juice
1 teaspoon sugar
1 cup shaved ice

1—Blend all ingredients in an electric blender.

2—Serve *frappé* in chilled cocktail glass.

DAIQUIRI ON-THE-ROCKS
Daiquirí en la Roca
(Serves 6)

1 cup fresh lime juice
1 cup sugar
2 cups white Puerto Rican rum
Ice cubes

1—Dissolve sugar in lime juice over *low* heat. Remove and allow to cool.

2—Add rum and chill in refrigerator a few hours before serving.

3—Mix well before serving over ice cubes in Old-Fashioned glasses.

BANANA DAIQUIRI
Daiquirí de Guineo

2 ounces (4 tablespoons) white Puerto Rican rum
1 ounce (2 tablespoons) fresh lime juice
1 teaspoon sugar
⅓ ripe banana, peeled
1 cup shaved ice

1—Blend all ingredients in an electric blender.

2—Serve *frappé* in cocktail glass.

> **Note:** Recipe can be varied by substituting the banana with other ripe fruits.

SANGRIA

A—1 bottle (4/5 quart) red dry wine
   1 cup sugar
   1 cup dark Puerto Rican rum
   1 cup orange juice
   ½ cup lime juice

B—1 can (1 pound) sliced peaches

1—In a large pot, mix **thoroughly,** with a rubber spatula, ingredients included in *A,* until sugar dissolves.

2—Add the contents of the can of sliced peaches, **including** the syrup, and stir. Pour into a glass pitcher and set in refrigerator. When ready to serve, pour over ice in tall glasses.

3—Garnish with orange and lime wedges and peach slices. (*Optional*)

PIÑA COLADA

A—1 can (15 ounces) Cream of Coconut
4 cups (32 ounces) white Puerto Rican rum
6 cups (48 ounces) canned pineapple juice

B—Ice

1—Mix **thoroughly** ingredients included in A and set in refrigerator.

2—Serve in highball glasses over ice cubes, or **frappé** in electric blender, and spoon into cocktail glasses.

GRAPEFRUIT HIGHBALL

Toron-ron
(Serves 1)

1 jigger (1½ ounces) dark Puerto Rican rum
Grapefruit juice
Ice cubes

1—In a highball glass, pour rum over ice cubes. Fill glass with grapefuit juice and mix.

CARIBE COCKTAIL

Coctel Caribe
(Serves 1)

1 jigger (1½ ounces) white Puerto Rican rum
4½ teaspoons fresh lime juice
1 ounce (2 tablespoons) pineapple juice
Ice

1—In a cocktail shaker, shake all ingredients.

2—Strain and serve into cocktail glass.

WHITE DOVE

Palomita Blanca

(Serves 1)

2 jiggers (1½ ounces each) white Puerto Rican rum
2 jiggers (1½ ounces each) anisette
Crushed ice

1—Fill a highball glass with crushed ice.

2—Pour anisette over ice. Add rum and stir.

Note: Carbonated water can be added, if desired.

HOT BUTTERED RUM

Ponche de Ron Caliente con Mantequilla

(Serves 1)

A—1 teaspoon brown sugar
   Hot water

B—1 jigger (1½ ounces) dark Puerto Rican rum
   Pinch of nutmeg

C—Cinnamon stick
   Butter slice

1—Preheat 6-ounce mug with boiling water and drain.

2—Dissolve sugar with small amount of hot water in the mug.

3—Add ingredients included in B. Mix and fill mug with boiling water.

4—Insert cinnamon stick and top with butter slice. Allow to melt. Drink hot.

Note: To prepare Hot Buttered Rum Cow, substitute water with milk.

CRUZAN SWIZZLE
(Serves 6)

1 bottle (4/5 quart) St. Croix rum
4 ounces fresh lime juice
¼ cup (4 tablespoons) sugar
½ teaspoon Angostura bitters
3 cups crushed ice

1—Pour all ingredients in a large pitcher and mix well with swizzle stick, until pitcher frosts.

2—Serve, *unstrained,* in tall glasses.

Note: Dark Puerto Rican rum can be used instead of St. Croix rum.

RUM HIGHBALL

1½ ounces dark Puerto Rican rum
Carbonated soft drink

1—In a highball glass, pour rum over ice cubes. Fill glass with favorite mixer (soda, cola, ginger ale, limeade, etc.), stir and serve.

RUM BLOODY MARY

1½ ounces dark Puerto Rican rum
4½ ounces tomato juice
¾ ounce lime juice
4 dashes Worcestershire sauce
4 drops Tabasco sauce
Pinch of salt

1—In a cocktail shaker, shake ingredients with ice cubes. Strain into a Burgundy-type wine glass.

RUM COLLINS

2 ounces white Puerto Rican rum
1 fresh lime, halved
1 teaspoon sugar
Soda water

1—Squeeze half a lime and drop into a highball glass. Add and dissolve sugar. Add ice cubes and rum. Stir and fill with soda water.

RUM MARTINI

2 ounces white Puerto Rican rum
Dash of dry vermouth (*to taste*)
1 fresh lime peel
Small white onion or stuffed olive

1—In a cocktail shaker, stir rum and vermouth with ice and pour. Add twist of lime peel and onion or olive. (If desired, can be served on-the-rocks.)

RUM OLD FASHIONED

1½ ounces dark Puerto Rican rum
6 drops Angostura bitters
1 fresh lime peel
½ lump sugar
Orange slice
Maraschino cherry

1—In an Old Fashioned glass, muddle the lime peel in a splash of water with sugar and Angostura bitters. Add ice cubes and rum. Garnish with orange slice and cherry.

RUM RICKEY

1½ ounces white Puerto Rican rum
1 fresh lime
Soda water

1—In a highball glass, pour rum over ice cubes. Squeeze and drop half a lime and fill with soda water.

RUM SCREWDRIVER

1½ ounces dark Puerto Rican rum
Orange juice

1—In a highball glass, pour rum over ice cubes. Fill glass with orange juice.

RUM SOUR

1½ ounces dark Puerto Rican rum
1 ounce fresh lime juice
1 teaspoon sugar
Orange slice
Maraschino cherry

1—In a cocktail shaker, shake rum, lime juice and sugar with ice cubes. Strain into sour glass and garnish with orange slice and cherry.

RUM AND TONIC

1½ ounces white Puerto Rican rum
1 fresh lime, halved
Tonic water

1—In a highball glass, pour rum over ice cubes. Squeeze and drop half a lime and fill with tonic water. Stir and serve.

Glossary

Acerola, West Indian cherry (*Malpighia punicifolia*)
A small cherry-like fruit of a shrub; very rich in vitamin C.

Achiote Coloring
Used to give color to food, obtained by heating lard or vegetable oil in a saucepan at *low* heat, together with whole *achiote* seeds, to yield a rich, orange-yellow color.

Achiote Seeds, annato seeds (*Bixa Orellana*)
The seeds of the annato tree, used for coloring lard or vegetable oil a bright orange-yellow. Paprika or saffron may be used as a substitute.

Aguacate, avocado (*Persea americana*)
The tropical pear-shaped fruit also called *"alligator pear,"* is usually marketed unripe. Rich in oil content, is nutritious, and used chiefly as a salad. When ripe and ready to eat, the flesh should yield when gentle pressure is applied to the skin.

Ají Dulce, sweet chili pepper (*Capsicum annuum*)
The dwarf green pepper which has a mild, sweet, and distinct flavor; ideal for seasoning dishes. It should not be confused with the hot pepper.

Ajonjolí, sesame seeds (*Sesamum orientale*)
The small, flat seeds of a tropical plant used in making beverages and candies.

Amarillo, ripe plantain
When the plantain is ripe, it is called **plátano amarillo,** or **amarillo,** referring to the yellowish-brown skin.

Aniseed, *semilla de anís* (*Pimpinella Anisum*)
The tiny, aromatic seed of a plant which grows extensively in Spain.

Apio, arracacha (*Arracacia xantorrhiza*)
The thick, edible rootstock of a tropical plant.

Bacalao, salt codfish
An inexpensive fish very popular in fritters and salads.

Batata Dulce, sweet potato (*Ipomoea batatas*)
Not to be confused with the Louisiana yam. The flesh of the tropical sweet potato changes in color from white through yellow to deep orange. A valuable source of vitamins A and C, as well as thiamine and riboflavin.

Berza, collard green, colewart (*Brassica* variety)
A variety of cabbage which does not heart. The leaf is used to flavor soups.

Breadfruit, *pana, panapén* (*Artocarpus communis*)
The large, roundish fruit of a tropical tree. A thick greenish rind covers the sweet, starchy flesh which is reminiscent in flavor and texture of a sweet potato. The **panapén** *is not edible raw.* Boiled breadfruit is served as a substitute for potato. Fried green breadfruit slices are served as **tostones** to accompany drinks or with meats, poultry or fish as a vegetable.

Breadnut, *semilla de pana* (*Artocaps communis*)
A variety of the tropical breadfruit tree; the fruit contains a large number of seeds resembling chestnuts. The seeds are eaten boiled.

Butifarras, pork sausages
A highly seasoned dry pork sausage native to the Caribbean. It can be substituted with country sausage or canned Vienna sausages.

Caldero, cauldron
A heavy cast-iron or cast-aluminum kettle or casserole, with round bottom and straight sides. A heavy kettle or Dutch oven may be used as a substitute.

Casabe, cassava cakes (*Manihot utilissima*)
Flat, dry cakes made from the grated roots of the cassava plant. It is used for soups and in the preparation of other native dishes.

Chayote, christophine, pear-shape (*Sechium edule*), also known as *mirliton*
The roundish or pear-shaped vegetable of a climbing plant which grows extensively in the Caribbean and to some extent in Florida and Louisiana. The flesh is delicately flavored and similar to summer squash.

Chicharrón, fried pork cracklings
See Index for recipe.

China, *naranja dulce,* orange (*Citrus sinensis*)
The most important fresh fruit of international commerce, this citrus fruit is grown in numerous varieties, the most common are Washington navel, Valencia, Hamlin, Pineapple and Parson Brown. Its juice is an important source of vitamin C.

Chorizo, Spanish sausage
A highly seasoned Spanish pork sausage; sun-dried and hot to the palate.

Culantro, *cilantro*
The long, serrated leaves of a small plant which grows wild in the Caribbean. It is used for flavoring.

Escabeche, pickled
Applies to the method of marinating cooked fish, poultry, game, etc. in oil, vinegar, onions and garlic marinade.

Gandul, pigeon pea (*Cajanus Cajan*)
This legume is generally cooked when green.

Garbanzo, chick-pea (*Cicer arietinum*)
A legume popular in Mediterranean countries and in the Caribbean. It is used in soups and stews.

Granos, legumes (see Index)

Grelo, turnip green (*Brassica Napus*)
The leaf of the turnip, a biennial cruciferous plant used to flavor soups.

Guanábana, soursop (*Annona muricata*)
A large tropical fruit with a soft white and aromatic flesh. When ripe, it is eaten raw or used in preparing sherbet and beverages.

Guayaba, guava (*Psidium Guajava*)
The round or pear-shaped fruit of the guava tree, which grows abundantly in tropical countries. The slightly acid flesh is enclosed by a yellowish-red thin skin. The fruit makes delicious jams, jellies, and preserves. It is also eaten raw; very high in vitamin C.

Guineito niño, finger banana
A variety of banana. It is small, resembling a thumb finger. The flesh, when ripe, is very sweet. Not to be used when unripe, it is delicious when ripe, fried in butter with fresh grated Parmesan cheese or in wine or butter sauce.

Guingambó, okra, gumbo (*Abelmoschus, esculentus*)
A tapering, angular, mucilaginous pod used as a vegetable when cooked, specially for gumbo soups or stews. Also known as **guingambós.**

Hicaco, coco-plum (*Chrysobalanus icaco*)
The fruit of a West Indian tree. Also the tree.

Lechosa, papaw, *papaya (Carica papaya)*
The fruit of a tropical soft-stemmed tree. Its flavor is very similar to that of a melon. The green fruit is used in preserves. When ripe, the yellow flesh is sweet and musky, and is delicious eaten raw. Its high content of papain enzyme, similar to pepsin, makes it valuable for its digestant action.

Lerenes, sweet corn root *(Calathea Allouia)*
The small, white tuber of a tropical plant very common in Puerto Rico and other islands of the Caribbean. *Always eaten boiled.*

Mabí, naked-wood *(Colubrina reclinata)*
The bark of the naked-wood tree, which is used to prepare a fermented beverage very popular in the Caribbean.

Malta, Non-alcoholic malt beverage
A non-alcoholic malt beverage extensively used for its nutritional value. Contains barley malt, cane sugar, corn grits, hops, water and preservatives.

Mamey, mammee apple *(Mammea americana)*
The fruit of a large tropical tree with bright yellow, juicy flesh. When ripe, it is eaten both raw or in preserves.

Mangó, mango *(Mangifera indica)*
One of the most delicious of tropical fruits which is being shipped in large quantities to northern markets, especially in April and May. When ripe, the orange flesh is sweet, juicy, and aromatic. Unripe or green mangoes form the basis of many chutneys. Ripe mangoes may be eaten raw or used for making jams, preserves and sherbet.

Naranja Agria, sour orange *(Citrus Aurantium)*
A very sour orange, not to be confused with the bitter orange grown in the South. The juice is used for flavoring meat and poultry dishes and to make marmalade.

Naranja dulce, (see *China*)

Níspero, sapodilla *(Sapota Achras)*
The fruit of a tropical tree. The smooth, aromatic tan pulp is covered by a thin, brown skin. Eaten *only* when ripe, it has a very delicate and distinct flavor.

Ñame, yam *(Dioscorea alata)*
The irregular-shaped, starchy, tuberous roots of a tropical plant. It is either baked, boiled or ground to a flour.

Orégano, Puerto Rican marjoram (*Lippia Helleri*)
The small aromatic downy, oval-leaf herb is a variety of the sweet marjoram used in seasoning. It is very abundant in the Caribbean and throughout the recipes in this book is used as **whole dried** orégano, not to be confused with **ground** orégano.

Paellera, *paella* pan
A shallow skillet, originally from Spain, used expressly to prepare the typical **paella.** Garnished, the food is served in the pan. Can be substituted by a large, deep heavy skillet.

Pajuil, *cajuil,* cashew (*Anacardium occidentale*)
The kidney-shaped fruit of the cashew-nut tree. The kernels or nuts are roasted for marketing, while the fruit is used in preparing preserves and candies.

Pana, *panapén* (see Breadfruit and Breadnut)

Papaya (see *Lechosa*)

Plátano, plantain (*Musa paradisiaca*)
A variety of the banana which **cannot be eaten raw.** Coarser in texture than the ordinary banana, it is harvested while green and is either baked, fried, or boiled. When ripe, it is called **amarillo.**

Quingombó (see *Guingambó*)

Sofrito
A seasoning sauce extensively used in cooking. See Index for recipe.

Tamarindo, tamarind (*Tamarindus indica*)
The thin, brown pods of a large tropical tree. The pods, containing from one to four seeds, are filled with a sweet-sour brown pulp. When ripe, the pulp is used in the making of beverages and chutneys.

Tostones, fried plantain slices
Slices of green or medium-ripe plantains partly fried, flattened and fried again until crispy and brown. Very popular as appetizers to accompany drinks, or served to replace vegetables with meats, poultry or fish. Also made of green breadfruit slices.

Whole dried orégano (see *Orégano*)

Yautía, tanier (*Xanthosoma atrovirens and sagittaefolium*)
The starchy roots of a tropical large-leaved plant. The flesh is usually creamy white or yellow and is similar in flavor and texture to a mealy Irish or Idaho potato.

Yuca, cassava (*Manihot Manihot*)
A tropical plant with fleshy rootstock yielding a nutritious starch. It is used as a food and in the making of tapioca, farina and **casabe** cakes.

INDEX

Index

Indice Alfabético

CAPITULO XV—BEBIDAS CON RON